CW00819335

SCHOLAR Study Guide

National 5 ESOL

Authored and reviewed by:

Mark Watson

Susan Paton

Heriot-Watt University

Edinburgh EH14 4AS, United Kingdom.

Distributed by the SCHOLAR Forum.

SCHOLAR Study Guide National 5 ESOL

National 5 ESOL Course Code: C827 75

ISBN 978-1-911057-29-1

Print Production and Fulfilment in UK by Print Trail www.printtrail.com

Acknowledgements

Thanks are due to the members of Heriot-Watt University's SCHOLAR team who planned and created these materials, and to the many colleagues who reviewed the content.

We would like to acknowledge the assistance of the education authorities, colleges, teachers and students who contributed to the SCHOLAR programme and who evaluated these materials.

Grateful acknowledgement is made for permission to use the following material in the SCHOLAR programme:

The Scottish Qualifications Authority for permission to use Past Papers assessments.

The Scottish Government for financial support.

The content of this Study Guide is aligned to the Scottish Qualifications Authority (SQA) curriculum.

All brand names, product names, logos and related devices are used for identification purposes only and are trademarks, registered trademarks or service marks of their respective holders.

Contents

Contents

Unit 1: ESOL in Everyday Life

Unit 1 Topic 1

Personal profile

Contents

Learning objective

By the end of this topic you will be better able to:

- ask polite questions and provide personal information when meeting new people;

- identify and produce specific phrases used in polite conversation with strangers;

- identify the features of biographical writing and write a short biography;

- identify the features of autobiography and write a short autobiography.

1.1   Vocabulary: Introductions/salutations

Think about how people introduce themselves when they first meet. There are the basic greetings of "Hello. My name is. . ." but as you progress in English you will meet many people who use different expressions to greet strangers.

Introductions/salutations (10 min)   Go online

Q1:   Rearrange the words to make correct sentences/questions used in introductory conversations.

   a) Do do you how?

   b) Meet to pleased you.

   c) A to it's meet you pleasure.

   d) You how are?

   e) Things are how?

Responses (5 min)   Go online

Q2:   Match the questions from the previous activity to the correct response.

a)	Pleased to meet you.	1)	Very well, thanks. And you?
b)	It's a pleasure to meet you.	2)	Everything is fine, thanks.
c)	How are you?	3)	Likewise
d)	How are things?	4)	Likewise

1.2   Listening: Introducing others

In certain situations you may find that you have to introduce a friend or colleague. Here are some examples of common language used in introductions.

- I'd like to introduce you to...
- There's someone I'd like you to meet, this is...
- Have you met...?

Introducing others (30 min) Go online 🔊

You are at a party with your friend, Steve. Steve knows a lot of people at this party and he keeps introducing them to you. Listen to the recordings and try to remember what each person says. Once you have listened to the recordings answer the following questions.

You will require the following sound file in order to complete this activity: n5-esl1-1-1listening.mp3

Q3: Where is Michelle from? She's from _____.
....

Q4: What is Michelle's job? She's a _____ in a university.
....

Q5: How does Steve know Karen? They met _____.
....

Q6: How old is Karen? (type out the number)
....

Q7: Why is Jenny at the party? Because her father knows _____.
....

Q8: Who is Mike? He's Steve's _____.
....

Q9: What does Mike do? He's an _____.
....

Q10: What nationality is Jenny? She's _____.
....

Q11: What's the name of the last person Steve introduces?
....

Q12: Why is this an awkward situation? Because she's Steve's _____.

1.3 Speaking: Discussion: Introductions

Introductions (30 min)

Work with a partner. Imagine you have just met each other at a party for the first time. You have both come to the party with a friend. Prepare a short conversation in which you:

- Introduce yourself and respond to your partner's introduction

- Introduce your friend and continue a short conversation for 3 minutes

If possible, practise this with your teacher or record it. Repeat the conversation a few times, until you are able to perform it without using any notes.

> **Top tip**
>
> Before you speak, you should make notes about:
>
> - How to introduce yourself
>
> - How to introduce your friend
>
> - What kind of questions to ask to continue the conversation
>   *e.g. questions to find out why the person is at the party / personal information about where he / she is from etc.*
>   *NB. Two examples would be sufficient*

1.4 Listening: Social Interaction

Listening activity: social interaction   Go online

To complete this activity, you will need the following sound file:
n5-esl1-1-2listening.mp3

Q13:
Listen to the recording and complete the sentences. Use **no more than four** words in each text box.

1. The speakers meet . . . .
2. Steve likes Spain because the weather is better and the people are more. . . . .
3. Chris thinks Steve is benefitting from the . . . . and . . . .
4. Anna was brought up in . . . .
5. Anna says she and her friends always planned to . . . .
6. Anna describes Edinburgh as . . . .

7. Chris says village life encourages . . . .
8. Anna says a disadvantage of village life is . . . .
9. Anna and Steve both enjoy an . . . . lifestyle
10. Anna and Steve find Edinburgh people . . . .

1.5 Grammar: Question formation

Question formation (15 min)   Go online

Yes/no questions are constructed so as to provoke a yes or no response. These questions may consist of auxiliary verb, subject/complement, main verb and object/adverbial phrase. The respondent may add more information after saying yes/no.

- Did you enjoy your holiday? Yes. I had a wonderful time.

Look at the information in the circles in the diagram. The information is based on *Listening comprehension: social interaction*. Think of questions you might ask using this information to provoke yes/no responses.

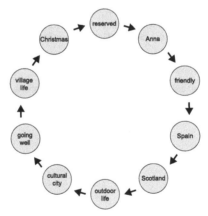

are you : business : Spanish people are : better in : a job in : is the weather : do you like : met : is Edinburgh a : is your : do you : do you think : have you : in Edinburgh : enjoy : home for : do you have : are people

Q14: Use the words/phrases above together with the words from the diagram to make 10 questions, ending in each of the responses from the image.

1.	Is the weather better in Spain?
2.	
3.	
4.	
5.	
6.	
7.	
8.	
9.	
10.	

1.6   Speaking: Forming your own questions and responses

Forming your own questions and responses (15 min)

This exercise is similar to the one you have just completed. Take a blank sheet of paper and draw a diagram containing ten pieces of information about your own life.

Exchange your diagram with another student in the class (or your teacher) but do not tell them what the words and numbers mean.

Your partner/teacher must ask you YES/NO answerable questions about your diagram until they have successfully guessed the meaning of all your information.

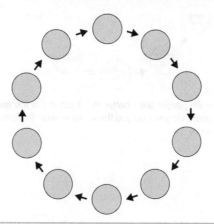

1.7   Writing: A biography

Biography (60 min)

Following on from the previous exercise, use the information you have learned about your partner to create a short biography (200 words). Change the list of information into sentences and try to add extra language and further details you have learned from your conversation with your partner.

Q15: Use the information you have acquired about your partner from the previous exercise to write a short biography. Use your notes and also try to add extra language and further details from the conversation you had. If you are working alone then write ten statements about someone you know well such as a friend or family member. Use the example below to help you get started:

- Thirty-eight
- Hotel manager
- London

1.8   Speaking: Lifestyles

Pre-reading discussion (15 min)

With a partner discuss the following questions.

- Where do you live?
- Why did you choose to live there?
- Do you like your lifestyle? Would you change it if you could? How?

1.9   Reading: A lifestyle choice

Where do you live? (45 min)

Read the following passage about Brian, someone who lives an interesting and unusual lifestyle. Answer the questions that follow.

One day you just might wake up and realise that your life is not the way you want it any more. Your thoughts are full of **logos**, advertisements and products, and your body is a slave to fizzy drinks, fried food and chocolate. You look at your home and realise it is **complicit** in this self-destructive, **conformist** lifestyle, and you smile to yourself in the dawning realisation that your constant **pursuit** of a perfect existence has brought you anything but that. Your dreams and **aspirations** have been **trodden** on to the point that they are only ever going to remain as dreams, and your **capitulation** to the consumer society is complete.

Former accountant Brian Doherty found himself in exactly this place. **Plagued** by a lack of fulfilment and his underlying sense of **discontentment**, Brian decided to part from society as a whole and withdraw into a world where he could be master of his own **domain**. Brian was earning a six figure sum in the city, driving an Italian sports car, dating a model and living in a luxury penthouse flat but none of that was offering him the spiritual well-being he sought. He found himself working eighteen or nineteen hour days but he barely had time to enjoy the all the **trappings** he acquired. It was a **vicious circle**; the more he worked, the more he earned and the more he **purchased**, thus requiring him to work harder to maintain his increasingly expensive lifestyle.

Four years ago, Brian walked out of the office one Tuesday lunchtime and never returned. He gave his car keys and **deeds** to his flat to his **bewildered** girlfriend and wished her good luck for the future. Since that time, Brian has lived silently, like an invisible **spectre**, in a one room shack near Grand Beach. It was the last purchase he made, costing him only two thousand pounds, but he insists it was the only worthwhile one he has ever made.

Brian doesn't dine out at the Ritz or the Central Hotel these days, but exists mostly on a diet of the **kelp** he collects, and the fruit and vegetables he trades with market sellers, in return for helping them sell produce at their fairs once a week. He is happy in the moment, there is no outside interference, no schedule to **adhere** to and nobody tells him what to do. He no longer worries about the rat race, or the **acquisition** of **material goods**. He has no money worries because he has no money.

One habit Brian has retained from his previous life is reading the newspaper, something he will do in the local lifeboat centre if he passes by and feels like a little company. He feels sorry for most of the people in the stories he reads, and wishes they could reach the realisation he did. Nowadays, Brian is content to live with the stillness and calm that the **isolation** of his new life brings him. Far more than in the past as an ambitious graduate, climbing the career ladder in the city and **splashing out** on whatever the latest 'must have' was, Brian now feels that in his new life, he is truly living the dream.

Q16: Brian was spending too much money and couldn't afford his lifestyle.

a) True
b) False

....

Q17: Brian left his job because he hated feeling trapped.

a) True
b) False

....

Q18: Brian's girlfriend couldn't understand his decision.

a) True
b) False

....

Q19: Brian's current house was a better purchase than his sports car.

a) True
b) False

....

Q20: What does Brian eat?

....

Q21: What aspect of his old life has Brian maintained?

....

Q22: Which of these terms best describe Brian? (Use a dictionary to help you.)

a) Hermit
b) Private Tenant
c) Anti-social citizen

....

Q23: Find a word or phrase in the story which means 'surrender; giving in'.

....

Q24: Find a word or phrase in the story which means 'loneliness; being alone'.

....

Q25: Find a word or phrase in the story which means 'the daily competition in life'.

1.10   Listening: An enjoyable lifestyle

Pre-listening speaking activity

Ask and answer the following questions where appropriate with a partner:

1. Where were you born?

2. What do you do for a living?

3. Do you enjoy your job/studies?

4. What are the negative aspects of your job/studies?

5. What is the best thing about your job/studies?

6. Are you married/single?

7. Do you have any children?

8. What are your hobbies and interests?

Listening activity   Go online

Now listen to a speaker responding to the same questions. After listening, answer the questions using **no more than four** words.

You will need the following sound file to complete this activity:
n5-esl1-1-3listening.mp3.

Q26: Where was she born?

....

Q27: What does she do for a living?

....

Q28: Does she enjoy her job/studies?

....

Q29: What are the negative aspects of her job/studies?

....

Q30: What is the best thing about her job/studies?

....

Q31: Is she married/single?

....

Q32: Does she have any children?

....

Q33: What are her hobbies and interests?

1.11   Writing: Autobiography

Where and how I live (60 min)

Write a short autobiographical essay. Include information about where you live and what your lifestyle is like.

Make notes about the following points to help you:

- What is your home like - can you describe it?

- Describe the area you live in.

- Are you happy with where you live?

- Do you think your lifestyle would be very different in another country? In what ways?

- Describe yourself - career, family, job - and how you feel about these things.

- What would be an ideal lifestyle in your opinion?

Top tip

Before you begin, consider the following questions:

* What is the purpose of the communication?
* What level of formality (register) would be appropriate?

Make some notes or a mind map to help plan out your writing before you begin. Try to write between 200-250 words. Ask your teacher to check your work.

1.12   Reading comprehension: Language learning

Reading comprehension: Language learning   Go online

The decline in language learning in schools in the UK may be the consequence of government legislation. In England in recent years, language subjects have not been compulsory for pupils. The uptake of languages as a subject of choice at schools and universities has also fallen dramatically, which may put young people looking for jobs at a serious disadvantage in the future. In an attempt to address this situation, the government plans to reintroduce compulsory language learning starting in primary schools with children around aged five.

It is clear that the reluctance to learn languages among young people in the UK is partly due to laziness and complacency. There is a mistaken belief among young Brits that most people in other countries speak, or at least understand, English. In reality, 75% of people in the world do not speak English. Indeed, the notion of English as a world language is in no longer realistic and while ". . . in the mid-20th century, nearly 9 percent of the world's population grew up speaking English as their first language, in 2050, the number is expected to be 5 percent."

Analysis of worldwide trends suggest that in the future, English is likely to have a strong profile as a second language and become an essential skill in the same way that computing is. At the same time, while English is likely to be the lingua franca in Science, it seems that dominance in other spheres is far from guaranteed. International communication may continue to be accomplished through common language; but with the rise in numbers of Mandarin speakers the latter is likely to be a strong contender in the race for domination.

By choosing not to learn another language, young people are disadvantaged in the job market. Having an additional language on a curriculum vitae undoubtedly raises an applicant's profile above others. By refusing to acquire an additional language, young Brits put themselves in an inferior position when compared to international peers. However, learning a language is not just about the words on the page, but also about enabling young people to learn more about culture and belief systems. Translation can provide some insight, but a fuller picture is conveyed through reading the native language.

Encouraging school pupils to choose languages may perhaps involve analysis of school accreditation systems. At the moment, young people often opt for subjects which are

---

perceived as easier, in order to acquire a greater number of exam passes. Teaching is perhaps also an issue. Traditional approaches to language learning may need to be abandoned in favour of more communicative approaches designed to enthuse learners at an earlier stage.

Q34: What kind of text is this?

a) A magazine/newspaper article
b) A literary review
c) A report

. . . .

Q35: What is the text mainly about? Choose **two** answers.

1. Trends in language learning in the UK
2. The future of the English language
3. Global attitudes to language learning
4. Migration
5. The curriculum in UK schools

. . . .

Q36: Pupils in schools in the UK have never been required to learn languages.

a) True
b) False

. . . .

Q37: The writer thinks that young people in the UK lack interest and enthusiasm in learning English.

a) True
b) False

. . . .

Q38: The status of the English language is changing.

a) True
b) False

. . . .

Q39: Learning a language won't help young people get jobs.

a) True
b) False

. . . .

Q40: The writer thinks that in the future, the English language will dominate in some fields.

a) True
b) False

....

Q41: Many pupils nowadays think it is easy to pass language exams.

a) True
b) False

....

Q42: Find a word in the text with the same meaning as 'people of the same age or social group'.

....

Q43: Find a phrase in the text with the same meaning as 'description of someone's qualifications, experience and character for a job'.

....

Q44: Find a phrase in the text with the same meaning as 'ways of teaching which emphasise speaking'.

1.13   Listening comprehension: Bilingualism

Listening comprehension: Bilingualism	Go online

To complete this exercise, you will need access to the following sound file:
n5-esl1-1-5listening.mp3

Q45: Daisy learned Italian at school.

1. True
2. False

....

Q46: Daisy found a job quite easily in Italy.

1. True
2. False

....

Q47: Daisy found translating quite challenging at first.

1. True
2. False

....

Q48: Tamsin planned to be a teacher.

1. True
2. False

....

Q49: The job with the tour company increased Tamsin's confidence.

1. True
2. False

....

Q50: Tamsin found teaching stressful

1. True
2. False

....

Q51: Both speakers have formal teaching qualifications.

1. True
2. False

....

Q52: What **three** factors enhanced Daisy's language skills when she was in Italy?

....

Q53: What aspect of working as a translator does Daisy say is a bonus?

....

Q54: Why does Daisy think that being in a country helps in language learning?

....

Q55: What does Tamsin say helps one to advance in a country?

....

Q56: What is the recording about?

1. School systems in the UK
2. Teaching languages effectively
3. Using languages at work

Unit 1 Topic 2

Lifestyle

Contents

Learning objective

By the end of this topic you will be better able to:

- participate in a conversation about Sport and Leisure;

- identify the prevalent use of emotive language in sporting contexts and produce this language;

- pick out key information from texts;

- write an article suitable for inclusion in a magazine.

2.1   Grammar: Verb and Noun combinations: Describing sporting activities

Example : Do, play or go

In English, we can generally categorise most sports and hobbies into three main groupings, those that we DO, those we PLAY and those which we use the verb GO with.

*Sarah **does** aerobics every Saturday morning.*
*Barry **plays** football for the local team.*
*Lucinda **goes** sailing during the summer months.*

Do, play or go (20 min)

Q1:   Look at the list of the following sports and try to decide if they would be used with DO, PLAY or GO. Place each under the correct heading.

Golf	Basketball	Cycling	Taekwondo
Zumba	Badminton	Fishing	Hill walking
Bowling	Volleyball	Diving	Hockey

Do, play or go: The rules   Go online

What are the rules?

Q2:   From the previous activity, can you summarise the general grammar rules for using DO, PLAY or GO...

We use DO with...	Sports which end in the letters '-ing'
We use PLAY with...	Sports which do not end in the letters '-ing'
We use GO with...	Many sports which involve the use of a ball

2.2 Grammar: Phrasal verbs

Phrasal verbs, sometimes known as multi-word verbs, contain two or more words and have the following structure:

Verb + preposition or adverb

The addition of a preposition/adverb to the standard verb creates a new expression with meaning which differs from that of the original verb.

Phrasal verbs: Sport (1) (15 min)   Go online

Q3: Complete the sentences below using the correct phrasal verb. You may need to change the tense (e.g. make it continuous or past tense etc).

e.g. I was so tired yesterday that I felt like giving up before the race had started!

catch up   warm up   work out   kick off   knock out

send off   give up   join in   take part   take up

a) Jones repeatedly fouled players in the other team and argued with the referee all the way through the first half. I'm amazed that he hasn't been _____.

b) Sports physiotherapists think that a lot of injuries are caused by people not _____ correctly or for long enough before they start exercising.

c) Kirsty's never believed that sport is just about _____ . She always wants to win in everything she does!

d) Alonso tried his best, but with the car seriously underpowered he wasn't able to _____ with the Mercedes and Ferrari ahead of him.

e) Gail keeps herself in shape by going to the gym three times a week to _____.

f) Since he wasn't getting any younger and he had a recurring problem with his knees, Jenas reluctantly _____ professional football three years ago.

g) Everyone in the tennis world was shocked when Nadal was _____ of Wimbledon in the early rounds last year.

h) The surprising thing about the winning athlete was that he didn't even _____ running until he was eleven years old. Before that he played rugby.

i) Chelsea vs. Barcelona in the Champions League final will _____ at 7.45pm on Saturday.

j) The great thing about amateur sport is that more or less anyone can get down to their local sports centre and _____ the activities.

Phrasal verbs: Sport (2) (15 min)   Go online

Look again at your answers to the previous exercise. Can you think of a word or expression which has the same or a similar meaning to the phrasal verbs used?

© HERIOT-WATT UNIVERSITY

Q4: Match the definitions given with the similar phrasal verb.

1. catch up	a. participate
2. warm up	b. expel/remove
3. work out	c. begin (a game)
4. kick off	d. stop
5. knock out	e. exercise
6. send off	f. prepare for exercise
7. give up	g. eliminate
8. join in	h. try/start
9. take part	i. participate/get involved
10. take up	j. become level/equal

2.3 Vocabulary: Sports crossword

Sports crossword (30 min)   Go online

Q5: Complete the crossword using the following sport vocabulary clues.

ACROSS

2. An unreturned tennis serve is called this.

4. Six points in American Football is known as this.

7. Indoor cycling events take place in this kind of arena.

9. It's the fastest sport in the world, with speeds of over 200mph, and surprisingly, it's a racquet game!

11. Originally a popular game with the upper classes of England, this uses wooden mallets and balls and is often played in large country gardens.

12. Movie stars Dolph Lundgren and Jean Claude Van Damme were both successful in this sport before their acting careers started.

13. An equestrian sport which needs the animal and the rider to work together and have perfect timing.

14. Another name for ping pong.

DOWN

1. Jahangir Khan was one of the most famous players in this sport which needs a racquet and some walls.

3. They play a World Series in this game, but only in America!

5. A sport which is played in a pool, but it isn't swimming and there is a ball!

6. This is the object used in the game in one across; like a ball but with feathers.

8. Ten sports make up this athletic event.

10. This is a famous British motor racing team, traditionally driving green cars.

2.4 Speaking: Hobbies and pastimes

Hobbies and pastimes are enjoyable activities that people like to do in their free time. Sport, film and music are very popular hobbies for people of all ages, but there are hundreds of other activities which people do.

Hobbies and pastimes (15 min)

Talk to your partner. Do you know these hobbies? Try to explain them to your partner.

gardening	life drawing	cross stitch	scrapbooks	pottery
coin collecting	role playing games	rambling	genealogy	stamp collecting

Example

gardening - "This is a hobby where people spend a lot of time outdoors, either in their own garden or an allotment, and they plant various seeds and take care of plants and flowers all year round. It is a hobby favoured by older people, but anyone of any age can do it."

2.5   Vocabulary: Hobbies and pastimes

Hobbies and pastimes (15 min)   Go online ❄

Q6:   Complete the following sentences using the hobbies and pastimes mentioned from the previous discussion activity.

gardening	life drawing	cross stitch	scrapbooks	pottery
coin collecting	role playing games	rambling	genealogy	stamp collecting

a) Jackie was never the best at painting when she was young, but she always maintained an interest in art. Recently she decided to take a course in _____ .

b) The map of the world took her about two years to complete, and a lot of material! Now, Linda is working on a new _____ pattern for her friend's grandchildren. . . pictures of farm animals!

c) It can take a few months to become familiar with using the equipment and trying to keep all the clay off your clothes when you're learning _____ .

d) Shannon's grandmother has a fascinating _____ ; hundreds of newspaper articles and cuttings of the royal family from the 1940s to 1980s.

e) People often laughed at Peter when he was young because he enjoyed _____, but he's made a successful career out of it, and earned himself a lot of money selling some of the rarest ones available at auction.

f) The difficulty with _____ is that there are so many variants of the same one, perhaps with a slightly different picture for heads or tails, that it can actually end up being quite expensive to collect all of the different versions!

g) Lucy was really disappointed that a window box was all she could have in her new flat. She had been so used to all that space for _____ when she lived with her parents in the detached house.

h) Every month, about fifty like-minded fans of Middle Earth meet together and take on the personas of Elves, Goblins and Werewolves, as they enjoy _____.

i) In spite of the often overcast weather which means a good waterproof jacket and boots are a necessity, _____ remains one of the most popular pastimes in Scotland.

j) There is a misperception that only elderly people are interested in _____ and that it is some kind of dull, isolated pastime for those who love the inside of libraries.

2.6   Writing: Hobbies and pastimes

My favourite hobby (60 min)

Your college/university student magazine has asked you to write a feature article about your favourite hobby. You should write around 200-250 words. Include information about:

* How you got started in this hobby.

* Cost and time involved in training or equipment for this hobby.

* Reasons why it is an enjoyable hobby and why you would encourage others to do it.

Before you begin, consider the following questions:

1. What is the purpose of the communication?

2. Who is the intended audience?

3. What level of formality and register would be appropriate?

2.7   Vocabulary: Identifying emotive language

Emotive words are words that tend to arouse an emotion in the mind of the reader. For example, a win by a popular local football team may be reported as a 'victory' or a 'success', instead of using the neutral and simple word, 'win'. Similarly, instead of saying a 'loss', the failure to win may be described as a 'catastrophe'.

The tabloid press often uses emotive language to emphasise positive or negative features about a person or event.

Emotive language (1) (15 min)

Go online

Q7: Organise the neutral sporting word(s), on the left, and the emotive counterparts by matching them into pairs.

1) Opponent	a) Slump
2) Defeat	b) Glittering
3) Winner	c) Soar
4) Rise	d) Capitulation
5) Fall	e) Defining moment
6) Important match	f) Adverse
7) Embarrassment	g) Champion
8) Impressive	h) Success
9) Negative	i) Rival
10) Win	j) Disgrace

Emotive language (2) (25 min)

Work with a partner, and use a dictionary or thesaurus if necessary.

Q8: Add the emotive words from the previous exercise to the first column adjacent to the appropriate neutral words. Then add two more EMOTIVE words for each neutral word in the additional emotive columns. Ask your teacher to check your work.

NEUTRAL	EMOTIVE 1	EMOTIVE 2	EMOTIVE 3
Opponent			
Defeat			
Winner			
Rise			
Fall			
Important match			
Embarrassment			
Impressive			
Negative			
Win			

Identifying emotive language (20 min)

Q9: Read the following piece of writing and highlight any emotive words.

The Swedish ice hockey team had a disastrous collapse in their heroic effort to secure the ultimate prize of the Olympic gold medal. The fall out of the humiliation was plastered all over the front covers of shameless tabloid newspapers all week.
. . . .

Q10: Rewrite the short text above in a NEUTRAL register. Sometimes it may be possible just to remove the emotive word. Ask your teacher to check your work.

2.8   Pronunciation: Syllables and word stress

Syllables and word stress   Go online

You will need the following sound files to complete this activity:
n5-esl1-2-1pronunc1.mp3 to *n5-esl1-2-1pronunc12.mp3*

Look at the following list of words from this unit. They are all related to the topic of Sport and Leisure.

Q11: For each word complete the table by answering these two questions:

1. How many syllables does each word have?
2. Where is the stress?

	Syllables and word stress
e.g. Leisure	*Oo*
Opponent	
Rival	
Capitulation	
Champion	
Eliminate	
Badminton	
Croquet	
Shuttlecock	
Zumba	
Genealogy	
Participant	
Velodrome	

2.9   Reading comprehension: Olympic parents

Reading comprehension: Olympic parents (45 min)   Go online

Read the passage of text and then answer the questions that follow.

Olympic Parents

The increasing amount of technology around today, from the multitude of cameras pointing solely at the audience of sporting events to the social networking sites that athletes' friends and families can all post updates on, means that nowadays staying out of the limelight can be almost as hard for the entourage as it is for the sports star. For the television producers, the action in the crowd can be almost as good TV as the event on the track or in the pool. Parents tend to live out the event with their offspring, covering their eyes and peering out, clapping, shouting, jumping up and down - there is nearly as much athletic action from the family as there is in the event! If the parents cap it all by crying, whether it is tears of sadness or joy, then you can bet that the newspapers will be queuing up to run those pictures the following day.

For the parents themselves, there are differing ways of dealing with the rollercoaster of emotion. One mother we spoke to, who did not want to be named, said that it was just "another aspect of life". For her son, born two months prematurely, then diagnosed with a rare form of leukaemia which he fought through, there have always been battles and hurdles to overcome. "He was the shortest kid in his class until the age of nine... and to be honest, although he loved swimming then, nobody foresaw either his sprout in height or the successes that followed in the pool. He's always been a real battler though. We had a car accident when he was eleven, two broken legs that we thought would finish his swimming... but no, it just made him work harder and longer when he had recovered... then we had the disappointment of losing his place on the national junior team due to a false start in the trials. Again, it just fuelled his desire further to reach the very top at the next opportunity."

The challenges of being a parent of an athlete are compensated for by sporting achievement. "That's how we have dealt with it. Seeing your child sick, injured or in pain is almost unbearable, and seeing them so disappointed is also really tough... but, for every one of these hard or unpleasant experiences we have also seen him elated as he won his way through school trials, regional finals and then, international meetings. You have to take the rough with the smooth and just be there to support them... I mean, they are your kids after all, the worst thing you could do would be to discourage them from achieving their dreams."

It's not just the emotional journey that Olympic families go through. There are serious financial implications for many as well. "It depends on the sport your child takes up", one parent told us. "We used to be fairly well off as a family, I was working as an accountant and my wife was a lawyer, but as we invested more of our time in our daughter's career, we also discovered we needed to invest more of our own money". This family have sold their four bedroom villa and now live in a more modest two bedroom flat, and they operate on a tight monthly budget to help finance their daughter's aspiring badminton career. "She travels all over Europe and goes to Asia a few times a year. These trips don't pay for themselves, and the prize money in badminton just doesn't compare with what you can earn in, say, tennis. But she's got a talent, she has a chance at an Olympic medal... and that's something that makes you forget how much it's all costing."

Q12: Where do you think you might read this kind of text?

a) broadsheet newspaper

b) sports journal

c) tabloid newspaper

....

Q13: Which features of language used in the text support your answer? Select four from the list below.

1. Formal language

2. Informal language

3. Reported speech

4. Direct speech

5. Short sentences

6. Long sentences

7. Idiomatic phrases

8. Inversion

....

Q14: What reason does the writer suggest for the high profile given to families of sports stars today?

....

Q15: Give a word or phrase from the text which suggests that being the parent of a sports star is:

a) a turbulent experience

b) a role which involves coping with success and failure

....

Q16: What are the main issues affecting sporting families discussed in the text? Give two answers.

....

Q17: List three physical challenges that the swimmer had to conquer.

....

Q18: What sacrifice have the parents of the badminton player made?

2.10   Listening comprehension: Video games

Listening comprehension: Video games (30 min)	Go online

You will need the following sound file to complete this listening assessment: *n5-esl1-2-2listening.mp3*

Q19: Professor Connors is a professor of child _____
....

Q20: He has spent _____ years researching the effects of video games on the young.
....

Q21: The media are generally highly critical of the impact of video games on young people.

1. True
2. False

....

Q22: Professor Connors believes that there are three main elements involved in assessing the impact of video games.

1. True
2. False

....

Q23: Professor Connors believes that those studying the impact of video games need to consider other factors in children's lives.

1. True
2. False

....

Q24: Pick three correct answers. Professor Connors suggests that children might use video games when they:

1. feel unhappy.
2. feel powerful.
3. do not fit in.
4. are getting good grades.
5. have no friends.

....

Q25: Where do you think you might hear this kind of discussion?
....

Q26: Professor Connors is currently exploring the consequences of using controls for video games.

1. True
2. False

....

Q27: Professor Connors is unrealistic about the need for a lot more research.

1. True
2. False

....

Q28: Professor Connors thinks that the arguments around video games lack sufficient analysis.

1. True
2. False

Unit 1 Topic 3

Physical environment

Contents

Learning objective

By the end of this topic you will be better able to:

- participate in a conversation about society; contemporary culture and more;

- express obligation, possibility and ability and make polite requests using modal auxiliary verbs;

- identify and distinguish between formal and informal language;

- identify features of organisation in letters of complaint;

- prepare and write a formal letter of complaint;

- listen to and understand spoken language through a focus on elision as a feature of connected speech.

3.1   Speaking: Discussion: Leisure activities

Leisure activities (10 min)

Discuss the following questions with a partner if possible.

1. What kind of things do you like to do in your spare time?

2. Where do you go when you want to relax?

3. Do you spend your free time with your family? What kinds of things do you do?

Parks are popular venues for families in the UK. Write a list of things you would expect to see in a park.

3.2   Vocabulary: Parks

Vocabulary: Parks (15 min)

Q1: Try to unscramble the vocabulary list below of things you may find in a park.

1. ndop

2. ssgra

3. eetrs

4. lwfoser

5. ngswis

6. cildehrn

7. cei / rcaem / nav

8. iptutgn / negre

9. blionwg / negre

10. dsog

3.3 Listening activity: British parks

Post listening activity: Answer the questions (15 min) Go online 🔊

You will need the following sound file to complete this exercise:
n5-esl1-3-1listening.mp3

Q2: Name the amenities which are available in the park.
....

Q3: What does each interviewee do there?

Post-listening activity: Match words and phrases to the correct speaker Go online 🔊
(20 min)

You will need the following sound file for this activity:
n5-esl1-3-1listening.mp3

Listen to the passage again and answer these questions.

Q4: Match the words and phrases to the correct speaker.

dapper	teacher	energetic	mum
retired	busy	tweed jacket	fitness gear
carrying papers	hat	young	trainer

Find phrases and idiomatic expressions from the dialogue to match the following definitions:

Q5: Become involved in things (perhaps after a quiet period in one's life)
....

Q6: Talk to someone briefly
....

Q7: Full (of life)
....

Q8: Analyse/Discuss
....

Q9: A habit which is intended to improve health
....

Q10: Considered too old to be useful or attractive
....

Q11: Something which is a well-established behaviour

....

Q12: Relax/allow yourself much more freedom than usual

....

Q13: Enjoy something very much/get fun from something

....

Q14: Clothes designed to be used for exercising

Post-listening activity: Which speaker?   Go online

Q15: Select the appropriate speaker (speaker 1, speaker 2 or speaker 3) for each statement. Who...?

a) Goes to the park every day?

b) Is trying to manage his/her weight?

c) Appreciates the games available in the park?

d) Appreciates nature in the park?

e) Takes a family member with them?

f) Does not live near the park?

g) Found out about an activity through the internet?

h) Was introduced to their activity through a friend?

i) Eats in the park?

3.4   Vocabulary: Using idiomatic expressions

Sentences using idiomatic expressions (15 min)

Now write example sentences of your own, using each of the phrases below which are taken from the previous activity and if possible ask your teacher to check them.

- To get out there

- Have a quick chat

- Teeming with life

- Chew over (something)

- Daily constitutional

- Over the hill
- An institution
- Let your hair down
- Get a kick out of something
- Fitness gear

3.5 Grammar: Modal auxiliary verbs

Modal auxiliary verbs (10 min)

The following sentences are from the earlier listening activity.

1. I must dash
2. You may feel a little over the hill
3. I can see
4. (they) should try it

Q16: Underline the modal auxiliary verb in each of the sentences above.

. . . .

Q17: Match each of the modal auxiliary verbs with the general meanings given in this table.

a) Recommendation/advice
b) Necessity
c) Possibility
d) Ability

3.6 Grammar: Modal auxiliary verbs: Choosing the correct modal

Positive or negative form (15 min)   Go online ❄

Complete the following sentences using either must, may, can or should in either positive or negative form.

Q18:

1. I _____ stop smoking as the doctor has told me it is contributing to my high blood pressure.
2. She does not enjoy walking in the park as she _____ see the point in it.
3. I think my husband _____ try jogging. He really wants to lose weight.
4. If you pick up a local newspaper you _____ be able to find out about activities available in your area.
5. You _____ take your dog out for a walk if you want to meet people.
6. There are lots of amazing films on this month. We really _____ go to the cinema.
7. I _____ understand why he is lonely, after all his wife has only just passed away.
8. I think you _____ be surprised at how many people pass through the park, even on rainy days.
9. She really _____ spend so much time on her own. I think it's bad for her.
10. I have been told by my family that I _____ overdo it, but I can't resist going to fitness classes.

3.7 Grammar: Modal auxiliary verbs: Meaning, form and use

Modal auxiliary verbs are used in conjunction with other verbs (the main verb) to provide further information about the attitude of the speaker or about what is being said.

Examples

1. Certain modal verbs are linked to particular situations such as when we wish to indicate that something is a good idea, is necessary or to make a polite request .

- *I should exercise more (I think it is a good idea)*
- *I must eat less (it is necessary)*
- *Can I have a coffee please? (I am making a polite request)*

....

2. Some modal verbs have more than one meaning.

- *I can play the piano (to express ability)*

- *Can I play the piano? (to ask permission)*

....

3. In other cases different modal verbs may be very close in meaning.

   a) *I must lose weight I want to be healthier*
   b) *The doctor says I have to lose weight*

....

In the first example the obligation is apparently self imposed while in the second example the obligation is imposed upon the speaker. This distinction is not necessarily always clear and the two forms are sometimes used interchangeably.

The following are known as pure modals: may, might, must, can, could, shall, should, will and would.

The features of pure modals are as follows:

1. Modals do not have a third person' s' e.g. *'she must eat less'* **not** *'she musts eat less'*

2. Modals are followed by the base or infinitive verb without to e.g. *'he must eat less'* **not** *'he must to eat less'*
   Key Point: Exceptions are 'ought' and 'have (got)' which are considered semi-modal or modal in form and are followed by a 'to' infinitive e.g. *she ought to lose weight, she has (got) to lose weight.*

3. The negative is formed using not or a contraction e.g. *I should not (shouldn't) eat chocolate*

4. In general modals are not used in a past form.
   Key Point: It is possible to use 'can' in the past, by changing it to 'could' e.g. *he can play piano, he could play piano*

5. With pure modals a past tense may be formed using have + the past participle e.g. *he should exercise more* becomes *he should have exercised more*

Examples

1. Where we wish to refer to the past and are using a modal, a different modal is often more appropriate.

- *We can go shopping today / we were able to go shopping (earlier).*
- *I must go out / I had to go out.*

....

2. In some situations 'could' for ability is not used.
'I was able to pick up my car from the mechanic yesterday'

3.7.1 Grammar: Practice: Referring to the past

Modal verbs: Referring to the past (25 min)   Go online

Replace the modals in the following sentences with past tense equivalents.

e.g. She must leave or she will miss the plane / she had to leave or she would have missed the plane

Q19:

  a) You can see the whole of the city from my window. You _____ see the whole of the city from my window.
  b) I must lose weigh before the summer holidays. I _____ lose weight before the summer holidays.
  c) I should try and meet new people and change my lifestyle a bit. I _____ to meet new people and change my lifestyle a bit.
  d) I may enjoy life more if I make more of an effort. I _____ enjoyed life more if I had made more of an effort.
  e) She can get her results today. She _____ to get her results yesterday.
  f) He may be late because of the traffic. He _____ late because of traffic.
  g) He shouldn't smoke but he is addicted. He _____ smoked but he was addicted.
  h) You mustn't get worked up - it's bad for your blood pressure. You _____ got worked up - it's bad for your blood pressure.
  i) They can't understand the questions. They _____ understand the questions.
  j) We must do more exercise. We _____ do more exercise.

3.8 Reading activity: Three mysteries

Three mysteries (20 min)

Modal verbs such as *may, might, must, can* and their negative forms can be used to indicate a degree of certainty in a given situation.

Imagine the following scenarios. Using a range of suitable modal auxiliary verbs, think about and if possible discuss with a partner what has /could have happened in each case. e.g. he can't have escaped because the doors and windows were locked.

Decide what happened in each of these scenarios.

Mary lives alone in a two bedroom flat. She has a cat which is not allowed to go out because Mary is afraid that it will run away. Mary leaves early for work, locking the door behind her as she goes. She meets her friend after work and finally returns home at ten o'clock. There is nothing particularly unusual about the appearance of the flat when she gets home, although the blind is open and Mary usually leaves it closed when she is planning to be home late. She looks at the blind and the curtains for a moment wondering why they look so untidy. She walks into the kitchen there is cat food all over the floor. She calls Sooty the cat. He usually comes to greet her but not tonight. She calls his name again and starts to look around for him but there is no response and he is nowhere to be seen. What has happened?

a) The cat had been stolen.

b) The cat had hidden.

c) The cat had escaped.

Sharon and Sally are friends. Once a week they go to an evening class. After the class they always go for dinner in a café. Sharon and Sally always have a lot to talk about, especially after the Spanish class because in the class they are too embarrassed to say anything. They chat and laugh without taking a breath and without paying much attention to what is going on around them. On this particular evening, they find the area near the café very busy. Their favourite parking place is taken and as they start to look for another parking place they realise that there are lots of parking restrictions. Eventually they manage to find a place near a church not too far from the café. They are so busy laughing and practising their Spanish pronunciation that they hardly notice when Sally drops her phone. A passing stranger stops them to hand the phone over to her. They walk to the café and then go inside where they have great food and a really good chat. After eating they leave and walk to their parking place. There is no sign of the car. What has happened?

a) They have forgotten where they parked.

b) They have parked in a prohibited area and the police have towed the car away.

c) The car has been stolen.

Pam was really excited about moving house. She was particularly looking forward to sitting on the bench in the front garden. She was really disappointed when she moved in to discover that the bench was not sitting where it had been. In fact there was no bench anywhere in the front garden or to the rear of the house. The next door neighbours seemed to have acquired a bench which was sitting in their back garden and this made Pam a little envious. Pam and her husband had a lot of expenditure that first year in their new home, so they didn't really want to buy a new bench. Pam tried not to think about it. Just over a year later she came home from work one day to discover a bench sitting in the front garden exactly as it had been when she first saw the house. What had happened?

a) The owners had taken the bench when they moved out but were now returning it.

b) The neighbours had taken Pam's bench but felt guilty so were now returning it.

c) Pam's husband had decided to surprise her as he knew that she had liked the bench so much.

3.9   Listening activity: Listening: Three mysteries

Listening comprehension: Three mysteries (20 min)   Go online

You will require the following sound file for this activity:
n5-esl1-3-2listening1.mp3, *n5-esl1-3-2listening2.mp3* and *n5-esl1-3-2listening3.mp3*

Listen again to three speakers describing what actually happened.

Q20: How did Speaker 1 feel at each stage of the events described? Give **three** answers.

....

Q21: How did Speaker 2 feel? Give **two** answers.

....

Q22: How did Speaker 3 feel at each stage of the events described? There are **five** possible answers.

3.10   Pronunciation: Features of connected speech: Elision

Features of connected speech: Elision   Go online

You will need the following sound files to complete this activity:
n5-esl1-3-3listening1.mp3 to *n5-esl1-3-3listening9.mp3*

Q23: Read out loud the following phrases and try to stress the appropriate words. Indicate the stress in the appropriate place for each sentence.

1. He must've escaped
2. He can't have escaped
3. He must be hiding
4. We can't have parked here
5. It may have been towed away
6. It must've been stolen
7. It may have been the previous owners
8. It can't have just appeared
9. It must've been a friend who put it there

Now **listen** and compare your pronunciation with that of the speaker. Note the way in which the 'h' sound following each modal is lost. This is known as **elision** and is quite a common feature of connected speech. This process of dropping a sound makes phrases easier to say.

3.11   Speaking: Discussion: Letters of complaint

Letters of complaint (10 min)

Consider the following questions and if possible discuss them with a partner or group. Make notes on the different types of answers you and your group/partner give.

1. Have you ever written a formal letter of complaint? Who did you write to and why?

2. In what situations might you be prompted to write a letter of complaint and to whom would you write?

3.12 Reading comprehension: Letters of complaint

Dear Sir/Madam

I have lived in the Mary Bridge area of the city for nearly twenty years and have always been happy here. However, recently I have become aware of a steady increase in the amount of litter which seems to be amassing in public places. I think that something should be done to rectify this situation as a matter of urgency.

Last week I was walking in the Botanic Gardens. I was horrified to find a stream of litter from the entrance on George Terrace to the top of the hill. This included sweet wrappers, empty drink cans and other debris. This is not only unsightly but it is also a hazard. Elderly people could easily trip over cans or slip on wrappers. Toddlers and dogs are also at risk from sharp edges of empty drink cans and the toxic remains of food packages.

Many tourists choose to come and visit our historic city. I am convinced that they must depart with a very poor **impression**. Recently we were awarded City of Culture status. Despite this, many residents are apparently completely disinterested in the impression we give to visitors. I find this extremely embarrassing and puzzling. Surely it is imperative that we encourage tourists to enhance our **dwindling** economy.

I would recommend local government **initiate** a campaign to encourage both adults and children to pick up their waste and introduce stricter **penalties** for those who contravene. At the moment many fines for this misdemeanour remain unpaid. This is a situation which must be corrected forthwith.

I look forward to your early response.

Yours faithfully

Reading comprehension: Letters of complaint (20 min)

Read the letter and answer the questions.

Dear Sir/Madam

I have lived in the Mary Bridge area of the city for nearly twenty years and have always been happy here. However, recently I have become aware of a steady increase in the amount of litter which seems to be amassing in public places. I think that something should be done to rectify this situation as a matter of urgency.

Last week I was walking in the Botanic Gardens. I was horrified to find a stream of litter from the entrance on George Terrace to the top of the hill. This included sweet wrappers, empty drink cans and other debris. This is not only unsightly but it is also a hazard. Elderly people could easily trip over cans or slip on wrappers. Toddlers and dogs are also at risk from sharp edges of empty drink cans and the toxic remains of food packages.

Many tourists choose to come and visit our historic city. I am convinced that they must depart with a very poor impression. Recently we were awarded City of Culture status. Despite this, many residents are apparently completely disinterested in the impression we give to visitors. I find this extremely embarrassing and puzzling. Surely it is imperative that we encourage tourists to enhance our dwindling economy.

I would recommend local government initiate a campaign to encourage both adults and children to pick up their waste and introduce stricter penalties for those who contravene.

At the moment many fines for this misdemeanour remain unpaid. This is a situation which must be corrected forthwith.

I look forward to your early response.

Yours faithfully

Q24: What is the writer angry about?

....

Q25: What are the writer's main objections? Give 3 answers.

....

Q26: To whom do you think the letter is written?

....

Q27: What solutions does the writer offer for the problem? Give 2 answers.

....

Q28: Match descriptions of content to the appropriate paragraph.

- Possible solutions
- Conclusion
- Discussion of why litter creates a bad impression
- Introduction
- Description of the problem and why it is a hazard

3.13   Vocabulary: Formal language

Formal language (20 min)

Dear Sir/Madam

I have lived in the Mary Bridge area of the city for nearly twenty years and have always been happy here. However, recently I have become aware of a steady increase in the amount of litter which seems to be amassing in public places. I think that something should be done to rectify this situation as a matter of some urgency.

Last week I was walking in the Botanic Gardens. I was horrified to find a stream of litter from the entrance on George Terrace to the top of the hill. This included sweet wrappers, empty drink cans and other debris. This is not only unsightly but it is also a hazard. Elderly people could easily trip over cans or slip on wrappers. Toddlers and dogs are also at risk from sharp edges of empty drink cans and toxic remains of food packages.

Many tourists choose to come and visit our historic city. I am convinced that they must depart with a very poor impression. Recently we were awarded City of Culture status. Despite this, many residents are apparently completely disinterested in the impression we give to visitors. I find this extremely embarrassing and puzzling. Surely it is imperative that we encourage tourists to enhance our dwindling economy.

I would recommend local government initiate a campaign to encourage both adults and children to pick up their waste and introduce stricter penalties for those who contravene. At the moment many fines for this misdemeanour remain unpaid. This is a situation which must be corrected forthwith.

I look forward to your early response.

Yours faithfully

Q29: The writer of the letter of complaint uses formal language. Look at the list of informal/neutral words below and find **formal** equivalents in the text.

Informal/Neutral	Formal
1. Building up	
2. Fixed/sorted	
3. Rubbish	
4. Ugly	
5. Sure	
6. Go/leave	
7. Idea	
8. Vital	
9. Start	
10. Disobey	
11. Crime	
12. Immediately	

3.14 Writing Activity: Genre analysis: Letters of complaint

A letter of complaint (60 min)

You have noticed that there is a lot of **graffiti** on bus shelters, park benches and garages in your local area. You are concerned because it looks unsightly and because you feel slightly threatened by the idea that gangs of youths are responsible for this vandalism. Write to your local authority asking them to step up the police presence in the area and also increase **penalties** for offenders.

You should write around 250 words.

Before you begin, consider the following questions:

1. What is the purpose of the communication?
2. Who is the intended audience?
3. What level of formality and register would be appropriate?

3.15 Study skills: Note taking

In pairs or groups think about the following questions:

1. What is the purpose behind note taking while you are reading or listening?
2. What are the most effective ways of taking notes?
3. How should you organise your notes?
4. What should you do with notes you have taken at lectures / seminars or while reading?

Note taking in study situations (20 min)

The following words have been extracted from the text below on note taking. Read and try to complete the gaps.

distinguish; possible; passive; learning; subject; focus; receive; approaches; process; active; revision; speaker; comfortable; rewrite

Q30:
There are many reasons why it is really important to learn how to take notes effectively, regardless of the 1._____ which we are studying. In the first place taking notes helps us to 2._____ more effectively on the context. This prevents us from allowing our minds to wander in different directions; thinking about our plans for later or what we are going to have for lunch.

It has been found that the 3._____ of doing more than one thing at a time, such as listening or reading as well as taking notes is more stimulating and, as a result, more conducive to 4._____. When we take notes we are processing information as we 5._____ it, organising ideas in our heads as we do so. Therefore the process of note taking is 6._____ rather than 7._____ which we also know is a more effective approach to learning. Finally, the notes which we take can be revisited at a later date and can be the basis of 8._____ for exams or assignments which can take a lot of pressure off!

There are a number of different ways in which our notes may be organised in order to support our study. We should 9._____ between fact and opinion in our minds and summarise what we read or hear accordingly. Summaries are more useful than noting down the words of the reader or 10._____ exactly since this process engages our mind. Different people have different 11._____ to taking notes such as drawing maps, pictures or tables or using coloured pens. It is important to find a method that you are 12._____ with and that works for you and then stick to this.

When you have taken notes it is important not to put them away and forget about them. Revisit your notes as soon as 13._____ after you have written them. At this stage you should also 14._____ the notes if possible and then organise them so that you can easily find them again. Don't forget to review your notes as often as possible to keep the ideas fresh in your mind. Good luck!!

3.16   Reading comprehension: The National Trust

Reading comprehension: The National Trust   Go online

The National Trust in Scotland is a charitable organisation which maintains land and property.

"Our responsibility is to retain the significance of all that has been entrusted to us for the benefit of future generations.   We achieve this by promoting conservation, access and enjoyment as a single experience."[1]

A prime example of this work is Pollok House in Glasgow, which is set in around 360 acres of land in Pollok Park. Although Glasgow, Gaelic for 'dear green place', is privileged to have around 90 parks, Pollok Park is the only park with extensive woods and land. Just three miles from the city centre, it offers a peaceful contrast to the busy industrial city beyond its gardens and woodlands.

Pollok House was commissioned by the Maxwell family who had been established in the area for several hundred years. The house was completed in 1752. The identity of the architect is unknown, but the exterior of the building is in a simple style. The interior, which is more decorative and ornate, is thought to be the responsibility of the Clayton family. They were also involved in the spectacular plaster work at Blair castle.

The house we see today includes an extension which was added in the late 1900s. This enabled a fine collection of paintings including work by Goya and El Greco and around 7000 books owned by the family to be accommodated. Later, during the First World War, the house was used as a hospital. It is fitting that it was it was here in 1931 that Sir John Stirling Maxwell arranged a meeting which led to the National Trust for Scotland being established. After Maxwell's death in 1956, the house, land, artwork and books were all passed to the city of Glasgow, and in 1998 they became the property of the National Trust.

Today, the property is open to the public. Visitors can enjoy the experience of wandering around the house and gardens and looking round the old sawmill which is part of the estate. Pollok Park was chosen as Britain's best park in 2006 and Europe's best park in 2008. It is very much a part of everyday life for those who live in the surrounding area. A big effort is made to involve the community around family days, which feature face painting, farmer's markets and Shire horses. Families are also encouraged to visit whenever the Shire horses have their shoes changed. Guided walks are available too, and these cover information on all things food and all things wood. Pollok Estate is also home to the Burrell Gallery which houses the private collection of around 9000 works of art that belonged to Sir William Burrell and his wife.

Whether you are interested in history or art or simply enjoy nature walks in beautiful surroundings, Pollok estate has lots to offer.

(1) http://www.nts.org.uk/Conserve/

Q31: 1. Where might you read this kind of text?

a) In a daily newspaper

b) In a personal letter

c) In a leaflet promoting the park

Are the following statements true or false?

Q32: The National Trust is a profiteering organisation
....

Q33: The National Trust secures properties through gifts
....

Q34: The building of Pollok House was instructed by:

1. an unknown architect.

2. the Maxwell family.

3. the Clayton family.
....

Q35: Find a word or phrase in the text with the following meaning "made something possible".
....

Q36: Find a word or phrase in the text with the following meaning "set-up".
....

Q37: Find a word or phrase in the text with the following meaning "it is appropriate".

3.17   Speaking: Discussion: Food and diet

Before beginning the next listening assessment, do this supplementary exercise. You should spend approximately 15 minutes on this.

Food and diet

Interview your partner using the following questions:

1. Would you describe yourself as a gourmand or gourmet? (Use a dictionary to look up these terms if necessary)

2. Do you eat to live or live to eat?

3. What is your favourite food?

4. Do you think you are a healthy weight?

5. Have you ever been on a diet?

3.18   Listening comprehension: Recycling

Listening comprehension: Recycling (30 min)   Go online

You will need the following sound file to complete this assessment activity:
n5-esl1-3-4listening.mp3

Q38: How do the speakers know each other?

....

Q39: Where did Magnus get his compost bin?

....

Q40: What two processes for composting does Magnus describe?

....

Q41: What method of composting is Magnus planning to use?

....

Q42: Why has he chosen this method?

....

Q43: What are the two categories of rubbish called?

....

Q44: What kind of waste is slow to rot?

....

Q45: Why should people not put cooked food on a compost heap?

....

Q46: What is the difference between fertiliser and compost?

....

Q47: Give **three** reasons why Magnus has decided start composting.

....

Q48: Who are Victoria and Sarah?

Unit 1 Topic 4

Goods and services

Contents

Learning objective

By the end of this topic you will be better able to:

- participate in a conversation about obtaining and providing goods and services in the context of shopping, the food industry, the health service and relocating;

- identify prevalent use of conditional sentences in conversation;

- identify the use of informal language in writing emails;

- write an informal email.

4.1   Reading activity: Shopping

Discuss the following questions with a partner (if possible):

* Do you prefer to visit shops and shopping centres or do you prefer shopping online?
* What are the advantages and disadvantages of shops / online shopping?

Reading activity: Shopping

Read the text and then answer the questions which follow.

Paragraph 1

Footfall in UK high streets has been in steady decline over the last fifteen to twenty years, and the impact on small businesses has been well documented. The change can be attributed to several factors which have undermined trade in a series of body blows, including: increased traffic congestion, the rise of out-of-town shopping centres and growth in internet shopping. As the online retail industry continues to expand and refine, allowing for ever more sophisticated shopping options, it is perhaps surprising that we find anyone in 'bricks and mortar' shops at all these days.

Paragraph 2

The decline in popularity of the high street is obvious across the UK. It's reflected in boarded-up windows and seemingly endless charity shops, the latter of which are bolstered by tax benefits, enabling their survival. City centres may appear more equipped to deal with current trends than town centres, offering a wide variety of outlets which lure a range of customers. Nevertheless, statistics indicate that even here retailers are suffering.

Paragraph 3

Imagine my surprise then, when on a recent trip to my local city centre I emerged, mid-morning, from the underground station to witness a sea of bodies surging en masse along a pedestrian precinct. Closer inspection revealed a multitude of shoppers had already beaten me to the end of season sales, many armed with masses of carrier bags which testified to the seriousness of their expedition. These were not just window shoppers. As I squeezed myself into an already overcrowded department store, I wondered what it was about this type of experience that had attracted so many customers. Sales always lure bargain hunters but very similar sales also take place online these days. On a damp Saturday morning, what drew hordes of us from our comfy sofas and mugs of tea which internet shopping enables, in favour of traffic, noise and wet feet?

Paragraph 4

Arguments in favour of physical rather than virtual shops correspond to arguments levelled against technology in other contexts. Internet shopping is anti-social while going out is sociable, involves meeting real live people, is stimulating, inspiring and altogether more 'human'. For retailers, real live consumers are more likely to make a random or impulse purchase. Staying at home means there is no buzz, no chance encounter, and no opportunity to try on and experience an outfit or spot the perfect dining table and chairs.

Paragraph 5

In the last few years providers of internet shopping services have improved the provision of goods and services in line with consumer preference. Options available are more sophisticated now than in the past. Attractions surpass the ability to browse many stores without moving from an armchair. Issues around waiting times and inconvenient delivery times have been addressed. We can opt for express service, click to purchase and collect in-store or even pick up our purchases at a nominated local shop. More recently, larger providers have organised pickup points in lockable safes for those people who are out at work in the daytime. At the same time, options for returning unwanted goods also continue to improve.

Paragraph 6

In spite of the increased effectiveness of the internet to meet our shopping needs and the apparent disappearance of town centre shops, it appears that 90% of shopping today is in actual rather than virtual shops. Despite fears to the contrary, the internet has not yet succeeded in taking over.

Paragraph 7

My own preferences depend on what I am shopping for. On the Saturday in question I needed practical clothes and the bargain hunting mob was making this really difficult. I headed home to the comfort of my living room and my laptop, where I bought the necessary items in a more efficient way. Had I wanted a book or a sofa however, that would have been an entirely different matter.

Complete the sentences below with **no more than four words** from paragraphs 1-3 of the text:

Q1: The number of people going shopping in town is . . . .

. . . .

Q2: Internet shopping is a serious threat to shops because of the willingness among providers to . . . .

. . . .

Q3: Town centre . . . . owe their continuing existence to government assistance.

. . . .

Q4: The idea that city centres are failing was discredited for the writer when she witnessed . . . . one Saturday morning.

Find words or phrases **in paragraphs 4-5** with the following meanings:

Q5: A meeting which has not been planned (two words)

. . . .

Q6: Corresponding to (three words)

....

Q7: Exceed

....

Q8: Dealt with

Choose the correct answer for each question:

Q9: The writer suggests that the main opposition to internet shopping is that:

a) it is often inefficient.
b) it is often uncomfortable.
c) the experience is isolating.

....

Q10: Which of these statements best reflects the writer's approach to shopping?

a) She prefers to avoid crowded shopping areas.
b) She opts for a method that suits her purpose.
c) She much prefers online shopping.

4.2 Listening activity: Food shopping

Pre-listening: Speaking about shopping habits

Discuss the following questions with a partner (if possible):

- Do you 'eat to live' or 'live to eat'? How important is taste and quality of food to you?
- What options do you have for food shopping in your local area? For example; Do you have supermarkets, specialist shops and markets near where you live?
- Where do you do your food shopping?

Pre-listening: Vocabulary Go online

Match the words and phrases to their definitions / meanings.

Q11:

1. On the other hand	a. Pretend something is different from that which it really is
2. Specialist	b. Person who really savours food
3. Nutritious	c. Fashionable
4. Foodie (informal)	d. Keeping in supply / available for purchase
5. Stocking	e. Consuming food as fuel without much interest in the taste
6. Trendy	f. Cooking without using any pre-prepared ingredients
7. Eat to live	g. Introduces the opposite side of an argument / discussion
8. Make from scratch	h. Enjoyable to eat
9. Delicious	i. Food which is good for our health
10. To pass something off	j. Expert

Listening comprehension: Food shopping Go online

To complete this activity, you will need the following sound file:
n5-esl1-4-1listening.mp3

Complete the sentences below using **no more than four words** from the recording:

Q12: Kim is . . . . her local supermarket.

. . . .

Q13: Mandy says her local supermarket has a section . . . .

. . . .

Q14: Kim admits she should perhaps be . . . .

. . . .

Q15: It really upsets Mandy to see . . . .

Indicate whether the adjectives below describe Kim or Mandy:

Q16: Single

a) Kim
b) Mandy

....

Q17: Apologetic

a) Kim
b) Mandy

....

Q18: Considerate

a) Kim
b) Mandy

....

Q19: Sociable

a) Kim
b) Mandy

....

Q20: Family-oriented

a) Kim
b) Mandy

....

Q21: Carefree

a) Kim
b) Mandy

....

Q22: Choose the sentence which best describes the relationship between Kim and Mandy.

a) Polite but disinterested
b) Affectionate and tolerant
c) Hostile

4.3 Listening Activity: Provision of health care: Health care professionals

Pre-listening activity: Speaking: Health related employment (20 min)

Discuss the following with a partner if possible.

   a) How many jobs can you think of which are related to physical health?

   b) How many jobs can you think of which are related to mental health?

Q23: With a partner try to work out the meanings of the following phrases.

   a) Test the water

   b) A strong sense of camaraderie

   c) Work hard and play hard

   d) Better late than never

   e) It's not all plain sailing

   f) My job is very rewarding

   g) To my mind

4.4 Health care professionals

Listening comprehension: Health care professionals (30 min)   Go online

Task A

Listen to the following interviews in which three health care professionals were asked to talk about their work in response to questions. While listening try to work out what five questions they were asked.

You will need the following sound files to complete this activity:
n5-esl1-4-2listening1.mp3, n5-esl1-4-2listening2.mp3 and *n5-esl1-4-2listening3.mp3.*

Q24: What five questions were the speakers asked?

   a) What ....?

   b) How long ....?

   c) Do you ....?

   d) What are ....?

   e) Do you ....?

Task B

Now listen again and while listening take notes on the answers given by the health care professionals. How did the healthcare professionals respond?

Q25: How did speaker 1, Alison, answer the questions?

....

Q26: How did speaker 2, Campbell, answer the questions?

....

Q27: How did speaker 3, Delia, answer the questions?

4.5   Grammar: Conditional sentences: Focus on meaning

Conditional sentences: Focus on meaning (10 min)   Go online

Look at the following statements from the previous listening activity.

You will need the following sound files to complete this activity:
n5-esl1-4-2listening1.mp3, n5-esl1-4-2listening2.mp3 and *n5-esl1-4-2listening3.mp3*.

1. If I get a place, I will definitely go on and do the nursing course.
2. If you are an auxiliary nurse, you have to work shifts.
3. If I had known how much I would enjoy It , I would have trained a long time ago.
4. If I could trade places with anyone though, I would probably be a sports coach for an international athlete.

Q28: Match these statements to the definitions of purpose. Which of the statements above:

a) refers to a general truth?
b) refers to an unreal or hypothetical situation?
c) refers to a possible future outcome?
d) infers regret about a situation in the past and the impact that has had on the present?

4.6   Grammar: Conditional sentences: Meaning and form

When we wish to express the idea that one thing is contingent upon another, we often use conditional sentences. Conditional sentences generally consist of two clauses in which the subordinate clause begins with *if* and is often, though not necessarily, placed before the main clause. There are four general types or patterns of conditionals: zero, first, second and third.

Example : Zero Conditional

Meaning: The zero conditional is used to refer to general or universal truths.

If you want to study medicine, you have to pass a lot of exams.

Form: Subordinate Clause - If + present tense   Main Clause - present tense

Example : First Conditional

Meaning: the first conditional is used to refer to the future, to indicate ways in which the future is contingent upon present behaviour. This might take the form of warning or negotiating. As in other conditional sentences the subordinate clause or the main clause can come first.

If you pass all your exams, you will qualify for medical college.
You won't pass your exams if you don't study.

Form: Subordinate Clause - If + present tense   Main Clause - future tense

---
Key point

It is possible to use any form of the present tense i.e. simple, continuous or perfect in the 'if' clause. It is also possible to substitute 'should' for 'if'. Sometimes you can use an imperative in the main clause.

e.g.   *Should you pass all your exams, you will be accepted for medical college.*

         If you want to go to medical college, work hard!

Example : Second Conditional

Meaning: the second conditional is used to talk about hypothetical or unreal situations. We use this structure to talk about present or future where we know or believe that something is not or may not be possible.

If I knew how to resolve my insomnia, I would be relieved.
If I got a chance to go to medical college, I would jump at it.

Form: Subordinate Clause - If + past tense   Main Clause - would + bare infinitive

Example : Third Conditional

Meaning: the third conditional is used to talk about things that have or have not happened in

---

the past and the impact of these on other aspects of the past or on the present.

If I hadn't broken my leg, I wouldn't have met and married a nurse!
If I had studied nursing when I left school, I wouldn't be trying to get qualified now I am thirty.

Form: Subordinate Clause - If + past perfect tense   Main Clause - would + have + past participle

---

Key point

1. It is possible to substitute other conjunctions for *if* such as *unless, provided* e.g.

    - *I won't go to exercise classes unless you promise to come as well.*
    - *I will help you with your diet provided you promise to stick to it.*

2. It is possible to use different modal verbs at various points in conditional sentences e.g.

    - *If you feel ill, you should go to the doctor.*
    - *If you break a limb, you might need physiotherapy.*
    - *If I went to the gym more regularly, I might be more fit.*
    - *If we had guessed the food was bad, we might not have contracted food poisoning.*

3. It is often possible to mix conditionals in sentences e.g.

    - *If I attended a chiropractor I might have recovered from backache. **(mixes 2nd and 3rd conditional)***

4.7   Grammar: Conditional sentences: Practice

Conditional sentences: Practice (20 min)

Q29: Complete the sentences using the correct form of the verb *to be*.

a) If I _____ so tired I would help you with your work.
b) I wouldn't have fallen asleep if I _____ so tired.
c) If I _____ tired but can't sleep, I drink hot milk.
d) If you _____ sufficiently tired, you will fall asleep.
e) I wouldn't have had such a terrible nightmare if I _____ unnerved by that film I watched.
f) Provided I do enough exercise in the day I _____ sleepy in the evening.
g) If I _____ a less agitated person I am sure I would sleep better.
h) Unless he _____ in bed and asleep by eight I can't get him up for school in the morning
i) Should you _____ home late please _____ quiet and don't waken us all up.
j) If I _____ a doctor I would like to _____ a vet.

Grammar practice (1)

Go online

Consider the following scenario: Lauren fell and hurt her head. She seemed to recover very quickly but developed a bad headache later in the day. Lauren's mother decided to take her to the emergency ward at the hospital for sick children. After waiting an hour, Lauren was given a quick examination then told to go home. She is to be given painkillers as necessary.

Q30:

Compare and contrast the meaning of the following sentences which refer to this situation. Discuss what you think each sentence means with a partner before checking your answers.

1a. If she hadn't been in pain, she wouldn't have gone to the hospital.

1b. If she wasn't in pain, she wouldn't have gone to the hospital.

2a. If the headaches continue, Lauren's mother will give her painkillers.

2b. If the headaches had continued, Lauren's mother would have given her painkillers.

3a. If Lauren's mother hadn't been worried, she wouldn't have taken Lauren to hospital.

3b. If Lauren's mother wasn't worried, she wouldn't have taken Lauren to hospital.

Grammar practice (2)   Go online

Q31: Match clauses in 1-10 with suitable clauses a-j to make appropriate sentences.

1. If you are unable to sleep	a) you wouldn't have had a problem dropping off.
2. If you wanted to sleep well	b) you could have been suffering migraine.
3. If you hadn't been so stressed	c) I would go to the doctor.
4. Should the doctor offer you sleeping tablets	d) you would be advised to continue taking painkillers.
5. If you had a problem with headaches	e) you might benefit from meditation.
6. If your backache continues	f) I would probably have fewer problems.
7. Unless the pain subsides	g) you wouldn't have been referred to a specialist.
8. If you hadn't gone to the doctor	h) you will have to stop working.
9. If I thought I had a serious medical problem	i) you will be tempted to take them.
10. If I had a healthier lifestyle	j) you shouldn't have used your computer late at night.

4.8   Writing activity: An informal email

Writing: An informal email (60 min)

Your friend is coming to stay in your home for a week while you are away. Write an email to your friend giving details of local services.

You should include:

- Where to buy essential goods
- What to do in an emergency
- Information about internet services
- Name of a local contact

You should write between 200-250 words.

4.9 Reading comprehension: Headaches

Reading comprehension: Headaches Go online

Recent research has shown that headache sufferers may be making things worse through treatment of their headaches with painkillers. There are around 200 different types of headache ranging from mild to severe and many people suffer from debilitating headaches for much of their lives. However it seems that a cure for some headaches may lie in resisting temptation to take medication.

Most people will experience headaches at some point in their life. The most common type of headache is the stress or tension related headache which many describe as a dull ache around the head. Some people say a tension headache is like a rubber band becoming tighter around the head. This kind of headache is associated with lack of sleep, lack of regular food and dehydration.

Migraine affects around 15% of the population of the UK and is an extremely debilitating condition. These headaches are associated with chemical changes in the brain and can last for hours or days. Migraine sufferers experience severe pain, nausea and frequently have light sensitivity as well. The causes of migraine are not clear but they can be exacerbated by alcohol, stress, lack of sleep, hunger, hormones, caffeine, nitrates, physical exercise, weather and altitude.

A rarer type of headache is the cluster headache in which pain is located behind one eye. These headaches are sometimes seasonal and experienced only in spring and autumn. Cluster headaches seem to arise when a nerve pathway at the base of the brain is activated. People who suffer these headaches are badly affected by smoking or alcohol though it is reported that during a headache free period sufferers can drink alcohol without any problem.

Although these are the main types of headache, it appears that around 5-10% of the population of the UK suffer from what are known as medication overuse headaches. This type of headache is caused by taking too many painkillers. It is thought that people with a history of tension type headaches may be more susceptible to the effect of painkillers. The problem is not that people overdose, but they overuse. After several months of taking painkillers two to three times a week, people then become addicted to the painkillers and experience rebound headaches if they do not take them.

The solution to this is apparently to avoid painkillers altogether, especially those containing codeine. It is now being recommended that sufferers of migraine try to go without the painkillers they are used to. Clearly this will be a painful process but it is thought that after some time the overall result will be that the number and intensity of headaches will be reduced by this action. Those who have used codeine routinely for a long period of time may need to reduce consumption gradually rather than stop altogether. As a general rule, it is not recommended that anyone should take painkillers for any more than two days a week or for two or more consecutive days.

Headaches are unpleasant and incapacitating. It is disturbing to realise that the imagined cure is often a part of the problem. However, it is encouraging to discover that there may be a partial solution. A reduction in painkillers may reduce the overall number of headaches. This may also enable the bodily systems of the addicts to readjust and once again be responsive to occasional use of painkilling drugs.

Q32: What is the function of the text?

a) Entertainment

b) Education

c) Advertising

....

Q33: Which two headache types are associated with changes in the brain?

....

Q34: Which of the headaches described is the least common?

....

Q35: Which type of headache might force people to seek darkness?

Decide whether these statements are true, false or the text does not say.

Q36: Cluster headache sufferers need to give up alcohol.

....

Q37: Those with a history of tension headaches are most likely to be affected by medication overdose.

....

Q38: People who have become addicted to codeine should stop taking it at once.

....

Q39: People who give up use of pain killers for headaches are likely to notice an immediate improvement.

....

Q40: Find a word or phrase in the last paragraph of the text with the meaning: "making one unable to live or work properly".

....

Q41: Find a word or phrase in the last paragraph of the text with the meaning "reacting quickly and in a positive way".

4.10 Listening comprehension: Food nowadays

Listening Comprehension: Food nowadays Go online

You will need the following sound file for this listening comprehension:
n5-esl1-4-3listening.mp3

Q42: How do Laura and Paul know each other? They are

a) friends
b) colleagues
c) siblings

....

Q43: Which of the following are discussed? Choose 3, indicate by ticking your choices.

a) Healthy menus
b) Content of food
c) Keep fit classes
d) Advertising of food products
e) Obesity
f) Metabolism

....

Q44: Complete the notes below on the content of the discussion. Use no more than four words in each space.

Laura thinks that we have a 1. _____ problem with obesity. She thinks that the nation is 2. _____ with food, that children eat too much and don't 3. _____ Paul doesn't think we have 4. _____ .

He thinks that 5. _____ is the biggest problem we face. He suggests two possible reasons for lack of information on this topic which are 6. the _____ and _____ .

Unit 1 Topic 5

Entertainment and leisure

Contents

Learning objective

By the end of this topic you will be better able to:

- participate in a conversation about entertainment, leisure, technology and the relationship between technology and society;

- recognise and produce a range of future forms;

- write an informal email;

- distinguish between, and produce, strong and weak forms;

- maximise opportunities for experiencing authentic English.

5.1   Reading activity: Art

Pre-reading activity: Speaking: Art (15 min)

Discuss the following with your partner or group:

1. Are you interested in art? Who is your favourite artist?
2. Do you paint or draw, or are you interested in any other artistic pursuits?
3. Are you familiar with the work of any artist from your own country?

Pre-reading activity: Vocabulary quiz: Art (30 min)   Go online

Q1:   Using the internet, find answers to the following questions:

1. What is the name given to a three dimensional work of art in stone, metal, wood or clay?
2. What is the name of the wooden board used for mixing paint?
3. What is the name of the style of painting associated with the French painter Monet?
4. What is the first name of the Spanish painter Picasso?
5. What is the name of the artist famous for painting the ceiling of the Sistine Chapel in Rome?
6. Which American artist was famous for painting iconic American images such as soup cans?
7. Which Norwegian artist painted The Scream?
8. Which female Mexican artist was born and died in the 'Blue House'?
9. Which artist born in Russia is credited with producing the first purely abstract paintings?
10. What is the name of the artist who painted 'The Starry Night'?

Reading activity: Text and questions: Art (45 min)

Read the following passage and then answer the questions that follow.

J.D. Fergusson is considered part of a group of painters now known as the Scottish Colourists, a group which includes G.L. Hunter, S.J. Peploe and F.C.B Cadell. Fergusson was born 1874 in Edinburgh although his family who were wine merchants had originally come from Perthshire. During the 1880s Fergusson trained as a naval surgeon for a short period of time, but his first love was art. He was accepted as a student at the Trustees Academy in Edinburgh, which later became the Edinburgh College of Art, but he was not comfortable with the style of training there; he found it very rigid and he decided he would teach himself to paint.

During the 1890s Fergusson travelled to Spain, Morocco and France, and he developed a particular fondness for France where he was influenced by artists such as Claude Monet, Edouard Manet and the Fauves (a group of post-impressionist painters). He became friends with Samuel Peploe, another Scottish painter, and they travelled to France frequently together to paint. Eventually in 1907, Fergusson moved to Paris and Peploe did the same in 1910.

In France the two spent time in the company of other artists such as Matisse and Derain who were central to the Fauve movement. The latter were interested in the use of bold colour which was not always associated with the object painted, vivid brushstrokes and the suggestion of movement and rhythm. This clearly had a strong influence on Fergusson, and while the other Scottish colourists grew more interested in still life painting as time passed, Fergusson retained a keen interest in representation of the human form throughout his life.

In 1913 Fergusson met Margaret Morris, a woman who was born in London but who had spent her early childhood in France. Morris was dynamic, exciting and successful, and had a flourishing career in dance and choreography. She had a theatrical background and had studied classical dance. Like Fergusson, Morris was an independent thinker and had rejected classical ballet technique in favour of her own system of movement. She held strong convictions about the remedial possibilities of exercise and in 1930 gained a distinction when she studied Physiotherapy at St Thomas's hospital in London.

In the same year that he met Morris, Fergusson had moved to the south of France and, although her dance school was in London, Morris would regularly visit him there. Fergusson was totally enchanted by Morris who became his muse as well as his partner. They had much in common, including an interest in the physical form; dancers are a recurrent theme in Fergusson's work, and they collaborated on many dance projects. In 1917 they opened a summer dance school in Devon. In many ways the couple had an idyllic lifestyle until the outbreak of the Second World War in 1939, when they moved back to Britain.

Fergusson and Morris lived together until Fergusson's death in 1961, aged 86. Although they travelled back to France for holidays, they spent their later years in Glasgow where they continued to work creatively. Margaret, who was seventeen years younger than her partner, outlived him by nearly twenty years. She was still working as a dance teacher in her eighties. In 1968, a small collection of fourteen Fergusson paintings were given by Margaret Morris to the University of Stirling. A larger collection is held in Perth in the Fergusson Gallery. Margaret Morris died in Glasgow on 29 February 1980, aged 89.

Q2:   Find antonyms within the text for the following words.

1. excludes	
2. rejected	
3. flexible	
4. seldom	
5. vivid	
6. lifeless	
7. dull	
8. failing	
9. conventional	
10. foreground	

....

Are the statements true or false?

Q3:   Fergusson found the methods of teaching in the Trustees Academy relaxed.

a) True
b) False

....

Q4:   Fergusson did not focus on still life painting.

a) True
b) False

....

Q5:   Margaret Morris was certain that exercise could improve health.

a) True
b) False

....

Q6:   Fergusson was very impressed with Margaret Morris.

a) True
b) False

Q7:   In France, J.D. Fergusson enjoyed the company of post-impressionist painters. They painted objects in unexpected ways using bold **a)**_____ and vivid **b)**_____.   Their paintings give a sense of **c)**_____ and **d)**_____. Fergusson and Morris who met in 1913 had much in common. They were both **e)**_____ thinkers, had a connection with France and a fascination with the **f)**_____ form.

Find words or phrases in the text with the following meaning:

Q8: Important/key (paragraph 2)

....

Q9: Someone who gives an artist inspiration to create (paragraph 4)

....

Q10: Worked together on projects (paragraph 4)

....

Q11: Close to perfection/perfect (paragraph 4)

5.2 Pronunciation: Strong and weak forms

Some words in English have strong and weak forms. This means that part of the word is not always stressed. Listen to the following sentences for example:

You will need the following sound files to complete this exercise: *n5-esl1-5-1listening1.mp3* and *n5-esl1-5-1listening2.mp3*

- *Why don't you go to the cinema?*
- *I just don't want to*

In the first sentence the weak form of the vowel *o* is used while in the second the vowel in the word *to* is stressed.

Pronunciation: Strong and weak forms	Go online

You will need the following sound files to complete this activity: *n5-esl1-5-2listening1.mp3* to *n5-esl1-5-2listening7.mp3*

Q12: Play the recorded sentences and write down what you hear. Count the number of words in each sentence and indicate where you think the speaker used strong or weak forms.

5.3 Study skills: Sources of 'Authentic English'

'Authentic English' describes English as it is used by native speakers. 'Authentic use' of English describes the ways in which the language is used in real life situations such as to get information or to share ideas.

When you are studying English language in a country where English is not the first language, it might seem difficult to find opportunities to experience authentic English.

Sources of 'Authentic English'

Q13: Work with a partner or in a group. Write a list of ways in which you might be able to experience authentic English.

Interview a partner if possible to find out what he/she already does to study more authentic English and how much time they spend doing this each week. Make notes on your discussion.

Make a decision about how to improve your access to authentic English using the ideas discussed through this activity.

5.4   Listening activity: Films

Pre-listening activity: Speaking: Films

Discuss the following questions with a partner:

1. Do you enjoy watching films?

2. Do you prefer to watch films at the cinema or at home?

3. Do you always watch contemporary films or do you watch old films too?

Pre-listening activity: Vocabulary: Films (30 min) Go online

Q14: Complete the crossword using the film vocabulary clues below.

DOWN

1. Particular style or type of film.

2. More obscure films usually made by smaller companies and seen by a smaller audience.

3. Films made by larger companies and seen by a wide audience.

5. Type of film with an exciting story about spying or crime for example.

7. Written language which appears at the foot of a movie screen.

8. Person whose job it is to perform in a film.

ACROSS

4. Person who has the most important role in a film.

6. The storyline.

9. Famous film industry in India.

10. Cinema in which a large number of films are screened at any one time.

11. Group of people performing in film or play.

12. Person whose job it is to decide on what is included in a film.

Listening activities: Note taking: Films (30 min) Go online

You will need the following sound file to complete this activity:
n5-esl1-5-3listening.mp3

Listen to the following dialogue in which two people are talking about an old movie that one of them has just watched.

Q15: While you are listening take notes on the following:

Plot	
Characters	
Director	
Cast	
Star	
Genre	
Why the film was good/bad	

....

Complete the notes based on what you have heard about the film.

Q16: All about Eve is a film starring Betty **1.**_____ as Margo Channing. Eve played by Ann Baxter wants Margot's life and all that is in it. She **2.**_____ all around her and almost **3.**_____ Margot's life in her attempt to get to the top. Margot is **4.**_____ about her age and her relationship, she realises that parts are often given to **5.**_____ actresses. The film has great actors and scripts and although the film is quite old, many of the issues explored are **6** _____.

5.5   Writing: Informal email

Writing: Informal email (60 min)

Your friend wrote you an email inviting you to the cinema at the weekend. Write an email in response to explain that you can't go to the cinema, but mention a film you have watched recently and recommend that they watch it too.

Write between 90-120 words.

In your email, you should:

- apologise for not being able to go to the cinema.

- explain why you cannot go.

- recommend a film that your friend can watch and tell them where or how they can view it.

Before you begin, you should also consider the following questions:

1. What is the purpose of the communication?

2. Who is the intended audience?

3. What level of formality and register would be appropriate?

5.6 Listening activity: Technology

Pre-listening activity: Vocabulary: Technology (15 min) Go online

Q17: Rearrange the letters given to make words associated with technology.

1. K R E W T O N
2. A E S A T B A D
3. E N R C E S
4. T H Y E X R E P T
5. A S H C R E
6. O M Y E M R
7. W O T A S E F R
8. U S E M O
9. B E T L A T
10. O S R P S E C O R

Pre-listening activity: Speaking: Technology (15 min)

Work with a partner (if possible). Discuss the following questions:

1. What significant technological enhancements have we seen over the last thirty to forty years?

2. What is your favourite item of technology? What do you think you couldn't live without?

3. What technological advancements do you think we might see over the next 40-50 years?

4. Do you think that all technological changes bring benefits to society and improve our lives?

5. What role do you think technology has in science fiction novels or movies?

Pre-Listening activity: Vocabulary: Collocations: Technology (15 min)   Go online

Match a word on the left hand side with one on the right to make common collocations.

Q18:

1) Technological	a) Dilemmas
2) Electronic	b) Domain
3) Genetic	c) Networking
4) Moral	d) Level
5) Fundamental	e) Health
6) Fierce	f) Sources
7) Social	g) Lives
8) Public	h) Display
9) Headline	i) Lesson
10) Direct	j) Competition
11) Information	k) Access
12) Salutary	l) Engineering
13) Mental	m) News
14) Private	n) Advancements

Listening activity: Note taking: Technology (25 min)   Go online

You will require the following sound file for this activity:
n5-esl1-5-4listening.mp3

While you are listening take notes to allow you to answer the following questions.

Q19: What is the context of the conversation?
....

Q20: Which works of fiction are mentioned (films and novels)

Discuss your answers with a partner or group if possible.

Post-listening activity: Responding to questions: Technology (20 min)   Go online

You will require the following sound file for this activity: *in5-esl1-5-4listening.mp3*

Q21: How does Anderton, the police officer, control his 3D hologram computer?

....

Q22: What device replaced newspapers?

....

Q23: What kind of products is Anderton offered in the first film?

Complete the following sentences in no more than three words:

Q24: The second film was released in 1982 and at the time seemed _____ .

....

Q25: Deckard, played by Harrison Ford, is employed to remove _____ creatures.

....

Q26: Deckard discovers that he and the creatures known as replicants are _____ .

Decide whether the following statements are true or false according to the script.

Q27: Gus thinks that nowadays technological experts battle to make great new discoveries.

a) True
b) False

....

Q28: Gus believes that the internet is a harmless invention.

a) True
b) False

....

Q29: Gus says that it can be dangerous to make our private lives public.

a) True
b) False

Discuss your answers in pairs or groups (if possible).

5.7 Pronunciation

Pronunciation: The phonemic script (20 min)   Go online

The Phonemic Alphabet

vowels: iː ɪ ʊ uː   diphthongs: ɪə eə
e ə ɜː ɔː   əʊ aʊ
æ ʌ ɑː ɒ   eɪ ɪə ɔɪ

consonants:
p f t θ tʃ s ʃ k
b v d ð dʒ z ʒ g
h m n ŋ r l w j

Q30: Transcribe each item of lexis in the table using the phonemic alphabet.

1) Technological	n) Advancements
2) Electronic	h) Display
3) Genetic	l) Engineering
4) Moral	a) Dilemmas
5) Fundamental	d) Level
6) Fierce	j) Competition
7) Social	c) Networking
8) Public	b) Domain
9) Headline	m) News
10) Direct	k) Access
11) Information	f) Sources
12) Salutary	i) Lesson
13) Mental	e) Health
14) Private	g) Lives

Pronunciation: Phonemic collocations   Go online

Q31: Match the phonemic transcriptions to their collocations.

1.	Technological Advancements	a.	/fɪərs kɒmpɪˈtɪʃən/
2.	Electronic Display	b.	/ˈsəʊʃəl ˈnɛtwəːrkɪŋ/
3.	Genetic Engineering	c.	/ˈpraɪvət laɪvz/
4.	Moral Dilemmas	d.	/fʌndəˈmɛntəl ˈlɛvəl/
5.	Fundamental Level	e.	/dʒəˈnɛtɪk ɛndʒɪˈnɪərɪŋ/
6.	Fierce Competition	f.	/ˈpʌblɪk dəʊˈmeɪn/
7.	Social Networking	g.	/ˈmɒrəl dɪˈlɛməs/
8.	Public Domain	h.	/tɛknəˈlɒdʒɪkəl ədˈvɑːnsmənts/
9.	Headline News	i.	/daɪˈrɛkt ˈaksɛs/
10.	Direct Access	j.	/ˈhɛdlaɪn njuːz/
11.	Information Sources	k.	/ˈsaljʊtəri ˈlɛsən/
12.	Salutary Lesson	l.	/ˈmɛntəl hɛlθ/
13.	Mental Health	m.	/ɛlɛkˈtrɒnɪk dɪˈspleɪ/
14.	Private Lives	n.	/ɪnfəˈmeɪʃən sɔːrsɛs/

Pronunciation: Syllables and word stress (20 min)   Go online

You will require the following sound files to complete this activity:
*n5-esl1-5-6pronunc1.mp3*to *n5-esl1-5-6pronunc14.mp3*

Q32: Listen to each word being spoken and while listening mark the number of syllables and indicate the stressed syllable.

Word	Syllables and word stress
e.g. Computer	*oOo*
Technological	
Electronic	
Genetic	
Moral	
Fundamental	
Fierce	
Social	
Public	
Headline	
Direct	
Information	
Salutary	
Mental	
Private	

5.8   Pre-Reading: Questions

Pre-Reading: Questions

Q33: What is the name of the man who co-founded Microsoft and is currently Microsoft's chairman?

....

Q34: What is the name of the man who co-founded Apple and was its Chief Executive Officer until his death in 2011?

Discuss what you know about Apple and Microsoft with a partner. Ask your partner if they know who invented the internet.

5.9 Reading: Tim Berners-Lee

Reading: Tim Berners-Lee (25 min) Go online

"It's hard to overstate the impact of the global system he created. It's almost Gutenbergian."
Time (1.)

1. Compared to Bill Gates or Steve Jobs, Tim Berners-Lee is relatively unknown. A rather modest and unassuming man, he did not set out to make a fortune or to become famous. Nevertheless, in creating the World Wide Web, he invented one of the most radical and powerful methods of communication and information sharing to date. The influence and power this innovation has had on our lives has been compared to the invention of the printing press by Gutenberg.

2. In 1989 Tim Berners-Lee wrote a memo to his boss asking to spend time on a project that would revolutionise information sharing. The idea was to link hypertext to the internet. This would involve creation of a hypertext protocol, which meant giving things a name that started with http; a unique resource locator (URL). At the time Lee's boss wrote on the memo "vague but exciting" but although he allowed Lee to work on it on the side, he didn't think it merited all Lee's attention. Ironically, this idea was the seed which eventually flowered to become the World Wide Web.

3. Today, we cannot imagine the obstacles which Lee overcame to develop his idea. Most of us couldn't function without the internet now, but in 1989 where there was interest it was often half hearted. There was also a complete lack of understanding of the potential of the technology, an inability to imagine what a hypertext link could look like and what it would do. Now we cannot conceive of using a computer without the facility to click on one word which takes us to another page of information. This was Lee's conceptual initiative, but it did not take off immediately.

4. Over twenty years later Lee has more ideas for the future. He believes that the next step should be 'linked data'. Lee believes that data sharing is crucial because this will give us more control over information. Currently data can be manipulated and shown to us in ways that suit those who hold the key to it. If everyone has access to data then everyone has the power that goes with that. This means that we are less vulnerable to misleading presentations of statistics.

5. Lee argues that linked data should give us greater awareness of what is happening in the world. This should also make it easier to do our own research instead of depending on someone else's analysis and presentation of facts. We will then be able to see relationships in our research. If for example we read that someone is suffering from Multiple Sclerosis we might then want to find out how many people suffer from this in that person's area. Such statistics could be invaluable. This could be the type of

link scientists need as they carry out research. Access to someone else's statistics could streamline study and make it more efficient. Medical research could greatly be enhanced by this progress.

6. Perhaps Tim Berners-Lee is not as well- known as some other innovative thinkers but then he was not chasing fame and fortune. Nevertheless he has been rewarded by society. He has been awarded several prizes including a Knighthood for pioneering work and for outstanding technical achievements.

1. http://www.ted.com/speakers/tim_berners_lee.html

Q35: Match the headings (a-f) to the paragraphs (1-6).

a) Joined up thinking
b) Planning ahead
c) Slow pedal
d) Understated
e) The Big idea
f) Sidelined

Find words/phrases in the text that suggest the following.

Q36: Tim Berners-Lee is not a show-off (paragraph 1).

....

Q37: Lee's boss thought Lee's idea was unclear (paragraph 2).

....

Q38: We are potentially victims of those who hold data (paragraph 4).

....

Q39: Linked data could make scientific process more effective (paragraph 5).

....

Q40: Lee's work is understood as ground-breaking (paragraph 6).

....

Decide whether the following statements are true or false.

Q41: The writer says that the majority of people do not need internet technology.

a) True
b) False

....

Q42: Lee's vision for the future involves information sharing.

a) True
b) False

. . . .

Q43: Lee thinks that without access to linked data we are more susceptible to influence and control of others.

a) True
b) False

. . . .

Q44: Lee insists that the future of medical science depends on linked data.

a) True
b) False

. . . .

Q45: The work of Tim Berners-Lee remains largely unacknowledged.

a) True
b) False

5.10   Grammar: Future forms

Look at the following phrases from the reading text:

1. *Before long we will probably all be experiencing it*

2. *It is going to happen to us very soon, if it hasn't already*

Q46: Both are predictions for the future. Which one is/is not based on present or past evidence?

There are several ways of talking about the future. The choices we make are based upon the meaning we want to express, although sometimes we use different forms to add variety or formality in particular text types.

Grammar: Future forms: Meaning (20 min)   Go online

Match the following sentences (1-8) with the descriptions of purpose (a-h).

Q47:

1. I am going to buy a new computer next Saturday afternoon.
2. It's going to have a bigger memory than the one I have at the moment.
3. It'll change my life.
4. I can't buy it this Saturday as I am meeting friends.
5. I can't buy it on Saturday morning as I play tennis on Saturday mornings.
6. I'll help you with your project when I get my new computer.
7. This time next month I'll have bought my new computer.
8. This time next month I'll have been using my computer for several weeks.

a) Prediction based on present evidence
b) Measure of duration of time based on point in the future
c) Future arrangement
d) Offer of help
e) Focus on completion of activity at a point in the future
f) Timetabled event
g) Prediction which is not based on evidence
h) Future plan

Grammar: Future forms: Understanding form

Read through the following overview of ways of talking about the future.

Examples

1. We use *be + going to + bare infinitive* when we are talking about future plans or decisions or to predict future events where there is evidence to suggest that something is likely.

*Children **are going to be** more effective users of technology than their parents.*

....

2. We use *will ('ll)* when we predict the future but have no particular evidence to suggest that something is likely. We also use *will* to talk about unplanned future events, to show willingness in a situation and to offer help.

***We'll** get better results if we change network provider. **I'll** investigate this and **I'll** help you set it up if necessary.*

....

3. We use present simple to talk about regular/timetabled events or activities.

We work with computers on Tuesday mornings.

....

4. We use present continuous where we are talking about arrangements.

We are working on presentations tomorrow.

....

5. We use future continuous when we want to talk about something which is expected to start at a particular point in the future and endure for a period of time. We also use this form when something is understood as part of the normal course of events.

- *She'll be working on her thesis all summer.*
- *We'll be seeing each other soon.*

....

6. We use future perfect simple or continuous to focus on the completion or duration of events from a point in the future.

- *I'll have finished working on my presentation by six o'clock.*
- *I'll have been working on my presentation for three hours by then.*

Grammar: Future Forms: Choosing the correct form (25 min)

Complete the following text using the most appropriate form.
going to : will/shall : present simple/continuous : future continuous/future perfect/future perfect continuous

Q48:
Good afternoon ladies and gentlemen. I am here today to show you around the university. Firstly, I 1. _____ (show) you around the academic departments. We 2. _____ (take) a tour of the library at 10 a.m. where you 3. _____ (able) to get library cards and have a look around. After this we 4. _____ (have) a look around a laboratory, a typical lecture theatre and seminar room. All lectures 5. _____ (finish) at twelve noon for lunch and the canteen 6. _____ (be) very busy. That is not a problem however as 7. _____ (eat) in an especially reserved section which 8.I _____ (direct) you to on arrival. We 9. _____ (meet) with the principal at one thirty and after the principal has spoken to you we 10. _____ (take) you to the residential area of campus where you 11. _____ (receive) keys and information on our social programme. We 12. _____ (finish) the tour by around three thirty and at that stage you 13. _____ (be) free to wander as you wish. Our more established students 14. _____ (hand) out tickets for various freshers' week activities later on today at the halls of residence and I believe they 15. _____ (give) away free drinks vouchers as well so look out for that. On the subject of drinks, you 16. _____ (be/ invite) to our first cocktail party of the season tonight. Cocktail parties 17. _____ (held) on the first Friday of every month. Just think by the time 18. _____ (attend) the second party, you 19. _____ (study) at this university for four whole weeks. Believe me the next three to four years 20. _____ (roll) by at a tremendous speed and before you know it you 21. _____ (finish) your degree and 22. _____ (look) for a job.

5.11   Reading comprehension: Technology

Reading comprehension: Technology (30 min)   Go online

The demands of today's hotel guests have changed considerably over the last fifty years. Gone are the days when a heated pool, a TV and minibar were seen as the height of sophistication. Technology has grown exponentially and consequently our requirements have become significantly more complex. As customers we "need" to read emails, see the latest news online, check weather forecasts, print out airline boarding passes and other such paraphernalia.

In response to the modern customer, many hotels have recently started to work alongside computer companies. It seems that in the face of economic downturn hotels must ensure that they remain competitive, and this means investing in all that modern technology can provide. The specific choices hotels make, in terms of technology, become part of their overall marketing brand and can be the deciding factor when we, the customers, book our stay.

My investigation into the extent to which supply currently matches demand was revealing. With respect to internet connection, customers want to have the same level of speed and functionality as they have in their own home. In view of the cost of this however, a layered system may be required which means that those of us willing and able to pay more for our stay will be rewarded with a faster and more effective connection. Many of us today are accustomed to sophisticated technology in the gym as well as in our homes, and with this in mind hotels are also investing in fitness technology such as the Nintendo Wii in their health suites to meet consumer demand.

According to one hotel representative I spoke to, the trick is to make the provision before the guests have realised they want it. Hence hotels are offering their high definition TVs with a huge number of channels as well in case a customer might decide they are missing a favourite channel. Hotels are also offering things we are unlikely to have at home such as mood lighting and sophisticated alarm systems which wake you up slowly with light and sound gradually escalating until you are fully awake. Arrival into a room can be accompanied by music and a welcome message.

While many hotels are embracing technology wholesale and investing heavily, others are going down the completely opposite path. The digital detox holiday offers escape from all the systems you have become accustomed to: a break from the mobile phone, computer and TV might sound like a holiday which has gone disastrously wrong, but this is exactly what some resorts are proposing. Often, with the help of a member of staff, you will be encouraged to surrender your technology at the door and will not be allowed to retrieve it until you leave. For those who are worried about their addiction to technology and feel they can't fight it alone, this may well offer a solution!

We generally embark on a detox to get us back on the straight and narrow, to cleanse our system of impurities with a view to relinquishing our unhealthy lifestyles once and for all. Whether you want the best of technology on holiday, or none at all, it is unlikely that you will achieve perfect technological harmony in your hotel room or decide to lose technology altogether when you leave your desert island. Perhaps the solution is to be realistic about technology in the first place and enjoy what is available, while taking heed of advice our grandparents might have once offered... moderation in all things.

Q49: What kind of text is this?

a) An advertisement

b) An article from a newspaper or magazine

c) A consumer review

. . . .

Q50: Are the following statements (a-f) True or False.

a) We are more sophisticated consumers now than we were in the past because of technology.

b) The current economic climate is forcing hotels to work harder to survive.

c) One hotelier says that hotels aim to anticipate customers desires.

d) People expect hotel wake-up systems to wake them gently because that is what they experience at home.

e) The purpose of a digital detox holiday is to support people who want to give up technology altogether.

f) The writer supports the total rejection of technology.

....

Find a word or phrase in the text with the following definition:

Q51: "objects needed for or associated with a particular activity"

....

Q52: "operations performed by or associated with a piece of equipment, computer hardware or software program"

....

Q53: Does the writer see addiction to technology as a serious problem? Yes/No (paragraph 5)

....

Q54: In the last line of paragraph 5 the writer's tone is:

1. serious.

2. ironic.

3. angry.

5.12 Listening comprehension: Keeping fit

Listening comprehension: Keeping fit Go online

You will need the following sound file in order to complete this listening comprehension: *n5-esl1-5-5listening.mp3*

Q55: Complete the gaps in the following notes based on the text using no more than four words:

The presenter suggests that the use of technology in diet and exercise programmes is 1. _____. Lisa is positive about technology and 2. _____ a few examples of what is available. The presenter describes 3. _____ as a more expensive version of a pedometer. Lisa says that some of the devices available are 4. _____ while some give 5. _____ . Lisa is 6. _____ about the value of technology in assisting exercise and fitness regimes.

....

Q56: Are the following statements True or False?

a) The presenter is initially cynical about the role of technology in diet and exercise regimes.

b) Lisa rejects the idea that input of calories and output of energy have a significant role in weight loss.

....

Q57: In what context does this conversation take place?

a) A university lecture

b) A radio news report

c) A TV interview

....

Q58: What is the purpose of the conversation?

a) To entertain

b) To educate/inform

c) To amuse

Unit 1 Topic 6

Planning a trip

Contents

Learning objective

By the end of this topic you will be better able to:

- participate in a conversation about travel and travel related subjects;

- recognise and produce idiomatic phrases in the context of travel;

- produce gerunds and infinitives;

- produce appropriate patterns of stress and intonation in polite, formal contexts;

- engage in independent learning;

- recognise features and organisation of informal emails and write an informal email.

6.1   Listening activity: Air travel

Pre-listening activity: Vocabulary: Song: Air travel (20 min)   Go online

Go to http://www.youtube.com/, search for Frank Sinatra's *'Come Fly with Me'*.

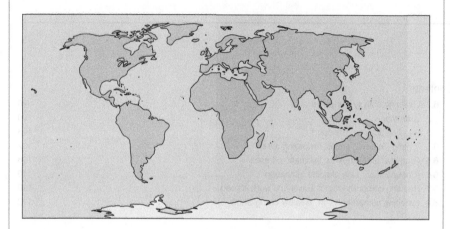

Q1:   Listen to the Frank Sinatra version of *'Come Fly with Me'*. Write down the names of all the destinations mentioned in the song.

You will need to listen to the song again for the following activity.

Go to http://www.youtube.com/, search for Frank Sinatra *'Come Fly with Me'* and listen to the sound clip.

Q2:   Listen again and then complete the song lyrics.

Come fly with me, let's fly, let's fly away
If you can use some 1._____ booze
There's a bar in far Bombay Come on.
Come fly with me, let's fly, let's fly away

Come fly with me, let's float down to Peru
In llama land there's a 2._____ band
And he'll toot his flute for you
Come fly with me, let's take off in the blue

Once I get you up there where the air is rarefied
We'll just 3._____, starry-eyed
Once I get you up there I'll be holding you so near
You may hear all the angels cheer because we're together

Weather-wise it's such a lovely day
Just say the 4._____ and we'll beat the birds
Down to Acapulco Bay
It's perfect for a flying honeymoon, they say
Come fly with me, let's fly, let's fly away

[instrumental]

Once I get you up there where the air is rarefied
We'll just 5._____, starry-eyed
Once I get you up there I'll be holding you so very near
You might even hear a whole gang of cheers 'cause we're together

Weather-wise it's such a cuckoo day
You just say those 6._____ and we'll take our birds
Down to Acapulco Bay
It's so perfect for a flying honeymoon, oh babe
Come fly with me, let's fly, let's fly
Pack up, let's fly away!!

Pre-listening activity: Vocabulary: Collocations: Air travel (10 min)   Go online

Q3: Match the nouns in column one with those in column two to make airline related compounds.

1. Cabin	a. luggage
2. Check in	b. handler
3. Hand	c. traffic control
4. Boarding	d. locker
5. Security	e. desk
6. Passport	f. demonstration
7. Baggage	g. crew
8. Air	h. gate
9. Safety	i. control
10. Overhead	j. pass

Speaking: Discussion: Air travel (20 min)

Discuss the following questions with a partner.

1. Do you know anyone who works for an airline? If so, what is their job?

2. Think about the job of cabin crew. What comes into your mind? What do you associate with that job?

Q4:   Reshuffle the following sentences to make questions.

a) Attracted what to work you airline?

b) Selection you process tell about us the can?

c) Training have you any did?

d) Glamorous you say is a it job would? So, if why?

e) Incidents have you or emergencies your flying career had any ever in?

Listening comprehension: Note taking: Air travel (40 min)   Go online

You will need the following sound file to complete this activity: *n5-esl1-6-1listening.mp3*.

Listen to the following interview and take notes in preparation for answering the questions. Compare notes with a partner, listen again if necessary.

Q5:   Which of the following does the speaker say attracted her to the job of cabin crew? Select **three** answers.

1. Finding out about other cultures

2. Meeting new people

3. Being in aeroplanes and airports

4. Staying in glamorous hotels

5. Earning a good salary

6. Variable working hours

Complete the following sentences with **no more than four words**:

Q6:   When Penny applied for the job it had been advertised in the press and . . . .

. . . .

Q7:   She was trained in . . . .

. . . .

Q8: Penny thinks it's a glamorous job but admits that at times it can be ....
....

Q9: Penny was involved in an incident when flying from Munich to ....

Listen again to the second part of the interview, and prepare to answer the questions which follow.

You will need the following sound file: *n5-esl1-6-1listening.mp3*

Q10: What was the cause of the problem?
....

Q11: What injury did Penny receive when the aircraft dropped 2000 feet?

a) She hit her head
b) She was not injured
c) She fell and hurt her leg

....

Q12: Why was no one prepared for what happened?

a) The pilots were not paying attention
b) There was no warning
c) The radar was broken

....

Q13: Penny compares her initial feelings during the incident to:

a) watching a film
b) being in a film
c) something unexpected

....

Q14: What helped Penny gain control of the situation?

a) watching a film
b) being in a film
c) something unexpected

....

Q15: Following the onboard incident:

a) many people were seriously injured.
b) some people were seriously injured.
c) there were no serious injuries.

....

Q16: With respect to the incident she describes, Penny thinks that:

a) she was very unfortunate to have had this experience.
b) she was lucky to have survived this experience.
c) dealing with experiences like this are part of her job.

6.2 Grammar

Grammar: Activity: Gerunds: Identifying structure (15 min)   Go online

These sentences/clauses below, which are extracted from the interview you listened to earlier, contain an '-ing' form of the verb (gerund). Look carefully at the form of each and then try the activity below.

1. I started shouting

2. Being in airports is fun for me

3. I was interested in finding out about different countries

4. Training is generally six weeks long

5. Inflating slides and jumping

6. ... eating in restaurants... shopping... visiting... famous landmarks

7. Everyone was screaming

8. ... risk putting us on a plane

9. I found it terrifying

10. I was watching a film

Q17: Match the sentences/clauses (1-10) with the examples of situations in which we use '-ing' forms of verbs (a-f):

a) past (continuous) tenses

b) As the subject of a sentence

c) After some verb / object combinations

d) After certain verbs

e) To list activities

f) After prepositions

Top tip

It is important to note that in certain situations we can/must use an infinitive rather than an '-ing' form. However, this can be confusing because we use infinitives in similar situations to those in which we use gerunds.

We use infinitives:

1. as the subject of a sentence;

2. after some verb/object combinations;

3. after certain verbs.

In general we have to learn when each form is appropriate i.e. which verbs are followed by gerund and which by an infinitive.

Examples

1. Note that some verbs can be followed by either a gerund or an infinitive without affecting meaning.

a) *I started training as a pilot ten years ago.*

b) *I started to train as a pilot ten years ago.*

. . . .

2. However, in some instances meaning is significantly different when the different forms are used.

a) *I stopped drinking coffee when I was working on planes.*

b) *I stopped to drink coffee when I was working on planes.*

Sentence a) suggests that I gave up the habit of drinking coffee while sentence b) suggests that I was in the habit of having a coffee break when I worked on planes.

Grammar: Activities: Verb patterns: Gerund or infinitive (15 min)   Go online

Q18: Decide in each case if you think the verbs are followed by a gerund or an infinitive.

a) *e.g. enjoy - gerund*
b) decide
c) expect
d) risk
e) mention
f) wish
g) imagine
h) want
i) consider
j) promise
k) involve
l) refuse
m) fail
n) dislike

Q19:

Complete the following sentences using a verb from the list in infinitive or gerund form.

travel, give, fly, eat, apply (x2), relocate, work, take, be, leave

Note: in some of the sentences the gerund/infinitive will follow a verb, and in some a verb/object combination.

a) She refuses _____ for a position as ground staff at the airport, only a flying job will please her.
b) She really dislikes _____ the food on planes.
c) His application has been accepted but he has been asked if he will consider _____ to London.
d) He enjoys _____ a pilot but he hates _____ his family.
e) I have decided _____ a year out of work and do some travelling.
f) 'I wish _____ wasn't so boring, I never enjoy being on a plane.'
g) She encouraged me _____ for a job in the travel industry because she enjoys it so much.
h) He said he didn't mind _____ me a lift to the airport because my car had broken down.
i) I would like _____ all over the world before I reach fifty.
j) I hate _____ shifts - nine to five is much better for me.

6.3   Reading activity: Transport

Pre-reading activity: Speaking: Transport

Before you continue with the reading activity discuss the following questions with a partner. Spend 5-10 minutes on these questions.

1. What is your favourite method of transport?

2. Is there any form of transport which you dislike?

3. Do you or does anyone you know suffer from anxiety when travelling?

Read the passage of text and then answer the questions that follow.

1. Do you jump for joy and start packing at the prospect of a long haul flight to the other side of the world, or does the prospect of boarding a plane leave you **quivering** like a jelly? If you are in the latter group, then fear of flying may already be seriously restricting your life.

2. It appears that a surprising number of people **undergo** severe distress when around planes. The results of a study carried out by researchers for Boeing were **revealing**.* The researchers in the USA found that 18.1% of adults were afraid of flying and 12.6 % described themselves as anxious about it. This means that one in three surveyed experienced negative feelings around flying. Interestingly, fear of flying is often related to other issues. This study also revealed that of those who avoided flying, only 6% did so because they thought planes were unsafe. The fear of flying can be something which grows through time. You may not have developed the particular fear yet, but if you have problems with small spaces, lack of privacy, the dark, heights, fear of attack or lack of control, you may be in the danger zone.

3. Fear of flying is an anxiety **disorder** that may have nothing to do with the actual fear of crashing, but which may be related to fears such as **claustrophobia** or of heights, lack of control, or the unknown. Captain Bunn, a former pilot and qualified therapist, has set up an organisation called SOAR to try and help people overcome their fear of flying. According to Bunn, the psychology behind the fear is quite complex. Most people have some ability to make themselves calm in stressful situations. This is something which stems from parental care-giving in childhood. The ease with which we are able to calm ourselves depends on our particular childhood experience. When we are faced with difficult situations we try either to control them or to escape from them and the extent to which we can do this depends on our ability to calm ourselves. Unfortunately, on a plane neither control nor escape is a viable option.

4. People with a high level of anxiety around flying may be tempted to avoid it altogether. Others try drugs or alcohol, but this can lead to abusive behaviour. A potentially more effective and more permanent cure might be to embark on one of the fear of flying courses which are available. The best of these courses offer help using recognised methods such as Cognitive Behavioural Therapy (CBT). Most courses offer a graduation flight but this can become another focus of anxiety or can create the illusion of cure. Course participants can become dependent on the group, managing to board a flight with experts and fellow sufferers but not alone. Captain Bunn says that allowing the sufferer to have some control over pace of the treatment brings a higher success rate.

5. If you are highly fearful, anxious or even have apparently unrelated concerns such as fear about lack of privacy when flying, help is available. Flying need not be the trauma you **anticipate** or have experienced. Sign up for a course or get your hands on some of the supportive materials available online or in print. There's a big wide world out there to discover, go and enjoy it.

* http:\\www.airsafe.com

Q20: Match five of the headings (a-g) with the paragraphs (1-5). Two headings are not necessary.

  a) Are you afraid of flying?

  b) Potential cures

  c) Seek help as soon as possible

  d) A common problem

  e) Early influences

Q21: Find words in the text to match the following definitions:

  a) Shaking slightly

  b) Limiting

  c) Area

  d) Fear of small or confined spaces

  e) Achievable

  f) Rude, offensive or violent

  g) False belief or idea

  h) Speed

  i) Not connected

  j) Expect

Reading activity: Fear of flying: Transport

Read the passage of text and then answer the questions that follow.

1. Do you jump for joy and start packing at the prospect of a long haul flight to the other side of the world, or does the prospect of boarding a plane leave you quivering like a jelly? If you are in the latter group, then fear of flying may already be seriously restricting your life.

2. It appears that a surprising number of people undergo severe distress when around planes. The results of a study carried out by researchers for Boeing were revealing.* The researchers in the USA found that 18.1% of adults were afraid of flying and 12.6 % described themselves as anxious about it. This means that one in three surveyed

experienced negative feelings around flying. Interestingly, fear of flying is often related to other issues. This study also revealed that of those who avoided flying, only 6% did so because they thought planes were unsafe. The fear of flying can be something which grows through time. You may not have developed the particular fear yet, but if you have problems with small spaces, lack of privacy, the dark, heights, fear of attack or lack of control, you may be in the danger zone.

3. Fear of flying is an anxiety disorder that may have nothing to do with the actual fear of crashing, but which may be related to fears such as claustrophobia or of heights, lack of control, or the unknown. Captain Bunn, a former pilot and qualified therapist, has set up an organisation called SOAR to try and help people overcome their fear of flying. According to Bunn, the psychology behind the fear is quite complex. Most people have some ability to make themselves calm in stressful situations. This is something which stems from parental care-giving in childhood. The ease with which we are able to calm ourselves depends on our particular childhood experience. When we are faced with difficult situations we try either to control them or to escape from them and the extent to which we can do this depends on our ability to calm ourselves. Unfortunately, on a plane neither control nor escape is a viable option.

4. People with a high level of anxiety around flying may be tempted to avoid it altogether. Others try drugs or alcohol, but this can lead to abusive behaviour. A potentially more effective and more permanent cure might be to embark on one of the fear of flying courses which are available. The best of these courses offer help using recognised methods such as Cognitive Behavioural Therapy (CBT). Most courses offer a graduation flight but this can become another focus of anxiety or can create the illusion of cure. Course participants can become dependent on the group, managing to board a flight with experts and fellow sufferers but not alone. Captain Bunn says that allowing the sufferer to have some control over pace of the treatment brings a higher success rate.

5. If you are highly fearful, anxious or even have apparently unrelated concerns such as fear about lack of privacy when flying, help is available. Flying need not be the trauma you anticipate or have experienced. Sign up for a course or get your hands on some of the supportive materials available online or in print. There's a big wide world out there to discover, go and enjoy it.

* http://www.airsafe.com

Are the following statements True or False according to the text?

Q22: Fear of flying is a condition which affects a large number of people.

a) True
b) False

. . . .

Q23: The condition always develops gradually.

a) True
b) False

Q24: Most people who are afraid of flying are concerned about the danger of crashing.

a) True
b) False

Q25: Psychological therapies do not help those who are afraid of flying.

a) True
b) False

Q26: Captain Bunn has experience of flying.

a) True
b) False

Q27: Caregivers can influence the way in which children react to stress.

a) True
b) False

Q28: Normal responses to stress are not possible on planes.

a) True
b) False

Are the following statements fact or opinion?

Q29: Research carried out showed that more than ten per cent of Americans surveyed were nervous about flying.

a) Fact
b) Opinion

Q30: The reasons why people develop a fear of flying can be complicated.

a) Fact
b) Opinion

Q31: The best treatment for fear of flying involves giving the sufferer some control over the process of cure.

a) Fact
b) Opinion

6.4 Writing: Informal email: Arranging a trip

Writing: Informal email: Arranging a trip

Q32: Read the text below written by a student who has started university in Scotland. Note the following:

a) What kind of text is this?

b) What kind of language is used?

c) What is the purpose of the communication?

d) Who is the intended audience?

....

Hi Joanne

I just wanted to confirm some of my travel details for when I come down to see you next week.

I have booked the train which leaves Glasgow at 1040. This is a direct service and will get me into Euston at 1513. I can then get a tube to Paddington and finally a train to Windsor which will arrive at 1707.

Will you be able to collect me at the train station around that time? Or would you prefer if I caught the bus to your flat? Let me know what suits you best.

I am really looking forward to seeing you and to spending some time in Windsor again after all these years!

Sue x

Q33:

Write an email response to your friend. In your email, you should:

• apologise because you have to work late on the day discussed.

• explain that you will be unable to pick your friend up.

• suggest an alternative plan for transport to your flat.

Write 90-120 words. Show your completed work to your teacher who will provide you with feedback.

6.5   Grammar and listening: Idiomatic phrases

Grammar and listening: Idiomatic phrases (25 min)   Go online

Look at the idiomatic phrases below. Do you know any of these phrases? Share ideas with your partner and try to work out the meaning of each.

1. Pigs might fly

2. Sparks fly

3. To fly off the handle

4. Fly by night

5. Get off to a flying start

6. Pass with flying colours

7. Fly the nest

8. Fly in the face of (something)

9. Flying high

10. Must fly

You will need the following sound file to complete this next part of the activity: *n5-esl1-6-3listening.mp3*

Q34: Now listen to a woman talking about her daughter who has always wanted to be an air hostess. Each of the phrases above have been used. Try to work out meaning from context.

Grammar and listening: Definitions: Idiomatic phrases around flying   Go online

Q35: Match the phrase to the correct explanation.

1. Pigs might fly	a. People clash and get angry
2. Sparks fly	b. To have to leave quickly
3. To fly off the handle	c. Begin very well
4. Fly by night	d. Doing well, living a successful life
5. Get off to a flying start	e. Be very successful
6. Pass with flying colours	f. Lose your temper quickly
7. Fly the nest	g. Do the opposite of what is expected
8. Fly in the face of (something)	h. Dishonest and keen to make a quick profit
9. Flying high	I. Leave home
10. Must fly	j. Something is unlikely to happen

Grammar and listening: Idiomatic phrases (10 min)

Q36: Choose the correct idiomatic phrase from the list to complete the sentences below. You may need to change the tense.

Pigs might fly	To fly off the handle	Get off to a flying start	Fly the nest	Flying high
Sparks fly	Fly by night	Pass with flying colours	Fly in the face of	Must fly

a) My mother thinks that the reason we haven't _____ is that she has made our home too comfortable.

b) We opened the travel agency on Monday and have been enormously busy all week. We really _____.

c) My son has just got all his Highers. He _____.

d) I warned my husband not to invest in the new airline. I had heard they were just a _____ company and wouldn't last.

e) I think I can become an aircraft engineer if I work hard, but my sister says "_____".

f) Whenever I see my sister's boyfriend _____. I just do not like him!

6.6   Pronunciation: Use of polite intonation

When we are travelling, especially in airports and by aeroplane, airline staff are trained to speak to us politely. This is achieved through variations in pitch. Levels can be high or low and tone can be rising or falling. Listen to the following example of polite questions which you might be asked in an airport or on an aeroplane.

Pronunciation: Use of polite intonation   Go online

You will need the following sound file to complete this activity: *n5-esl1-6-4listening1.mp3* to *n5-esl1-6-4listening4.mp3*

Q37: Decide if you think the speaker's voice tone is rising or falling. Which word in the sentence is stressed? Indicate by underlining the word.

a) Can I help you sir/madam?

b) Can I see your boarding card please?

c) Do you want an aisle or window seat?

d) Would you like something to drink?

Listen again and repeat the sentences. Practise with your partner or group.

6.7   Reading comprehension: Travel and work abroad

Reading comprehension: Travel and work abroad   Go online

Readers who have been following our "Travel and work abroad" series about some rather more unusual ways of getting away from it all have so far enjoyed finding out about life in a circus, volunteering and teaching. This week we go very upmarket and feature the life and work of Megan, an employee of Global Mobility. Megan looks after highly paid executives in the oil industry, ensuring that when they travel and work they experience as little inconvenience as possible. "I have been involved in Global Mobility for around fifteen years. It is not something that I had planned to do, as I had never heard of the job until I saw the position advertised in a newspaper. As a consequence, I was taken on by an oil company at a time when I had very little direct experience. I had the generic, administrative skills which enabled me to cope, but it was a challenge at the beginning. Nowadays I have the experience necessary to do the job more easily, but it still gives me a lot to think about. There is nothing routine about the job and no two days are the same."

"My job is essentially Human Resources and man management. The company I work for employs me to deal with the deployment of staff to our centres around the world. I arrange visas, negotiate work permits, arrange accommodation and pay utility bills for our staff over a range of projects worldwide. The volume of work this presents can be extremely high. I tend to deal with specialised, ambitious and highly paid individuals. As such, I rarely find my clients to be patient. Generally, the stress level of staff does not present a problem but occasionally I do have to placate some rather egotistical individuals."

"Overall, I really enjoy the work. I have a home base but I have close contact with teams in the UK, USA and Far East and I regularly have to travel and meet other teams. The wide range of time zones involved means that conference calls are sometimes arranged at very early or late hours, but that doesn't happen often. I accept these things because it's part of the job. I suffer a little from the lack of a permanent team around me sometimes. If any new systems are put in place for example, it can be more difficult to pick these up remotely. Nevertheless, because of having friends in the London office I am never at a loss for long."

"I feel that the advantages of my job far outweigh the disadvantages. I love being able to help people make a fresh start in a new country, help them feel settled and happy. Being part of the global team which makes this possible is amazing. The team is very important to me. I am part of a global network. Having a home base means I can also spend time with my family, which is very important to me as well."

"It seems to me that in life, we can rarely guess what is around the corner. At one stage in my career, having been made redundant, I took a job in a store selling Christmas turkeys. At that time I never thought that I would end up flying to the USA and Far East on business trips. I have always worked hard and now I am getting some rewards, but I don't take anything for granted."

Q38: Megan's job is mainly:

  a) repetitive and predictable.

  b) varied and interesting.

  c) sociable and fun.

                        ....

Q39: Most of Megan's clients are:

  a) easy-going.

  b) good-natured.

  c) tense.

                        ....

Q40: Decide if the following statements are true or false.

  a) Megan often has to work without assistance.

  b) Helping people gives Megan a great deal of job satisfaction.

  c) Success has come easily for Megan.

                        ....

Q41: Find a word in paragraph *1* with the following definition: "non-specific or typical of a whole group".

                        ....

Q42: Find a word in paragraph *2* with the following definition: "make someone less angry about something".

....

Q43: Find a word in paragraph *2* with the following definition: "thinking you are better than someone".

....

Q44: Find a word in the last paragraph with the following definition: "Having lost a job".

....

Q45: Which of the following best describe Megan's attitude to her current success:

a) Appreciative

b) Complacent

c) Dissatisfied

6.8   Listening comprehension: Healthy Living Show

Listening comprehension: Healthy Living Show (30 min)	Go online

You will need the following sound file to complete this assessment activity: *n5-esl1-6-5listening.mp3*

Q46: What background and experience does the main speaker have?

....

Q47: What are some of the main symptoms of jet lag? Select three answers from the list:

a) Confusion

b) Disorientation

c) Slurred speech

d) Dizziness

e) Insomnia

f) Fatigue

....

Q48: Complete the sentence using **no more than three** words:

Jet lag is caused by . . . .

....

Q49: Complete the sentence using **no more than three** words:

Jet lag is more problematic for our bodies when we travel . . . .

Decide whether the following statements are true or false.

Q50: Alcohol helps to overcome jet lag.

....

Q51: We should create a routine to match our new time zone when we travel.

....

Q52: A short nap on arrival in a new destination will help us cope better with jet lag.

....

Q53: Natural light is an important factor in maintaining natural body rhythms .

....

Q54: What is the context of the conversation?

1. A lecture
2. A radio broadcast
3. A TV debate

Unit 1 Topic 7

Current affairs

Contents

Learning objective

By the end of this topic you will be better able to:

- participate in a conversation about environmental issues;
- maintain the flow of conversation in formal and informal situations;
- identify the form and pronunciation of question tags and produce these;
- identify features of formal letters and write a formal letter.

7.1   Environmentally friendly homes

Pre-reading activity: Speaking: Discussion: Homes (10 min)

Work with a partner or in a group if possible.

Q1:   Talk about the difference between the following pairs of words.

1. Attic : cellar
2. Front door : door
3. Roof : ceiling
4. Lamp : light
5. Heater : fire

Environmentally friendly homes (15 min)   Go online

Q2:   Match the terms on the left with the definitions on the right. You may work with a partner.

1. Draught	a. Window panes consisting of two layers of glass with a space between.
2. Double glazing	b. Space below the roof of a house.
3. Cavity wall	c. Mixture of rotten food and plants used to make soil richer.
4. Compost	d. Process or method of building.
5. Construction	e. Use of material such as foam to prevent flow of air or sound.
6. Loft	f. Flow of cold air.
7. Insulation	g. Machines for use in the home.
8. Domestic appliances	h. Two walls with a space between them.

7.2   Vocabulary: Environmentally friendly homes

You are going to talk and read about environmentally friendly behaviour in the home in later topics. Before you begin, check your understanding of some of the vocabulary which will be used by attempting this activity.

Pre-reading activity: Speaking : Discussion: Environmentally friendly homes (15 min)

Is your home environmentally friendly? Interview your partner using the following questions:

1. Do you live in an old house/flat or a modern house/flat?

2. Do you suffer from draughts?

3. Are your windows single, double or triple glazed?

4. Do you have loft or cavity wall insulation?

5. Do you use energy smart light bulbs?

6. Is your washing machine generally set on a high or low temperature?

7. Do you have a compost heap?

Reading: Environmentally friendly homes

Read the following text and compare the information in the article with what you discussed with your partner. Do you think your home is environmentally friendly?

1. An important element in saving energy costs, and at the same time running a more environmentally friendly home, is heat conservation. Heat energy can be contained more effectively through insulated lofts and walls. If you have a modern home then the chances are that you will experience fewer problems in preserving energy. Design and building specifications have improved dramatically in recent years. As a result of this, most homes built post 1920 in the UK already have features such as cavity walls which are suitable for insulation. However, if you are living in a house which is older than this and feeling chilly, it is worth checking out whether or not you are properly insulated. Lagged pipes and boilers also save heat energy which can, in turn, save money.

2. It doesn't matter how well insulated your walls, pipes and boilers are, you may still suffer from draughts. If you can feel gales blowing through windows, gusts of air under doors and down chimneys then all the insulated heat may well be disappearing. These energy saboteurs can be cut down by taking some simple steps around the home. In many climates, single glazing on windows is simply not enough - double or even triple glazing will insulate your home, making it cosier and more efficient immediately. Again, an investment in glazing is of no real value if you continue to allow air to travel up and out of chimneys and through gaps under doors, for example. Fireplaces can be covered with screens and doors. Remember, simple steps such as thick window drapes across windows and draught excluders under doors may stop hot air escaping and cool air coming in. All these steps can be effective ways of conserving heat energy.

3. If you are serious about lowering energy costs it is important to think about domestic appliances. Older products are likely to be less environmentally friendly than newer models which are generally far more efficient. In the UK, more environmentally friendly

models of washing machines are graded accordingly. Consumers should also look for machines which use less than fifty litres of water per wash.

4. It is not only heat that we need to conserve if we really want to cut down our costs and our carbon footprint, it is also light. Many people already use energy efficient light bulbs and the benefits are enormous. Not only does an energy efficient light bulb use significantly less energy, but it also lasts for around ten times as long as a traditional light bulb. If you have outside lighting, it would be more energy efficient to replace this with motion sensors which will give you the security you want without costing the earth.

5. Environmentally friendly houses may involve some investment of cash. However, it won't necessarily cost any money to change our habits and start thinking more carefully about our behaviour, and this is perhaps equally important. For example, it may not be within your means to upgrade domestic appliances but you can consider how you use the appliances you have. Again, with respect to washing machines, it is far more energy efficient to wash full loads than partial loads and to wash at lower temperatures. Turning off lights, televisions and computers when we are not using them are all ways to help reduce our individual energy bills and our collective carbon footprint.

Post-reading activity: Matching paragraph headings: Environmentally Go online **friendly homes (30 min)**

Q3:   Match these headings to paragraphs of the text (one heading is not required).

a) 'Green' thinking

b) See the Light

c) Eliminate air flow

d) White Goods

e) Chill Out

f) Consider Insulation

Post-reading activity: Identifying informal language

Q4:   This text is written in a quite informal way. What features of informal writing can you find in the text?

Post-reading activity: informal to formal language: Environmentally Go online **friendly homes**

Q5: Look at the following language from the text and try to think of more formal substitutes.

a) Chilly (par.1)

b) Check out (par.1)

c) (It) doesn't matter (par.2)

d) Cut down on (par.2)

e) Enough (par.2)

f) Stop (par.2)

g) Around (par.4)

h) Want (par.4)

i) Investment of Cash (par.5)

j) Turn off (par.5)

Are the following statements True or False?

Q6: Conserving energy in older houses can be more problematic than in modern homes.

a) True

b) False

....

Q7: Good insulation will eliminate heating problems.

a) True

b) False

....

Q8: Domestic appliances in the UK are scored in terms of energy efficiency.

a) True

b) False

....

Q9: An investment in environmentally friendly homes is less worthwhile than making lifestyle changes.

a) True

b) False

Q10: Explain in your own words why the use of the phrase 'cost the earth' (paragraph 5) in this context is effective.

7.3 Vocabulary: Environmental issues

Pre-listening activity: Vocabulary: Environmental issues (10 min)   Go online

Q11: Add vowels to gaps below to make words and phrases associated with environmental issues.

a) F L _ S H / F L _ _ D S

b) C _ _ S T _ L / _ R _ S _ _ N

c) R _ S _ N G / T _ D _ S

d) M _ L T _ N G / G L _ C _ _ R S

e) F R _ _ K / W _ _ T H _ R

f) V _ _ L _ N T / S T _ R M S

g) W _ R M _ R / C L _ M _ T _

h) H _ _ T / W _ V _

Pre-listening activity: Speaking: Environmental issues (10 min)

Discuss the following questions with a partner or in a group.

- What do you understand by the term 'global warming'?
- What do you think are the causes of global warming?
- What do you think are the effects of global warming?
- What concerns do you have about global warming?
- Do you have any experience of the effects of global warming?

Listening activity: Note taking: Environmental issues (45 min)   Go online

You will need the following sound file to complete this activity: *n5-esl1-7-1listening.mp3*

Q12: Look at the following words and phrases from the recording which are examples of idiomatic use of language. Match the idiomatic phrases on the left with definitions on the right.

1. Strike a chord	a. become attached to something or someone
2. Latch on to	b. abandon a situation
3. Peak season	c. escape from a situation in which you no longer wish to be involved
4. Sit tight	d. something which reminds one of something and/ or makes one feel sympathy
5. Jump ship	e. time of the year when most tourists visit
6. Bail out	f. wait where you are

. . . .

Q13: Listen to the recorded conversation again. While listening, write down all the words / phrases that you hear which are used to express fear or are connected with being afraid. When you have finished, discuss your answers with your partner / group.

Match the speakers (Jeff, Louise or Samantha) with the ideas expressed.

Q14: Flash floods are frightening because we do not know when to expect them.

a) Jeff
b) Louise
c) Samantha

. . . .

Q15: The media sometimes make us worry when there is no real need.

a) Jeff
b) Louise
c) Samantha

. . . .

Q16: Living beside the seaside might not be possible in the future.

a) Jeff
b) Louise
c) Samantha

. . . .

Q17: We are experiencing a genuine environmental crisis.

a) Jeff
b) Louise
c) Samantha

Identify which of the speakers (Jeff, Louise or Samantha) expressed the following ideas.

Q18: Who was affected by a lack of snow?

a) Jeff
b) Louise
c) Samantha

....

Q19: Who was affected by floods?

a) Jeff
b) Louise
c) Samantha

....

Q20: Who does not talk about being affected by global warming?

a) Jeff
b) Louise
c) Samantha

Complete the following sentences in **no more than four words**:

Q21: Jeff saw images on the internet revealing .... over the Taj Mahal in India.

....

Q22: Louise's skiing holiday was disappointing because .... due to flooding.

....

Q23: When heavy rain threatened his home, Jeff was asked if he wanted ....

....

Q24: The speakers are:

a) friends.
b) relatives.
c) fellow students.

7.4   Grammar: Question tags

Look at the following extracts from the recording you listened to earlier. Each contains an example of a tag question (in bold).

a) They (Flash floods) are absolutely terrifying, **aren't they**?

b) ... we can't hide our heads in the sand any more, **can we**?

c) You live in a flood zone, **do you**?

Grammar: Discuss types of question tags (15 min)

If possible work with a partner to answer these questions.

Q25: In which of the examples has the speaker just realised / received new information about something?

a)   They (Flash floods) are absolutely terrifying, **aren't they**?
b)   ... we can't hide our heads in the sand any more, **can we**?
c)   You live in a flood zone, **do you**?

....

Q26: In which of the examples does the speaker expect agreement?

a) They (Flash floods) are absolutely terrifying, **aren't they**?

b) ... we can't hide our heads in the sand any more, **can we**?

c) You live in a flood zone, **do you**?

a)   a and b
b)   b and c
c)   a and c

....

Q27: Look at the structure of each sentence again. Can you think of the grammatical rules for different kinds of question tag?

A tag is a question added to the end of a sentence which we use when we seek agreement from the listener, when we are making a tentative request for agreement from the speaker or when we have just found out/realised something.

Example

We should all do our best to reduce carbon emissions, shouldn't we?
We don't have to stop using the car altogether, do we?
You live in an eco-hut, do you?

The tag takes the form - auxiliary (+ n't) + pronoun.

As a general rule, patterns of use are as follows:

Positive statement + Negative tag	We use when we seek/expect agreement from listener. *We have to recycle whenever possible, don't we?*
Negative statement + Positive tag	We use when we seek/expect agreement from listener although we may be less certain of agreement. We also use when to express surprise. *You don't throw away plastic bottles, do you?* *You don't still use plastic carrier bags, do you?*
Positive statement + Positive tag	We use when we are just informed of something or just realise something. *You can take rubbish to the recycle plant yourself, can you?*

Key point

Question tags

1. In sentences without an auxiliary verb we use 'do' in the tag.
   e.g. *We saved energy all last year by car sharing, **didn't** we?*

2. Where the main verb is 'be' in the first person we use 'aren't I' in the tag.
   e.g. *I'm very eco-friendly, **aren't I**?*

3. Where the pronoun is 'this', 'that', 'those' or 'these', we use 'it' or 'they' in the tag.
   e.g. *These cleaning products are environmentally friendly, aren't **they**?*
   *That car is extremely low on carbon emissions, isn't **it**?*

4. In formal (spoken) language, we might say 'is it not?' rather than 'isn't it'?
   e.g. *The best way forward is to work on enhancing policy agreements on climate change, **is it not**?*

Grammar: Choose the correct (10 min)   Go online

Q28: Complete the following sentences with the most appropriate tags.

a) Climate change is affecting all of us now, _____?

b) The planet isn't likely to survive if we don't make changes, _____?

c) We should all try to recycle our rubbish, _____?

d) Some countries are more eco-friendly than others, _____?

e) You live in a very eco-friendly way, _____?

f) The changes in climate have affected wildlife too, _____?

g) These old-fashioned houses certainly eat up energy, _____?

h) The new boiler we have installed wasn't very expensive, _____?

i) You've just installed solar panels, _____?

j) Mr Smith, you have been employed as an energy specialist for ten years, _____?

k) So you have never been to a bottle bank before, _____?

l) Madam, your party has only considered environmental issues worthwhile in the lead up to the election, _____?

7.5 Pronunciation: Question tags

Voice plays an important part in indicating how we are feeling. In question tags intonation generally follows the patterns described below. Read the examples and then listen and repeat the sentences.

You will need the following sound files to listen to these examples:
n5-esl1-7-2listening1.mp3 to *n5-esl1-7-2listening7.mp3*

Examples

1. We tend to use falling intonation where a negative tag follows a positive statement or where a positive tag follows a negative statement if we are fairly certain of agreement.

*n5-esl1-7-2listening1.mp3: We can start by using energy saving light bulbs, **can't we**?* ↘

*n5-esl1-7-2listening2.mp3: We can't stop using the car altogether, **can we**?* ↘

....

2. Where we are less certain of agreement we might use rising intonation. We might also use rising intonation if we were expressing indignation.

*n5-esl1-7-2listening3.mp3: We can definitely reduce our carbon footprint, **can't we**?* ↗

*n5-esl1-7-2listening4.mp3: We can't install **solar panels** on our roof, **can we**?* ↗

*n5-esl1-7-2listening5.mp3: You don't expect me to use public transport all the time, **do you**?* ↗

....

We tend to use rising intonation where a positive tag follows a positive statement to express surprise at new information.

n5-esl1-7-2listening6.mp3: Energy saving bulbs last ten times longer than traditional bulbs, do they?

> **Top tip**
>
> Be careful, because flat intonation in question tags can sound sarcastic intentionally or unintentionally e.g.
> *n5-esl1-7-2listening7.mp3:*
> *You are going to start cycling ten miles to work every day, **are you**?* →

Pronunciation: Question tags: Patterns of intonation

Go online

In pairs, mark the tags in the following statements with appropriate patterns of intonation; **rising** ↗ or **falling** ↘; to express the meaning (in brackets).

Example *The amount of carbon waste produced by industrial cities is dangerously high, isn't it? (expecting agreement)*

therefore
*The amount of carbon waste produced by industrial cities is dangerously high, **isn't it**?* ↘

Q29:

a) I don't think you give much thought to the future of the planet, do you? (tentative suggestion)

b) I don't think you give much thought to the future of the planet, do you? (expecting agreement)

c) She has given her heart and soul to designing sustainable homes, hasn't she? (expecting agreement)

d) She has given her heart and soul to designing sustainable homes, hasn't she? (tentatively)

e) So you think you are eco-friendly, do you? (sarcastically)

f) You are very eco-friendly, aren't you? (expecting agreement)

g) So you're saying I can't install solar panels on my roof, are you? (surprised)

h) So you're saying I can't install solar panels on my roof, are you? (expecting agreement)

i) The future of our wildlife is under threat if we don't take radical steps to reduce pollution, isn't it? (tentatively)

j) The future of our wildlife is under threat if we don't take radical steps to reduce pollution, isn't it? (expecting agreement)

k) You don't think my giving up driving a sports car will save the planet, do you? (expressing disbelief)

l) You don't think my giving up driving a sports car will save the planet, do you? (expecting agreement)

m) The state of the planet is our responsibility, isn't it? (expecting agreement)

n) The state of the planet is our responsibility, isn't it? (tentatively)

o) You are an eco-warrior, are you? (surprised)

p) You are an eco-warrior, are you? (sarcastic/disbelieving)

7.6 Study skills: Formal and informal language

When we are talking about the environment, for example with friends and fellow students, we would probably use quite informal language. In other less familiar contexts, particularly in writing, we would usually use more formal language.

Formal and informal language (60 min)

Q30: Look at the following words and phrases and try to replace them with more formal equivalents. There may be more than one appropriate answer.

1. For	
2. Worried	
3. Things we do	
4. Lots	
5. Like	
6. Started	
7. To get people to see	
8. To work together	
9. To pool	
10. To come up with (something)	
11. To start off	
12. The last thing	
13. About	
14. Giving (people) encouragement to do something	
15. Facts and figures	
16. Urge	
17. Get (attention)	
18. Think	

7.7   Writing: Use of formal language

Use of formal language (30 min)

Read the letter below which is intended for a Member of Parliament, and then try to rewrite it using more appropriate/formal language. Show it to your tutor if possible.

Dear Mr Robinson

I am writing for a group of students who are in the 'Go Green' society of the Student's Union at Western College. We are all really worried about global warming, climate change and the future of the planet. We know that lots of things we do, like using cars all the time instead of buses or trains, waste energy **resources**.

We have started doing a project to try and get students and staff to see that cars are a problem and to do things differently. We got together with another nearby college, pooled our resources and have come up with a plan to move forward on this.

To start off we think we will ask some lecturers and students about the ways they travel and then we are going to look carefully at the results to see what ideas we can come up with. The last thing we will do is decide how we can be kinder to the environment when we travel to college. We have been thinking about car share schemes and giving people good reason to cycle to work instead of driving.

We wanted to ask you if you could provide facts and figures about environmental problems that would get attention and urge people to think twice about what they are doing.

Thank you very much
Yours sincerely

7.8   Writing: Focus on formal letters

Focus on writing formal letters (30 min)

Write a follow-up letter to Mark Robinson MP, telling him about the progress you have made with the Go Green group in your attempts to persuade staff and students at your college to be more environmentally friendly. Include the following information:

- Thank Mr Robinson for statistics provided.

- Describe the work you have done to date.

- Invite Mr Robinson to visit the college and meet the 'Go Green' group.

You should write between 90 and 120 words.

7.9   Green fashion

Reading comprehension: Green fashion (40 min)   Go online

Read the text and then answer the questions which follow.

How often do you buy new clothes?
Are you a slave to fashion, buying the latest trendy, designer clothes and then throwing them out as soon as they are no longer in vogue? Well perhaps it's time to adopt a different attitude to clothes and shopping and try an alternative trend which is sweeping the nation. With an environmentally friendly approach to clothes you will find that you can save money as well as help save the planet.

Why fashion can be bad for the environment
If you are addicted to 'fast fashion'; clothes which are cheap to buy but soon replaced by new designs, then it might interest you to know that this behaviour can have a powerful and negative impact on the environment. In Britain it is estimated that 2 million tonnes of clothing is bought each year and at the same time 1.2 million tonnes of clothing is thrown away.* The problem with this is that a lot of waste clothing ends up in landfill sites which can cause pollution to the local environment as well as producing methane; significantly more dangerous than CO_2 in terms of damage to the environment. Fast fashion often means low cost clothes made by badly paid labourers, and implies a greater amount of energy to produce the clothes in the first place. Production of cotton uses a lot of water in areas where water may be in short supply. Growing cotton also involves the widespread use of pesticides - many of which are toxic to marine life.

How to make your clothes 'green'
There are many ways that you can turn things around and take a more ethical approach to clothes. In the first instance, you might like to think about whether you really do need so many new clothes. Look at what is in your wardrobe and you may be surprised to discover a number of things which can be revamped. Consider a visit to a vintage clothing or charity shop. In times of recession such as today, these shops are easy to find. Take clothes you no longer want but which others might like and at the same time perhaps pick up something 'new' to you. This is an ideal way to change your look and to help save the planet.

Stay Chic
If you are unimpressed with the concept of recycled clothes then do not despair. There are several companies around offering exciting new designs in clothes and shoes which are ethically produced. Fair-trade labelling is a standard agreed by a range of interested groups including producers, traders, academics and others to ensure ethical and sustainable production. The Fair-trade label can be found on clothes available in many high street outlets and ensures a more responsible approach has been taken in producing garments. Estethica is an organisation initiated by the British Fashion Council which brings together designers committed to concepts such as fair-trade and the use of organic or recycled materials. Members of Estethica are not only top class designers but they also consider sustainability.

Small steps
Remember you do not have to make an enormous effort to change your approach. Most towns and cities in the UK have recycle banks for unwanted clothing. At the same time, there are a number of small changes you can make at home. Try repairing old clothes rather than throwing them away. Buy clothes to last, rather than for a single season. Wash rather than

dry clean, because dry cleaning often involves use of harmful chemicals. Finally, remember to try to wash full loads in your washing machine at low temperatures, and don't forget about the good old fashioned hand wash.

http://www.direct.gov.uk/en/Environmentandgreenerliving/Greenerhomeandgarden/ Greenershopping/DG_064424

Q31: In what context might you read this text?

a) A daily newspaper

b) A magazine

c) An educational journal

....

Q32: What is the purpose of the text?

a) To entertain

b) To educate

c) To entertain and educate

....

Q33: Are the following statements True or False?

a) Fast fashion can contribute to environmental pollution.

b) Production of clothes can waste a lot of energy.

c) Methane is less damaging than CO_2 emissions.

d) Ethical clothes shopping means buying unattractive designs.

e) Many high street stores sell ethical clothes.

f) Designers working for Estethica care about the planet.

....

Q34: In what ways does the writer suggest clothes can be recycled? (give two answers)

....

Q35: In what ways is the production of cotton harmful to the environment? (give two answers)

....

Q36: Explain in your own words what a fair-trade label means.

....

Q37: Find three words in the text which mean 'fashionable'.

....

Q38: What message does the writer express?

a) The fashion industry is destroying the environment.

b) Ethical shopping and recycling can help to protect the environment.

c) Recycling is the latest fashion.

7.10 Listening Comprehension: Compost

Listening comprehension: Compost (30 min)   Go online

You will need the following sound file to complete this assessment activity:
n5-esl1-7-3listening.mp3

Complete the sentences by typing missing words or phrases into the boxes. Use **no more than four** words:

Q39: Magnus got his compost bin from . . . .

. . . .

Q40: Magnus describes the . . . . processes of composting.

. . . .

Q41: As he doesn't have . . . ., Magnus can only use one method of composting.

. . . .

Q42: The two categories of rubbish are called . . . . and . . . .

. . . .

Q43: People should not put cooked food on a compost heap because it . . . .

. . . .

Q44: Decide which **one** of the following statements is true according to Magnus:

a) Compost feeds the plants while fertiliser feeds the soil.
b) Compost feeds the soil while fertiliser feeds the plants.
c) Compost feeds both soil and plants.

. . . .

Q45: Select the **three** main reasons which prompted Magnus to start composting from the list below:

a) To nourish the soil
b) To share time with his wife
c) To help cut down on landfill waste
d) To keep gardening costs down
e) To avoid being in his wife's way

. . . .

Q46: Simon and Magnus are:

a) great friends.
b) neighbours.
c) colleagues.

Unit 1 Topic 8

Cultural awareness

Contents

Learning objective

By the end of this topic you will be better able to:

- recognise and discuss aspects of cultural variation;
- identify and produce present tenses in simple, continuous and perfect aspect;
- identify features of articles and write a short article;
- use study and free time more effectively in order to enhance language learning.

8.1   Vocabulary: Identification of stereotypes

Stereotypes (15 min)

Q1:

Think about your own country and the stereotypical habits/behaviour associated with it. Now think about the four countries listed in the table and try to complete the table with stereotypical habits/behaviour of each nationality.

E.g. Scottish people: Clothes: kilts, Food/Drink: haggis and whisky etc.

	Clothes	Food/Drink	Home/transport	Others
My country				
Japan				
England				
France				
Italy				

8.2   Speaking: Stereotypes

Challenge your thinking (5 min)

Think about your answers to the previous activity and share your thoughts with others if possible, in your group. How many of these stereotypical features of nationalities are accurate?

8.3 Reading and speaking: Cultural awareness

Interview a colleague using the following activity questions and then check answers to find out how culturally aware you are.

Cross cultural quiz (40 min)

Q2: You are invited to the home of an Iranian family. When you sit down you notice the children of the family staring at your feet. What is the reason for this?

a) Iranian children are taught to be humble.
b) It is polite for the stranger to make the first move in conversation with Iranians.
c) You have forgotten to remove your shoes before entering the home which is customary in Iranian homes.

. . . .

Q3: You are invited to a dinner party with some British people and the conversation gets around to work. You tell them that you are dissatisfied with your work because the job is dull and the salary is low. You ask for tips on finding a new job and ask how much everyone else earns. Why does another guest change the subject?

a) You should never tell British people you do not enjoy your work as it is considered shameful.
b) British people believe it is rude to discuss salaries.
c) British people do not talk about work at social gatherings.

. . . .

Q4: You are chatting to a Polish friend about her studies and she tells you that she has an exam the following day. You remind her to have a good night's rest, not to worry and wish her luck. She says, "No, thank you", which you find confusing. What upset her?

a) In Poland it is considered unlucky when someone wishes you luck.
b) Polish women do not appreciate being told what to do.
c) Your comments made her feel like she did not have a chance at succeeding in the exam.

. . . .

Q5: You are attending a business meeting with some Japanese people. Before you start negotiating you sit down at a table opposite them, remove your jacket and wait politely for their input. The meeting does not go well.

a) Japanese people do not conduct business across a table.
b) You should always take the initiative when doing business with Japanese people.
c) The removal of your jacket is an inappropriate lack of formality.

. . . .

Q6: You are conducting interviews for a position in your bank. Your final applicant is of Indian nationality. You are confused because when you ask questions this applicant often merely says 'yes'. What is the reason for this?

a) The applicant has no idea how to answer your questions.
b) The applicant is showing respect to you and your position.
c) The applicant is demonstrating full understanding of your questions.

....

Q7: You are introduced to a new colleague who is from France. You want to make him comfortable so you chat about the weather and the news and ask if he has a family. He is quite unresponsive. Why?

a) French people do not engage in conversations about the weather.
b) French people do not engage in conversations about current affairs.
c) It is not usual to make enquiries about the personal life of a French person if you do not know them well.

....

Q8: You have been invited to the home of a Turkish colleague and want to take a gift with you. What would be most appropriate?

a) A bottle of wine.
b) A selection of cakes.
c) A box of candles.

....

Q9: You are teaching some Spanish students and arrange to meet some of them in a local restaurant at 7 o'clock. At 8 o'clock you are still waiting for them so you give up and decide to go home. What is the reason for their behaviour?

a) It is not acceptable to socialise with Spanish students if you are a teacher.
b) When Spanish people make an arrangement it is not a definite agreement.
c) Spanish people are less rigid about punctuality than others and would not have thought this was insulting.

....

Q10: You are shopping in a department store in Scotland and trying on a coat. Another lady shopper, obviously Scottish, starts to chat to you about the quality and style of the coat, the price and whether or not the coat suits you. What is the reason for this?

a) She is being friendly. This is normal behaviour in Scotland.
b) She is a bit rude and has no sense of appropriate behaviour.
c) She is eccentric.

....

Q11: You are delivering a seminar in your subject area; you arrive a few minutes late due to heavy morning traffic. You apologise profusely for the slightly late arrival but begin the seminar immediately. The topic is controversial but seems well received. You call a break mid-morning during which you sit down next to a German lady who has always been supportive of your ideas. You ask for her opinion of the seminar so far but she seems a little hostile. What is the problem?

a) She does not like the controversial nature of the material and believes it is not appropriate to discuss such matters.
b) She does not think it is appropriate to chat socially during the break.
c) She is offended by your lack of punctuality. This is a big issue in Germany and she perceives your lateness as extremely rude.

8.4 Listening activity: Living in Scotland

Listen to the four speakers talking about their experience of living in Scotland. You will hear the recording more than once.

Living in Scotland (1) (15 min)   Go online

You will need the following sound files in order to complete this activity: *n5-esl1-8-1listening1.mp3, n5-esl1-8-1listening2.mp3, n5-esl1-8-1listening3.mp3* and *n5-esl1-8-1listening4.mp3*.

Listen to the sound files and take notes on the questions that follow.

1. *Speaker 1*: Brigida

2. *Speaker 2*: Claudia

3. *Speaker 3*: Justyna

4. *Speaker 4*: Nazhin

Q12: Where is speaker 1 from?

....

Q13: Where is speaker 2 from?

....

Q14: Where is speaker 3 from?

....

Q15: Where is speaker 4 from?

....

Q16: What was the reason that speaker 1 came to the UK?

....

Q17: What was the reason that speaker 2 came to the UK?

....

Q18: What was the reason that speaker 3 came to the UK?

....

Q19: What was the reason that speaker 4 came to the UK?

....

Living in Scotland (2) (25 min)   Go online 🔊

You will need the following sound files in order to complete this activity:
n5-esl1-8-1listening1.mp3, *n5-esl1-8-1listening2.mp3*, *n5-esl1-8-1listening3.mp3* and *n5-esl1-8-1listening4.mp3*.

Before listening to the sound files, read the following questions. While listening, try to answer the questions. After listening, type in answers in two or three words then check your answers (with a partner if possible) and listen again if necessary.

1. *Speaker 1*: Brigida

2. *Speaker 2*: Claudia

3. *Speaker 3*: Justyna

4. *Speaker 4*: Nazhin

Q20: What was the main problem which the first speaker had when she moved to Scotland? (2 words)

....

Q21: How does Brigida describe her husband? (2 words)

....

Q22: What benefit does Claudia's husband get from walking everywhere? (2 words)

....

Q23: What does Claudia suggest people should do in Scotland? (2 words)

....

Q24: What two things does Justyna think that Polish and Scots have in common? (4 words)

....

Q25: What feature of Justyna's speech sometimes makes it difficult for people to understand her? (2 words)

....

Q26: Nazhin says that currently women in Iran do two things which are different from women in the UK; what are they? (3 words, 3 words)

....

Q27: Why does Nazhin say that Scottish men find Iranian men unusual? (3 words)

8.5 Grammar: Review of tense and aspect

Grammar: Present simple and continuous (10 min)

Look at the table below, compare the sentences on the left with those on the right.

1a)	My husband walks to work	1b)	My husband is walking to work
2a)	I live in Edinburgh	2b)	I am living in Edinburgh

Q28: Discuss with a partner the difference between the sentences *1a)* and *1b)* and *2a)* and *2b)*. You should think about form and meaning. Make notes on your discussion.

Grammar: State verbs (10 min)

Look at the sentences below which are not normally used in the continuous form.

   a) *People in Edinburgh enjoy culture.*

   b) *Sometimes people don't understand me.*

Q29: Explain why these sentences are not normally used in the continuous form.

Grammar: Present perfect simple and continuous (10 min)

Look at the table below, compare the sentences on the left with those on the right.

1a)	I have lived in Scotland for ten years	1b)	I have been living in Scotland for ten years
2a)	I have cooked a traditional meal	2b)	I have been cooking a traditional meal

Q30: Discuss with a partner the differences in form and meaning. Make notes on your discussion.

Grammar: Activity: Identifying errors (15 min)

Go online

Read the following text which has been written by a student of English. He was asked to describe his experience of living in Glasgow. He has made some mistakes in use of grammar. There are 19 mistakes.

Q31: Underline the mistakes in the text.

I am living in Scotland for two years and I am very happy here. When I first arrived in the UK, I found the culture a little strange and I was a bit homesick. However, now I am relaxed and comfortable here as I am knowing a lot of people and have a lot of friends.

First I will telling you about the little problems because nowhere is perfect. A lot of people is complaining about the food in Scotland. This is really not a big problem. I find that although some Scottish people eating fried foods a lot, there are lots of very good shops and restaurants for buy or eat other foods. You don't have to eating chips. Also some people drink a lot of beer but not everyone drinks.

The weather in Scotland is not the best. If you are coming to Scotland there is something that it is very important to be bringing with you and that is waterproof clothes. I am buying lots of waterproof clothes now so I do not have a problem with the rain any more. It is raining here a lot. Last month it rained every day. The local people are used to rain but even they were upset because this is supposed to be summer.

Something that you should know about Scotland is that people in Scotland are very friendly. People in Glasgow are talking to you all the time, at bus stops, in shops and in the street. They are often talking about the bad weather. I am making lots of friends because the Scots like people from different countries and often want to help you.

Another really good thing about Scotland is the scenery. It is really important to visit the north of the country. I am visiting many towns and villages in the north of Scotland already and I visit three islands, Mull, Islay and Skye. The scenery is fantastic! I recommend you visiting them too.

Finally, I would like to say that I am not regretting the chance to be here and experience the Scottish culture. I think I am going back to Spain one day but for now I am glad to be here.

Grammar: Correcting grammatical errors (15 min)

Go online

Read the following text which has been written by a student of English. He was asked to describe his experience of living in Glasgow. He has made some mistakes in use of grammar.

Q32:
Correct the mistakes in the text that you identified in the previous question. This text contains the mistakes you have already identified.

I am living in Scotland for two years and I am very happy here. When I first arrived in the UK, I found the culture a little strange and I was a bit homesick. However, now I am relaxed and comfortable here as I am knowing a lot of people and have a lot of friends.

First I will telling you about the little problems because nowhere is perfect. A lot of people is complaining about the food in Scotland. This is really not a big problem. I find that although some Scottish people eating fried foods a lot, there are lots of very good shops and restaurants for buy or eat other foods. You don't have to eating chips. Also some people drink a lot of beer but not everyone drinks.

The weather in Scotland is not the best. If you are coming to Scotland there is something that it is very important to be bringing with you and that is waterproof clothes. I am buying lots of waterproof clothes now so I do not have a problem with the rain any more. It is raining here a lot. Last month it rained every day. The local people are used to rain but even they were upset because this is supposed to be summer.

Something that you should know about Scotland is that people in Scotland are very friendly. People in Glasgow are talking to you all the time, at bus stops, in shops and in the street. They are often talking about the bad weather. I am making lots of friends because the Scots like people from different countries and often want to help you.

Another really good thing about Scotland is the scenery. It is really important to visit the north of the country. I am visiting many towns and villages in the north of Scotland already and I visit three islands, Mull, Islay and Skye. The scenery is fantastic! I recommend you visiting them too.

Finally, I would like to say that I am not regretting the chance to be here and experience the Scottish culture. I think I am going back to Spain one day but for now I am glad to be here.

Grammar: Select the correct tense (15 min)   Go online

Q33: Complete the following sentences using the verb in brackets in either present simple/continuous/perfect.

a) I _____ in Aberdeen since 1999. **(lived)**

b) I _____ some new friends at the university bar tonight. **(meet)**

c) Today I **(work)** on an essay but I _____it yet. **(not finish)**

d) I _____ meeting new people but I am a little shy. **(enjoy)**

e) My family _____ a few times since I moved to this city. **(visited)**

f) I _____ into the city centre every day to buy food or have a coffee. **(walk)**

g) My friend Isabel _____ Psychology as well, so we work on projects together. **(study)**

h) I _____ being a student but sometimes I _____ in case I don't pass my exams. **(love), (worry)**

i) The principal of the university _____ a lecture at the start of every term. **(give)**

j) I have no idea about my future career but I know I _____ to work with people. **(want)**

8.6   Writing: Magazine article

Party Time

After months of preparation from original idea to final event, the student celebration finally happened last night.

We decided to organise an international evening for several reasons. Firstly, we had to complete a project which involved working with others. Secondly, we wanted to meet students from other classes. Finally, we thought it would be fun!

I went in a taxi because the weather was stormy but most people used public transport - we had included timetables with the tickets.

The hall was lit up with candles and looked magical. Despite the weather there was a fantastic turnout. The food provided by international students was marvellous. I enjoyed some delicious dishes and terrific music and dancing.

It really was a great event.

Writing: Genre analysis (20 min)

Read the following text then answer the questions that follow.

Party Time

After months of preparation from original idea to final event, the student celebration finally happened last night.

We decided to organise an international evening for several reasons. Firstly, we had to complete a project which involved working with others. Secondly, we wanted to meet students from other classes. Finally, we thought it would be fun!

I went in a taxi because the weather was stormy but most people used public transport - we had included timetables with the tickets.

The hall was lit up with candles and looked magical. Despite the weather there was a fantastic turnout. The food provided by international students was marvellous. I enjoyed some delicious dishes and terrific music and dancing.

It really was a great event.

Q34: Look at each paragraph. What information is contained in each?

....

Q35: Where would you find this type of text?

a) A student magazine
b) A newspaper article
c) A university textbook

....

Q36: What tone does the writer use?

a) Serious
b) Light-hearted
c) Amused
d) Sad

....

Q37: Who is the intended audience?

a) School teachers
b) Other students
c) The general public

....

Q38: What kind of language does the writer use?

a) Formal
b) Neutral
c) Informal

Writing: Article for student publication (60 min)

You have been asked to write an article for your college/university magazine about an event which you attended recently. You should write around 250 words and should include discussion of the following:

- Introduction and conclusion

- The choice of event

- The venue

- Food and entertainment

- Your experience - did you enjoy the event?

Show your completed work to your teacher.

8.7 Study skills: Approaches to learning English

Learner training (20 min)

Q39: Look at the following sentences which illustrate approaches to learning English, and decide if you agree or disagree with these (note the letter of the sentences if you agree with them). When you have finished, compare answers with your partner and discuss with your teacher the most useful ways to approach language learning.

a) It is important to read grammar books as often as possible. Grammar is the most important element in language learning.

b) It is important to do homework every day.

c) It is best to be quiet in class unless you are sure of your answers.

d) The teacher's definitions of vocabulary are not as useful as dictionary definitions.

e) Talking to other students is a waste of time.

f) If you are uncertain of pronunciation of a word then you should avoid using it.

g) There is no point in group work; the group will not be able to sit exams for you!

h) It is better to work out grammar rules by yourself than rely on books.

i) It is a waste of time watching movies in English.

j) Success in English depends upon quality of teaching and individual effort.

8.8 Reading Comprehension: Scandinavian drama

Reading comprehension: Scandinavian drama (30 min)   Go online

Read the following text and then answer the questions which follow.

Last night I watched the first episode of the latest offering of Scandinavian crime drama to hit the small screen here in the UK. As I prepared myself for the experience, I pondered upon this genre, sometimes referred to as Nordic noir, which has become almost an obsession in recent months in Britain. What is the appeal?

Perhaps one of the most important features of Scandinavian drama, as opposed to British drama, is the darkness of the subject matter. Scandinavians do not shy away from issues others might avoid. This may not be surprising from a country with long, dark, wet winters and landscapes that are highly conducive to brooding introspection. Grey and drizzly terrain and haunted characters found in remote and bleak areas are typical of the genre. In addition to this, much of the action takes place at night.

Another feature of the Scandinavian drama is the plot, which does not unfold in a linear fashion but twists and turns slowly toward a conclusion. We are often led along a particular path for a long time, convinced of a certain outcome, only to be dumped suddenly and unceremoniously when we realise we are wrong.

The characters are explored in great depth. The relationships carefully developed so that we become intimately involved with them and attached to them. We feel betrayed when the series abruptly ends leaving us to mourn their loss. It is also characteristic of the genre that women are given strong and interesting roles. At the same time, there is very little attention paid to the fact that it is a woman who is prime minister or gritty detective. This is not considered noteworthy.

Another interesting dimension of Scandinavian drama is the element of social commentary. It seems that countries such as Sweden are not what they once were. This is interesting and somewhat disappointing; we British used to respect these countries as examples of moral correctness and fine social policy. The fact that dramatists are willing to highlight this can only be seen as a point in their favour.

As for my own feelings about Nordic noir I am now hooked. My only concern is how to watch it. Should I watch the current series throughout the next couple of months or should I buy a box set of DVD's later on and watch them in one fell swoop?

Q40: What kind of text is this? (1 mark)

a) TV Review

b) Article

c) Letter

. . . .

Q41: What name is given to Scandinavian drama? (1 mark)

. . . .

Q42: The writer says that Scandinavian drama is different from drama from other countries. From the list below pick five areas of difference. (5 marks)

- Roles for men
- Roles for women
- Character
- Plot
- Sense of humour
- Social commentary
- Subject matter
- Levels of violence

. . . .

Q43: The writer says that the environment in Scandinavia makes people examine their thoughts and feelings. Find a four word phrase in the text which shows this. (1 mark)

. . . .

Q44: The writer suggests that Scandinavian drama sometimes leaves us feeling abandoned. Which word in the text suggests this? (1 mark)

. . . .

Q45: What five word phrase does the writer use to suggest that aspects of Scandinavian society are breaking down? (1 mark)

....

Q46: What features of Scandinavian countries does the writer believe that the British admired in the past? (1 mark)

....

Q47: What informal word does the writer use to suggest he/she is now addicted to the new show? (1 mark)

....

8.9   Listening comprehension: Holiday choices

Listening comprehension: Marion and Sandy   Go online

You will need the following audio file to complete this activity:
n5-esl1-8-2listening.mp3

Q48: Which adjective best describes Marion's feelings about her holiday?

a) Happy

b) Disappointed

c) Mixed

....

Q49: Which adjective best describes Sandy's feelings about her holiday?

a) Happy

b) Disappointed

c) Mixed

....

Q50: Marion and Sandy are agreed that staying with foreign relatives could be _____.

....

Q51: Sandy describes her parents-in-law as _____.

....

Q52: Marion thinks that Sandy and she should get _____ next year.

....

Q53: What solution does Sandy finally decide would overcome her problem?

....

Q54: Where do the two women meet?

....

Q55: Where does most of the conversation take place?

Unit 2: ESOL in Context : Work

Unit 2 Topic 1

Jobs

Contents

Learning objective

By the end of this topic you will be better able to:

- participate in a conversation about employment;

- discuss skills and qualities required in particular employment areas;

- take part in an interview for a job;

- identify the features of formal job applications;

- write a letter of application.

1.1   Vocabulary: A to Z of jobs

A to Z of jobs (30 min)

You have been given the first and last letter of common jobs beginning with each letter of the alphabet. You have also been given the number of letters. Complete the list of jobs as quickly as you can .

There are **NO** example answers for the letters K, Q, X or Z.

Q1:

A_____t (6)	B_____r (7)	C_____r (7)	D_____r (6)
E_____r (8)	F_____r (6)	G_____r (8)	H_____r (11)
I_____r (11)	J_____t (10)	K	L_____r (6)
M_____c (8)	N_____e (5)	O_____n (8)	P_____n (9)
Q	R_____t (12)	S_____r (7)	T_____r (7)
U_____r (10)	V___t (3)	W_____ (6)	X
Y_____h w_____r (5,6)	Z		

1.2   Speaking: Discussion: Careers

Pre-Listening discussion: Careers (15 min)

Think about these three different careers and discuss the following questions with your partner or teacher if possible.

Undertaker   Paramedic   Helicopter Pilot

1. What kinds of skills and abilities does each one require?
2. Do you need any particular educational background to do these jobs?

3. Do you need any training to do these jobs?

4. What kind of challenges and responsibilities do you think these jobs have?

1.3 Listening: Careers

Careers (30 min)   Go online

Listen to the information about three people who do these jobs discussed above and answer the questions that follow.

You will need the following sound files to complete this activity: *n5-esl2-1-1listening1.mp3*, *n5-esl2-1-1listening2.mp3* and *n5-esl2-1-1listening2.mp3*

Complete the following sentences using no more than three words:

Q2: Jonathan thinks he offers an essential _____ to his community.
....

Q3: Some people would find Jonathan's job disturbing because he works with _____.
....

Q4: Jonathan learned about the job through training and from his _____.
....

Q5: Jonathan finds his job satisfying because he gives the deceased respect and _____.

Listen to speaker two and then answer questions 6 - 8

Q6: Pick **three** correct answers from the list below. In her job, Melissa requires knowledge and skills in which areas?

A) Emergency medicine
B) Languages
C) Radio operating
D) Surgical procedures
E) Advanced driving
F) Customer service

Decide whether the next statements are true or false.

Q7: Melissa believes that nurses are unskilled workers.

a) True
b) False

....

Q8: Melissa would be unwilling to swap her job for more highly paid work .

a) True
b) False

Listen to speaker three and then answer questions 9 - 11

Q9: David became a pilot immediately after high school.

a) True
b) False

....

Q10: David felt that flying aeroplanes for commercial airlines was too competitive.

a) True
b) False

....

Q11: David has been doing his present job for ten years

a) True
b) False

1.4   Speaking: Volunteer work

Volunteer work

You are going to read a text about volunteer work. Before reading, think about the following questions. (If possible discuss your ideas with a fellow student or teacher).

1. Do opportunities for volunteering exist in your country?

2. Have you or has anyone you know worked as a volunteer?

3. In what context would you like to volunteer if you had the opportunity?

1.5   Reading activity: Volunteer work

Volunteering (1) (45 min)

Read the following paragraphs which come from a text about volunteer work. Note that the paragraphs are in the wrong order.

a) Of course, if you are an animal lover but not accustomed to spending time around the real, living, breathing creatures, or are not quite ready for that step yet, you could begin your volunteering role with an indirect role in animal welfare. For example, you could become involved in organising events or in taking photographs for an animal charity. As with any job nowadays, references for volunteer animal work are a **prerequisite**, as is a criminal record check, most likely to filter out anyone with **convictions** for cruelty.

b) What springs to most people's minds when considering volunteering activities with animals tends to be either dog walking, or helping out in an indeterminate role at the local cat and dog home. While these are both options, they barely scratch the surface of the range of opportunities available. Often it is a case of matching your existing skills and career ambitions to the type of volunteering that is available . Consider, for example, helping at the local zoo. This could involve a lot of cleaning, or it could be in an administrative role. If you are confident and outgoing, you could even be a guide to parties of school children. Quite often, in zoos, community farms or animal shelters, you will be given a demanding but **menial** task at first, and if you show a sufficient level of attentiveness to the task, you will be **entrusted** with more interesting and **diverse** tasks in due course. In that way, it isn't dissimilar to the **learning curve** involved in a paid career. Sometimes it can even turn into a contracted position with a regular salary.

c) I have always loved the company of animals. Ever since I can remember, my family had pets: cats, dogs, guinea pigs and hamsters. As a child, I never wanted for friends if my human playmates were not around. Growing up in such a fashion, it is perhaps unsurprising that I have continued to have a strong relationship with the animal kingdom in my adult life and in my career as a veterinarian. It took some time to qualify as a vet, and one of the questions I am most frequently asked by **aspiring** animal carers these days is, "How can I gain experience to help me in my application for vet school?"

d) One of my vet colleagues and two of the veterinary nurses at my practice started out as volunteer animal helpers. A skeletal stray cat, clinging to life, found in a tatty box in an alleyway led to Sally becoming involved in the Cats Protection League. Initially she manned their telephone line for 8 hours a week, gradually building up her experience and interest via more hands on duties. Eventually she was convinced that vet nursing was the route she wanted to pursue. Similarly, Derek made his way to our practice via a route that began with a volunteer role at Battersea Dogs Home, after losing his own Dog, Tanya, to cancer. Derek found that working in close proximity to qualified veterinary surgeons, initially as a receptionist, inspired him to study towards a degree in veterinary studies. It took eight years from that first volunteer role until his first day as a **fully-fledged** vet but he still maintains that the volunteering role was invaluable in launching his career.

e) A common error made by many potential volunteers is underestimating the amount of time their commitment could involve. Remember that wherever you work with animals, it is likely to involve unsocial hours, require physical exertion and could also involve a lengthy training programme. Animal rescue centres will not expect volunteer workers to be experts about all things animal but they will **appreciate** commitment. Those with a genuine love and passion for animals, coupled with a desire to learn more, tend to last the pace more often than the ones who are solely thinking about their career Find words from paragraphs 1,3 & 4 with the following meaningss. It is all about dedication.

f) There are a multitude of possibilities which will help the wannabe vet, including becoming a volunteer working with animals or working with environmentally friendly groups. Besides the obvious benefits to recruiters, volunteer work with animals is also a great way to meet like-minded people and acquire new skills.

Q12: The paragraphs are in the wrong order. Using the letters rearrange the paragraphs so they are in the correct, logical order. Assign each letter to the appropriate number of the correct order e.g. 1-d, 2-a and so on.

Volunteering (2) (45 min)

Read the text, now in the correct order, and answer the questions that follow.

1. I have always loved the company of animals. Ever since I can remember, my family had pets: cats, dogs, guinea pigs and hamsters. As a child, I never wanted for friends if my human playmates were not around. Growing up in such a fashion, it is perhaps unsurprising that I have continued to have a strong relationship with the animal kingdom in my adult life and in my career as a veterinarian. It took some time to qualify as a vet, and one of the questions I am most frequently asked by aspiring animal carers these days is, "How can I gain experience to help me in my application for vet school?"

2. There are a multitude of possibilities which will help the wannabe vet, including becoming a volunteer working with animals or working with environmentally friendly groups. Besides the obvious benefits to recruiters, volunteer work with animals is also a great way to meet like-minded people and acquire new skills.

3. What springs to most people's minds when considering volunteering activities with animals tends to be either dog walking, or helping out in an indeterminate role at the local cat and dog home. While these are both options, they barely scratch the surface of the range of opportunities available. Often it is a case of matching your existing skills and career ambitions to the type of volunteering that is available . Consider, for example, helping at the local zoo. This could involve a lot of cleaning, or it could be in an administrative role. If you are confident and outgoing, you could even be a guide to parties of school children. Quite often, in zoos, community farms or animal shelters, you will be given a demanding but menial task at first, and if you show a sufficient level of attentiveness to the task, you will be entrusted with more interesting and diverse tasks in due course. In that way, it isn't dissimilar to the learning curve involved in a paid career. Sometimes it can even turn into a contracted position with a regular salary.

4. A common error made by many potential volunteers is underestimating the amount of time their commitment could involve. Remember that wherever you work with animals, it is likely to involve unsocial hours, require physical exertion and could also involve a lengthy training programme. Animal rescue centres will not expect volunteer workers to be experts about all things animal but they will appreciate commitment. Those with a genuine love and passion for animals, coupled with a desire to learn more, tend to last the pace more often than the ones who are solely thinking about their career aspirations. It is all about dedication.

5. Of course, if you are an animal lover but not accustomed to spending time around the real, living, breathing creatures, or are not quite ready for that step yet, you could begin your volunteering role with an indirect role in animal welfare. For example, you could become involved in organising events or in taking photographs for an animal charity. As with any job nowadays, references for volunteer animal work are a prerequisite, as is a criminal record check, most likely to filter out any one with convictions for cruelty.

6. One of my vet colleagues and two of the veterinary nurses at my practice started out as volunteer animal helpers. A skeletal stray cat, clinging to life, found in a tatty box in an alleyway led to Sally becoming involved in the Cats Protection League. Initially she manned their telephone line for 8 hours a week, gradually building up her experience and interest via more hands on duties. Eventually she was convinced that vet nursing was the route she wanted to pursue. Similarly, Derek made his way to our practice via a route that began with a volunteer role at Battersea Dogs Home, after losing his own Dog, Tanya, to cancer. Derek found that working in close proximity to qualified veterinary surgeons, initially as a receptionist, inspired him to study towards a degree in veterinary studies. It took eight years from that first volunteer role until his first day as a fully-fledged vet but he still maintains that the volunteering role was invaluable in launching his career.

Q13: People who are keen to work in animal care regularly ask the writer for:

a) References
b) Advice
c) Work experience

....

Q14: Volunteering with animals:

a) mainly benefits the organisation.
b) mainly benefits those recruited.
c) helps both the organisation and the individual recruited.

Complete the sentences in no more than **three** words:

Q15: You should search for opportunities which correspond to your _____.

....

Q16: Volunteering is similar to _____ because dedication and responsibility will be rewarded.

....

Q17: People are often unprepared for _____ in volunteering.

....

Q18: According to the writer, volunteers should have _____ and a _____ (give two answers each with no more than three words)

....

Q19: The writer suggests that working _____ with experts can motivate people to embark on a career as a vet.

Find words or phrases in **paragraph 5** with the following meanings:

Q20: When something must happen before something else can happen (one word)

....

Q21: Unsuitable applicants are rejected (two word phrasal verb)

....

Q22: In this text, the writer wants to:

a) Recommend volunteering
b) Describe the life of a vet
c) Explain why he/she chose to become a vet

....

Q23: Which of the following is the best description of the text?

a) A scholarly article
b) An advertisement for jobseekers
c) A magazine article

1.6 Speaking: Ideal job

Ideal job (30 min)

Talk to your partner or teacher about a job you think you would like to do. You should take fifteen minutes to prepare to discuss the topic. You may write short notes if you require them (but do not read from a script!)

Consider the following ideas and then ask and answer questions on the topic for a conversation lasting 6 minutes:

- If you could choose to do any job in the world, what would it be?
- Why would you choose this job / what is the attraction of it?
- What skills and qualities do you think you would require to do this job?
- What would be difficult or challenging about this job?
- What do you think is the more important aspect of a job: how much you are paid or how much you enjoy the work?

1.7 Writing: A job application

A job application with a difference (60 min)

Look at the following job advertisement.

Wanted: Astronauts for Space Station Duty

With the demise of the US space shuttle program, the World Space Organisation (WSO) is recruiting new participants for the next phase of its own interplanetary study. Seven new astronauts are required to man the International Space Station for a period of up to five years.

The right candidate will have a background in a scientific field, a Master's degree is preferred but an undergraduate degree in a Biochemical or Engineering discipline will be considered.

Experience of flying small aircraft is desirable, or proof of other piloting skills and experience (such as flight simulator training).

Twenty-twenty vision is a necessity for this role and there will be a variety of visual tests, as well as more general aptitude tests to ensure you possess adequate problem solving skills. Multilingual candidates will be viewed favourably, particularly those that can speak English and Russian.

Physical fitness is another key factor.   You will be expected to have fitness levels equivalent to professional sports people.

Finally, we can only accept applications from candidates between the height of 5 feet 2 inches and 6 feet 3 inches, weighing between 50kg and 80kg, due to the limitations on physical space within the space station.

Write a letter of application explaining why you are a suitable candidate.   The best applicants will be selected for interview and contacted within the next six weeks.

Thank you for your interest. The World Space Organisation.

Write a formal email to apply for the position, addressing (and explaining) all the required points as mentioned in the advertisement.

Before you begin, consider the following questions:

- What is the purpose of the communication?

- What level of formality and register would be appropriate?

Make some notes or a mind map to help plan your writing before you begin. Try to write around 220 words. Ask your teacher to check your work when you have finished.

1.8   Reading comprehension: Ronan Abbey

Reading comprehension: Ronan Abbey   Go online

Read the passage of text and then answer the questions that follow.

a) Many readers will be familiar with the beautiful building and grounds of Ronan Abbey which featured in "Cloisters", the award-winning film adaptation of Jane Watson's novel released eighteen months ago.   Information officer Fiona Kelly has been employed at Ronan Abbey for seven years now. Her job, and indeed her entire life, changed dramatically with the release of Cloisters. We caught up with Fiona one Saturday morning. We wanted to know what life was like before the impact of the movie and find out how she is coping with the recent upsurge of interest in the abbey.

b) "There was always a fair amount of interest in the abbey and I have always been kept busy managing that.   There were many visitors among historians and teachers who wanted to learn more about the historical background of the site. We provided a lot of reading material and links to research. We also organised school trips and ran weekend events in our cafe".

c) While this may sound like enough work to contend with, according to Fiona it was nothing compared to the current workload. "We were quite unprepared for the massive response that there has been to Cloisters and the sheer volume of work which this has generated. We are not complaining, however! It is wonderful to see Ronan Abbey getting the attention it deserves, but we have had to learn very quickly how to be a major tourist attraction".

d) Fiona remained cautious in the immediate afterglow of the release of Cloisters and all the publicity they received. "My work has quadrupled, but at first we thought that the excitement might calm down after a few months and things would go back to normal. This did not happen at all, and in any case we really wanted to encourage the interest. Eventually I did have to insist on getting some assistance. I now have a small team to support me and we are doing just fine".

e) Being an information officer is not something that Fiona set out to do in life, but when she saw the job advertised she realised that it was perfect for her. "I was a teacher for a number of years before going into arts administration and I enjoyed both of these jobs, but I also like variety. When I saw there was a position at Ronan Abbey I realised it really combined all my interests and experience".

f) We wondered what an average day was like for Fiona following the film release, but she was quick to explain that there was no such thing as an average day. She is responsible for maintaining and updating the website, writing and printing publicity material, arranging visits and all aspects of staffing. "I have a lot of visitors, several groups and individuals as well. We have long and short-term projects which involve schools and the local community. We ensure maintenance of this beautiful building as well as its grounds and we liaise with marketing to ensure that the products we provide meet the needs of our customers. The success of Cloisters changed my work and with that my life. I have had to meet new challenges and learn new skills. My confidence has really grown as a consequence. All I can say is thank you Jane Watson for making it happen".

Q24: The main purpose of this text is to:

a) promote the movie "Cloisters".
b) talk about the work of Fiona Kelly.
c) describe Ronan Abbey.

Complete the sentences using no more than **three** words.

Q25: Academics have always been interested in _____of Ronan Abbey.

....

Q26: Fiona found _____to Cloisters quite unexpected.

....

Q27: The job at Ronan suits Fiona particularly well because it brings together her _____.

....

Q28: Fiona has to _____of Ronan Abbey so that its condition is preserved.

Find words from paragraphs 1,3 & 4 with the following meanings:

Q29: "an increase" or "expansion"

....

Q30: "created"

....

Q31: "the pleasant feeling after a good thing has happened"

....

Q32: Match each paragraph with the most suitable description of its content.

A) A day in the life
B) Fiona Kelly's background
C) Life before Cloisters
D) A cry for help
E) Connecting Fiona Kelly, Cloisters and Ronan Abbey
F) The glare of publicity

1.9   Listening comprehension: Small businesses

Listening comprehension: Small businesses	Go online

You will require the following sound file to complete this assessment activity:
n5-esl2-1-2listening.mp3

Q33: Decide if the statements are true or false.

a) The presenter says that the credit crunch has made people more cautious about spending money.
b) Jon rejected his father's business model.
c) Jon makes more money from accessories than from shoes.
d) Ken makes more money from repairs and accessories than new bicycles.
e) Geraldine found out about potential customers before opening the shop.

f) Geraldine thinks that the key to her success is enabling shopping excitement at reasonable prices.

g) Isabella's husband encourages everyone in the café to talk

....

Q34: Match the speaker - Jon, Ken, Geraldine or Isabella, to the statement of information. Which speaker:

1. acquired the business after someone's death?

2. involves family in the business?

3. has extended the business recently?

4. travels as part of their job?

5. is living someone else's dream?

....

Q35: Val suggests that viewers with aspirations to own a business should:

a) exercise caution.

b) acknowledge the fear but do it anyway.

c) be sensible, plan carefully and then try it.

....

Q36: What is the main purpose of the broadcast?

a) To explore Middlesfield High Street.

b) To analyse the success of local business in a financially difficult time.

c) To provide insights into effective business management strategies.

Unit 2 Topic 2

Preparing for work

Contents

Learning objective

By the end of this topic you will be better able to:

- talk about the process of searching for work, acquiring experience ;

- prepare for interviews;

- discuss the advantages and disadvantages of volunteering, work experience and internships.

2.1   Listening Activity: Finding a job

Pre-listening activity: Speaking

Discuss the following questions with a partner and note down some of your ideas:

- What is the best way to find out about job vacancies? What sources of information could you use?

- Do you have any experience of applying for a job?   Describe the stages of your application.

- What work (shift) patterns / arrangements are available in the UK job market?

Pre-listening activity: Vocabulary   Go online

Q1:
Match the vocabulary on the left with the correct definition on the right.

1. generic (adjective)	a. meeting with and / or talking to people who might be useful in your work
2. keen (adjective)	b. lasting forever, or for a long time
3. enterprising (adjective)	c. enquiry about a job where none has been advertised
4. to impress (verb)	d. someone who has the ability to succeed in using new ideas or projects
5. seasonal (adjective)	e. subject area / area of interest
6. permanent (adjective)	f. wanting very much to do something
7. tricky (adjective)	g. happening at a particular time of year
8. speculative application (adjective, noun)	h. typical of a whole group of things
9. networking (noun)	i. difficult to deal with
10. field (noun)	j. make others think highly of you

Listening Activity: Finding a job   Go online

To complete this exercise, you will need the following sound file:
n5-esl2-2-1listening.mp3

Complete the following sentences using no more than **three** words:

Q2:   Amir has been looking for a job for _ _ _ _ _ _ _ _ _ _ _ _ _ _ _ _ _ _ .

. . . .

Q3: Sam says that Amir only needs _____ for everything to change.

Choose **three** correct answers from the list below:

Q4: Amir is currently searching for a job on:

a) generic websites.
b) local government websites.
c) school websites.
d) online newspapers.
e) social networking sites.

....

Q5: Jamie got a full-time job in his local library.

a) True
b) False

....

Q6: Amir is worried that he will forget all that he has studied.

a) True
b) False

....

Q7: Sam thinks Jamie is very skilled at networking.

a) True
b) False

....

Q8: Amir and Sam:

a) studied librarianship together.
b) both know Katy.
c) both studied arts at university.

....

Q9: Which of the following best describe Sam's attitude to Amir?

a) Kind and supportive
b) Impatient and dismissive
c) Cool and interested

2.2   Reading Activity: Interviews

Pre-reading activity: Speaking: Job interviews (15 min)

Make a list of ideas with a partner on the following points.

- Have you ever had a job interview?

- How do you feel during job interviews?

- What kind of questions do interviewers ask during interviews?

- What kind of behaviour is expected from the interviewee before, during and after the interview?

Reading activity: Job interviews (25 min)

Read the text below which is about job interviews and then answer the questions which follow

The current economic recession has led to fierce competition for jobs up and down the country. It would seem that many employees are having contracts torn up and rewritten, while others are being made redundant in huge numbers. As a result, more people are in pursuit of each position advertised than has ever been the case before. A recent survey suggested that as many as fifty applicants are applying for individual vacancies in fields like teaching, nursing and the police. In such a climate, the importance of giving a good interview cannot be overstated. Nevertheless, the same survey revealed that employers currently find many interviewees suffering from stage fright at the time of interview as a result of poor preparation. Apparently, around seventy-five per cent of interviewees fall into this category.

Let's consider the type of behaviour at interview that could send us straight back to the job centre! Common mistakes made by interviewees include disclosing inappropriate information about themselves or their former places of employment. Instantaneous answers may show a degree of honesty, but that may not always be the best policy. If complete honesty involves making disparaging comments about former managers or colleagues then it should be avoided at all costs. While we would certainly not recommend lying to a potential employer, sometimes it is more helpful to divert attention. The direct questions which interviewers often ask are better answered by politician-style body swerves rather than open and hastily made responses.

Another topic of conversation to avoid is any talk of remuneration at the interview stage, unless of course it is brought up by the interviewer. It is best to be polite and tactful at all times. It is also advisable to resist any temptation to embellish your curriculum vitae. If you don't have a degree in science, or you have never managed twenty staff before, it's best not to pretend you have. The interviewer may call your bluff asking you a scientific question you can't answer. Worse still, think what might happen if you actually got the job you applied for and had to depend on your fictitious skills?

What kind of interview behaviour could get us hired? Showing a keen interest in the post you are applying for can pay dividends, particularly if you have an awareness of the duties and responsibilities the post will entail. Such preparations highlight research skills to interviewers, and keep the focus on what you, the interviewee, can offer the employer, as opposed to what they can do for you. Remember to remain positive and enthusiastic throughout and exploit opportunities to describe why you are a perfect candidate for this job, using examples from your experience. Keep these ideas in mind for your next interview and see if the results are more positive for you.

Q10: The demand for jobs is greater than ever before.

a) True
b) False

....

Q11: Interviewees do not care enough about the interview process and this is why they fail.

a) True
b) False

....

Q12: Interviewers are generally impressed by candidates who are completely honest about previous colleagues and workplaces.

a) True
b) False

....

Q13: At interviews, candidates should always ask how much money they can expect to be paid.

a) True
b) False

....

Q14: Candidates who can demonstrate knowledge about the responsibilities of the post at interview will be well received.

a) True
b) False

....

Q15: Lying in an interview is dangerous because the employer may question you further about this.

a) True
b) False

....

Q16: Pick **three** answers from the list below. In interviews, it is important to demonstrate:

a) a wide range of interests and hobbies.

b) an interest in maintaining a healthy lifestyle.

c) an interest in the post.

d) evidence of suitability for the job.

e) an awareness of the duties and responsibilities.

....

Q17: One of the most common mistakes interviewees make is:

a) Giving false information about their experience

b) Answering too quickly and without judgement

c) Being impolite during their interview

....

Q18: The main recommendation made by the writer is that candidates for interview should be:

a) serious and well informed.

b) well prepared.

c) relaxed and spontaneous.

....

Q19: This text is mainly intended to:

a) inform.

b) entertain.

c) both inform and entertain.

Post-reading activity: Vocabulary: Definitions (20 min)   Go online

The current economic recession has led to fierce competition for jobs up and down the country. It would seem that many employees are having contracts torn up and rewritten, while others are being made redundant in huge numbers. As a result, more people are in pursuit of each position advertised than has ever been the case before. A recent survey suggested that as many as fifty applicants are applying for individual vacancies in fields like teaching, nursing and the police. In such a climate, the importance of giving a good interview cannot be overstated. Nevertheless, the same survey revealed that employers currently find many interviewees suffering from stage fright at the time of interview as a result of poor preparation. Apparently, around seventy-five per cent of interviewees fall into this category.

Let's consider the type of behaviour at interview that could send us straight back to the job centre! Common mistakes made by interviewees include disclosing inappropriate information about themselves or their former places of employment. Instantaneous answers may show a degree of honesty, but that may not always be the best policy. If complete honesty involves making disparaging comments about former managers or colleagues then it should be avoided at all costs. While we would certainly not recommend lying to a potential employer, sometimes it is more helpful to divert attention. The direct questions which interviewers often ask are better answered by politician-style body swerves rather than open and hastily made responses.

Another topic of conversation to avoid is any talk of remuneration at the interview stage, unless of course it is brought up by the interviewer. It is best to be polite and tactful at all times. It is also advisable to resist any temptation to embellish your curriculum vitae. If you don't have a degree in science, or you have never managed twenty staff before, it's best not to pretend you have. The interviewer may call your bluff asking you a scientific question you can't answer. Worse still, think what might happen if you actually got the job you applied for and had to depend on your fictitious skills?

What kind of interview behaviour could get us hired? Showing a keen interest in the post you are applying for can pay dividends, particularly if you have an awareness of the duties and responsibilities the post will entail. Such preparations highlight research skills to interviewers, and keep the focus on what you, the interviewee, can offer the employer, as opposed to what they can do for you. Remember to remain positive and enthusiastic throughout and exploit opportunities to describe why you are a perfect candidate for this job, using examples from your experience. Keep these ideas in mind for your next interview and see if the results are more positive for you.

Q20: Highlight a word or phrase from the article which has the same meaning as the words listed.

a) strong or tough

b) fired or dismissed

c) fear or anxiety over a performance

d) revealing

e) immediate

f) unpleasant and dismissive

g) add extra (untrue) information

h) payment

i) considerate; careful

j) avoidance; evasions

2.3 Pronunciation: Syllables and word stress

Syllables and word stress (15 min)   Go online

You will need the following sound files to complete this activity:
n5-esl2-2-2listening.mp3 (1-5)

Listen to the sound files and complete the table by answer the following questions.

    a) How many syllables does each word have?

    b) Which syllable is stressed?

Q21:

Word	Syllables and word stress
e.g. Career	oO
Disclosing	
Instantaneous	
Disparaging	
Embellish	
Remuneration	

2.4 Listening comprehension: Interview feedback

Listening comprehension: Interview feedback   Go online

You will need the following sound file to complete this assessment:
n5-esl2-2-3listening.mp3

Q22: Complete the sentences in no more than **three** words.

    1. Roseanne prefers to _____soon after an interview.

    2. Tim is feeling _____.

    3. The permanent position was offered to someone with_____.

             . . . .

Q23: Tim believes his presentation skills are generally a strength.

a) True
b) False

....

Q24: Tim blames his brother and his brother's girlfriend for his lack of preparation.

a) True
b) False

....

Q25: Tim's interview was negatively affected by a lack of organisational awareness.

a) True
b) False

....

Q26: At the moment, Roseanne is unhappy with Tim's work.

a) True
b) False

....

Q27: Tim has already taken advantage of the shadowing scheme at work.

a) True
b) False

....

Q28: What is the best description of Tim as an employee?

A) Conscientious and hard-working

B) Confident and careless

C) Underprepared and inexperienced

....

Q29: In their meeting, Roseanne:

A) offers Tim support.

B) disciplines Tim.

C) sympathises with Tim.

2.5 Reading comprehension: Volunteering and internships

Reading comprehension: Volunteering and internships	Go online

1. As competition for jobs becomes more intense, many employers are keen to see that applicants have not only the qualifications required for a job but that they have also acquired some experience. In order to get this necessary experience, potential employees might consider voluntary work, job shadowing or applying for an internship.

2. Volunteering involves giving up some spare time to an organisation. Although not paid for their work, volunteers, in return for their time, will benefit from the opportunity to acquire new skills. In general, hours and duration of the work (as well as duties involved) are negotiated between volunteer and management rather than being imposed as they would be in a paid position.

3. It is clearly more beneficial to get involved in an organisation which you feel enthusiastic about. Select carefully from the lists of volunteering organisations which you will find on local volunteering websites. These include charities which support young people, the elderly, sick, poor or disabled. There are also a number which support animal welfare.

4. Volunteering is not confined to opportunities in the UK but also includes working overseas. Voluntary Service Overseas (VSO) is one of many organisations with websites supplying details about what to expect and how to apply. As well as allowing you to find out more about your chosen area, volunteering can provide an element of structure to an otherwise formless week while you are looking for a job. At the same time, there is a networking potential since you will come into contact with other volunteers as well as paid employees with whom you may be able to make lasting connections. Finally, these hours of work are viewed favourably by potential employers when included in a CV.

5. Work placements are another way to gain desirable experience. Some of the larger organisations offer formal work experience programmes. The British Broadcasting Corporation (BBC) programme, for example, offers opportunities to experience working life in one of various departments such as News and Current Affairs or Drama for a period of three to twenty days. This is a scheme which should be highly beneficial if the placement is sufficiently well organised. Individuals are given a placement manager who will be able to work with them to ensure that they are getting as much as possible out of their time. Such placements are highly competitive, so it is important to ensure that time and care is taken in the application stage to avoid disappointment.

6. An internship differs from volunteering since it is an opportunity to benefit from short term, paid employment in an organisation. Some industrial placements can be taken in a gap year from university and could involve placement in the UK or overseas. It is also possible to apply for an internship following graduation and many websites exist which offer details on what is available. When organising an internship, it is important to ensure that certain conditions are in place so that the experience is valuable. Initially a contract should be drawn up by the organisation involved so that expectations on both sides are clear. Not all organisations offer an induction but this is a distinct advantage. It is also an advantage to be offered the assistance of a mentor who can oversee your progress and provide feedback.

7. Whether you decide to volunteer, go for shadowing, work experience or an internship, it is important to ensure that you maximise the potential of the opportunity you have been presented with. Taking control of the process is likely to offer dividends. In the first place ensure that you feel positive and excited about the prospect, otherwise you are unlikely to benefit. Ensure that there is likely to be some challenge, it might feel comfortable to do quite little but in the long run this is not an advantage. Being underused will not add to your skills and experience or help you gain understanding of your potential. Even if feedback or mentoring is not available, set yourself some personal goals and then reflect on and review your progress.

Q30: Complete the sentences with no more than **four** words from the text:

1. To succeed in the job market today, potential employees require _____.
2. As a volunteer, you will be able to _____ various aspects of work with a manager.
3. Choosing volunteer positions which particularly attract you is likely to be _____.
4. Volunteering can give _____when you have fewer commitments in your life.
5. Work placements can really help you but they need to be _____.

....

Q31: Which word in paragraph 5 describes a situation where a lot of people want to do something?

....

Q32: Which word in paragraph 6 describes the process of being shown around when starting a new job?

....

Q33: Which word in paragraph 7 means advantages?

....

Q34: Which word in paragraph 7 means not having been given enough work to do?

....

Q35: An appropriate title for this text might be:

A) How to succeed in the job market

B) Making the most of unpaid employment

C) Gain work experience while searching for a full-time post

Unit 2 Topic 3

Communication

Contents

Learning objective

By the end of this topic you will be better able to:

- take part in a conversation about health and safety in the workplace;
- identify the features of health and safety documentation in the workplace;
- write a formal email requesting a health and safety review at work.

3.1 Listening activity: Describing pain

Pre-listening activity: Vocbulary/Speaking : Pain

There are times when we may need to describe pain in order to communicate with doctors or nurses. Pain can be described in terms of quality, duration and intensity.

With a partner make a list of the different words you know to describe pain. Check your list of words with other students or with your teacher.

Listening activity

Go online

Listen to some people discussing their aches and pains. While listening, make notes on what the problem is.

To complete this exercise, you will need the following sound files:
n5-esl2-3-1listening.mp3 (1-9)

Post listening activity: Vocabulary

Go online

Organise the words below into categories indicating whether they describe quality, duration or intensity of pain.

Q1:

Word	Category	Word	Category
Aching		Numbness	
Acute		Piercing	
Blinding		Pounding	
Chronic		Severe	
Cramping		Sharp	
Dull		Shooting	
Excruciating		Stinging	
Intermittent		Throbbing	
Mild		Twinge	

3.2 Reading Activity: RSI

Reading comprehension: RSI

Read the text and then try to answer the questions.

1. The increased use of technology in the workplace means that even those who would not consider their work to be desk-bound find that they are obliged to spend more time in front of a computer. This may be to manage emails, which are now the primary means of communication in most working environments, or to document aspects of work which in the past would have been handwritten.

2. Incidence of repetitive strain injury (RSI) has increased dramatically with the rise in the use of computers. RSI generally manifests itself as a stiffness or pain in the back, neck, shoulders, forearms, wrists and hands. RSI is the consequence of work-based activity such as using a computer or telephone. While symptoms may escalate and finally become severe, it often starts out as a mild, niggling complaint with low level cramping, tingling or numbness.

3. RSI is not something which an employee should struggle with alone. It is incumbent on employers to ensure that adequate provision is made to minimise the impact of technology on the ongoing health of staff. Even if this were not a legal obligation, it would still benefit the employer in the long term to address such issues. The comfort and safety of employees is likely to impact on their efficiency and productivity.

4. Each employee is entitled to a have a risk assessment of their area carried out by a health and safety inspector as a precautionary measure. Depending on the employer, this may include a training session on effective management of your workplace environment. The latter may be implemented by computer-based training with the employees being obliged to sit and pass an online assessment to prove that they have read and understood the content.

5. There are steps which can be taken to minimise RSI involving adjustments to equipment. In the first place, consider the ergonomics of your workstation. A good, comfortable chair which supports your back is of paramount importance. The height and position of your chair in relation to your desk and how this affects your posture is also key. You should ensure that you are sitting straight and that your feet are on the floor. The top of your screen should be at eye level with your keyboard positioned about six inches from the edge of your desk allowing you to rest your arms. Elbows should be held at the side of your body. It is also important to ensure you have adequate light and that your posture is not undermined by the need to bend your head to see the screen.

6. Changes in behaviour can also have a powerful impact on the frequency or intensity of pain often associated with working at computers. For example, it is important to take regular breaks - every half hour would be beneficial. The break need not be for long but standing and stretching or simply moving around should help. If you have to take telephone calls then consider the angle at which you hold the phone - cradling a phone between neck and shoulder is likely to exacerbate any problems.

7. Workplace stress is often cited as a factor in RSI. The need to meet deadlines can be a disincentive to taking regular breaks. At the same time, the experience of pain is in

itself stressful. Those affected could benefit from relaxation classes such as Yoga or Pilates. Such activities not only offer a means to calm the mind but they can also help to strengthen core muscles and posture and thereby help to build resistance to injury and support recovery.

Complete the sentence with an appropriate word or phrase (use no more than three words from the text) Refer to paragraphs 1-3:

Q2: Even employees who are not _____ are still affected by increased dependence on computers today.

....

Q3: RSI often starts out as a mild complaint but later ----------------------------------.

....

Q4: With respect to technology, employers should make sufficient effort to _____ on staff.

Find a word in paragraphs 4-5 for each of the following definitions:

Q5: Preventative

....

Q6: Applied

....

Q7: Factors contributing to the ease of use, efficiency and comfort in a workplace

....

Q8: Supreme

Give two short answers to this question (no more than **three** words for each):

Q9: What two approaches to RSI can alleviate many of the symptoms?

....

Choose **two** positive effects of Yoga/Pilates discussed from the list below.

Q10: Yoga and Pilates can:

 a) reduce anxiety.
 b) encourage weight loss.
 c) build muscles.
 d) provide pain relief.
 e) help fight disease.

. . . .

Choose **one** answer from the list:

Q11: This text is:

a)   an article form a newspaper or magazine.
b)   an article from a government public information brochure.
c)   a workplace bulletin.

3.3   Grammar: Tense review

Tense review	Go online

To listen to this converstation, you will need the following sound file: *n5-esl2-3-2listening.mp3*

Q12: Look at the extracts from the text and match them with the appropriate tense/aspect.

a. I **have started** working	1. Will future (spontaneous utterance)
b. I **am treating**	2. Going to future (plan)
c. The first month **was** really frightening	3. Past perfect
d. I **was worrying**	4. Present perfect simple
e. I **have been getting**	5. Present continuous
f. If I **had known** then	6. Present simple for future arrangement
g. I **am not going to be** complacent	7. Past continuous
h. I'**ll allow** myself	8. Present perfect continuous
i. I **leave** in three weeks	9. Past simple

3.4   Speaking: Technology and health

Speaking: Technology

Prepare to have a conversation with a partner on the subject of technology at work / in your school. The conversation should last five to six minutes. You should consider the following points:

- How often and for what purpose are you required to use computers at work or school?

- What do you think are the benefits and drawbacks of technology in each context?

- Do you know of anyone who has experienced RSI or another health issue associated with the use of technology?

- Do you think that the health of the nation is likely to suffer if the use of technology continues to increase?

3.5   Writing: Formal email : Health and safety

Writing: Health and safety

You have been suffering some pain in your neck and shoulders as well as occasional tingling in your fingers. You are concerned that the requirement to use a computer for several hours a day is causing the problem. Write an email to your line manager/head teacher asking that a review of your workstation is made by a health and safety officer in order to establish whether or not any changes need to be made. You should write around 220 words.

You should include some or all of the following:

- Information on your daily use of computers

- Symptoms you are experiencing

- Details of your workstation

- Suggestions regarding appropriate action

3.6 Listening comprehension: Healthy working lives

Listening comprehension: Healthy Working Lives Go online

Complete each gap using no more than **three** words:

Q13: Parvin's examples of abnormal working hours include _____and an _____hours.

....

Q14: In Europe _____employees is a shift worker while _____works extended hours.

....

Q15: We have become used to getting _____outside normal hours.

Decide whether the following statements are true or false.

Q16: Circadian rhythms adversely affect sleep patterns.

....

Q17: Shift workers sleep for as long as other workers.

....

Q18: Many shift workers complain that they feel stressed.

....

Q19: People who work shifts are protected by law.

....

Q20: This discussion is designed to:

A) advise against shift work.

B) encourage people to try shift work.

C) educate people about the health issues associated with shift work.

3.7 Reading comprehension: Accident and incident report form

Accident and Incident Report Form

Please complete this form in the event of an accident or incident in the workplace to include work related injuries, diseases or ill health. The form should be completed by the employee involved if possible or by a representative as soon as possible after the event or awareness of ill health. A copy should be emailed to your line manager who will be responsible for taking matters forward, ensuring continued care of those involved. With your permission, a copy will also be sent to your union representative where appropriate. Non-union members should ignore this instruction.

Please indicate by means of a tick in the box provided whether you wish a union official to be informed.

What do you wish to report?

I would like to report an accident at work in which I received an electric shock after plugging a laptop into a wall socket.

When did the accident/incident take place?

It happened on the 30th of January. One week ago.

Where did the accident/incident take place? (Please provide full details of the address)

At my office workstation at Unit 65, Block C, 130 Bath Road, London UB3 4HB

What happened?

I had just returned to the office following a lunch break. I had been giving a presentation earlier that day and had been using my laptop for that purpose. I was in a hurry to start work again as I wished to type up a report on the feedback I had received on my presentation. I also wanted to send some emails. I stooped down to plug the laptop into the wall, as the socket is located under my desk. As I did this there was bang and a flash of light. I felt a peculiar throbbing sensation radiating up my right arm. I was thrown back from the socket although it is unclear whether this was my instinct for self-preservation kicking in or whether the shock forced me back. Regardless, as I bounced backwards I smacked my head on the top of my desk and fell to the floor.

Was anyone else involved?

I work in quite a busy office and I would estimate that there were about twenty people in the office at the time. However, as it was just after lunch people were still chatting and getting organised for the afternoon so it is unlikely that any more than a couple of people who were very close by could really comment on the situation.

Please provide the names of any witnesses

Jason Cameron, Judy Speers

Details of action taken and treatment given where relevant

I came to and realised that there was blood on my head and I felt a bit weak and shocked. My colleagues Jason and Judy were beside me. They had, I later discovered, switched off the power source and started mopping up the blood. They were a little concerned about moving me and it was decided that I should be taken immediately to the accident and emergency department at the local hospital. I went in an ambulance, although I am not entirely convinced that this was necessary. It was probably best to err on the side of caution. I had a series of tests at the hospital including an ECG in case my heart had been affected. I also had a head x-ray.

Were you able to go straight back to work following the accident/incident?

No. I was told by staff at the hospital to go home and rest as I had sustained a mild head injury. I was also very shaken by what had happened.

Reading comprehension: Accident and incident report form   Go online

Accident and Incident Report Form

Please complete this form in the event of an accident or incident in the workplace to include work related injuries, diseases or ill health. The form should be completed by the employee involved if possible or by a representative as soon as possible after the event or awareness of ill health. A copy should be emailed to your line manager who will be responsible for taking matters forward, ensuring continued care of those involved. With your permission, a copy will also be sent to your union representative where appropriate. Non-union members should ignore this instruction.

Please indicate by means of a tick in the box provided whether you wish a union official to be informed.

What do you wish to report?

I would like to report an accident at work in which I received an electric shock after plugging a laptop into a wall socket.

When did the accident/incident take place?

It happened on the 30th of January. One week ago.

Where did the accident/incident take place? (Please provide full details of the address)

At my office workstation at Unit 65, Block C, 130 Bath Road, London UB3 4HB

What happened?

I had just returned to the office following a lunch break. I had been giving a presentation earlier that day and had been using my laptop for that purpose. I was in a hurry to start work again as I wished to type up a report on the feedback I had received on my presentation. I also wanted to send some emails. I stooped down to plug the laptop into the wall, as the socket is located under my desk. As I did this there was bang and a flash of light. I felt a peculiar throbbing sensation radiating up my right arm. I was thrown back from the socket although it is unclear whether this was my instinct for self-preservation kicking in or whether the shock forced me back. Regardless, as I bounced backwards I smacked my head on the top of my desk and fell to the floor.

Was anyone else involved?

I work in quite a busy office and I would estimate that there were about twenty people in the office at the time. However, as it was just after lunch people were still chatting and getting organised for the afternoon so it is unlikely that any more than a couple of people who were very close by could really comment on the situation.

Please provide the names of any witnesses

Jason Cameron, Judy Speers

Details of action taken and treatment given where relevant

I came to and realised that there was blood on my head and I felt a bit weak and shocked. My colleagues Jason and Judy were beside me. They had, I later discovered, switched off the power source and started mopping up the blood. They were a little concerned about moving

me and it was decided that I should be taken immediately to the accident and emergency department at the local hospital. I went in an ambulance, although I am not entirely convinced that this was necessary. It was probably best to err on the side of caution. I had a series of tests at the hospital including an ECG in case my heart had been affected. I also had a head x-ray.

Were you able to go straight back to work following the accident/incident?

No. I was told by staff at the hospital to go home and rest as I had sustained a mild head injury. I was also very shaken by what had happened.

Complete the sentence with an appropriate word or phrase. Use no more than **three** words from the text.

Q21: The form is designed to be used to record an _____.

. . . .

Q22: It is the responsibility of the line manager to _____.

. . . .

Q23: Employees who are not part of a union should _____.

Find words/phrases with the following definitions in the paragraph entitled **What happened?** Use no more than **three** words from the text.

Q24: Response

. . . .

Q25: Bent over

. . . .

Q26: Spreading out from a central point

. . . .

Q27: Protection of oneself from harm or death

Choose the correct answer.

Q28: The main impact of the incident on the writer's physical well-being was:

A) a head injury.
B) distress.
C) bleeding.

. . . .

Q29: The main purpose of the report is to:

A) ensure that the employee receives compensation.

B) ensure that the employee is fully supported.

C) encourage employers to renew equipment.

. . . .

Q30: The tone the writer has used in the report is:

A) angry.

B) conversational.

C) neutral.

Unit 2 Topic 4

Working with others

Contents

Learning objective

By the end of this topic you will be better able to:

- identify and use collocations relating to working life;

- understand how to utilise your note taking skills;

- write a formal report giving feedback on a staff event.

This topic presents the language used when discussing internet politics and note taking in the workplace. It revises tenses you should already be familiar with at National 5 level and introduces vocabulary relevant to the subjects discussed. It includes work on all four skills: reading, writing, speaking and listening. There are also supplementary pronunciation activities.

4.1   Pre-reading activity: Internet politics

Pre-reading activity: Speaking: Internet politics

Consider the following questions and discuss with a partner if possible:

1. Do you use social networking sites?
2. Have you ever used social media at work, college or school? If you answered yes, do you think this is acceptable?
3. When using social media do you control who can access your personal information?
4. Would you expect your manager at work to look at your online profiles?

Pre-reading activity: Collocations   Go online

Q1:   Match words from the column on the left (a-j) with a suitable word from the column on the right (1-10) to make common collocations.

a. uncharted	1. sense
b. lag	2. steam
c. social	3. behind
d. idle	4. remark
e. lend	5. tongues
f. blissfully	6. networking
g. loose	7. territory
h. common	8. gossip
i. throwaway	9. unaware
j. let off	10. support

Pre-reading activity: Definitions Go online

Q2: Try to match the phrases with meanings below:

a. uncharted territory	1. unguarded conversation
b. lag behind	2. To say or do something which allows you to get rid of feelings or excess energy
c. social networking	3 .give your time to help others
d. idle gossip	4. websites and computer programmes that allow people to communicate
e. lend support	5. practical knowledge and judgement
f. blissfully unaware	6. completely new area or situation
g. loose tongues	7. passing the time by talking about the lives of others
h. common sense	8. comment which is not intended to be taken seriously
i. throwaway remark	9. happy because you do not know the truth of a situation
j. let off steam	10. travel at a slower pace than others

4.2 Reading activity: Internet politics

Reading activity: Internet politics

While reading the following text, take notes on a) the main points of each paragraph and b) the overall purpose of the text. When you have done this try to answer the questions which follow.

1. Few areas of employment in the UK today remain unaffected by the massive growth in technology and more particularly the use of the internet. Most organisations now depend entirely upon email communication and employees pick up data at their own convenience, at work or elsewhere through mobile phones and tablets. As the seemingly unstoppable march of technology continues to impact on more areas of our private, social and working lives, we find that the divide between these areas has become less distinct. Unfortunately, policy in many organisations lags behind technological developments leaving both employers and employees struggling in uncharted territory.

2. Social networking sites appeal to all ages. The impulse to catch up on idle gossip, to find out who did what with whom and when, attracts parents and young people alike. Perhaps more unexpected is the fondness of academics for the potential of sites which frequently serve as a vehicle for showing pictures of 'fun' times; the family pet playing piano for example. For academics, Twitter, Facebook and various other sites

allow access to the world of academia, enabling updates on seminars, publications and reviews at the touch of a keyboard.

3. As the fascination with the internet and all that it can deliver continues unabated, many managers struggle to navigate this in the workplace. Various issues have arisen. As users, we advertise our interests, describe our lives in detail and lend support to various causes on websites, but how much consideration do we give to the image of ourselves that is thereby projected? Moreover, how many of us take care to preclude the attention of strangers by exercising control over privacy settings? A look at the average Facebook page suggests that many of us are still blissfully unaware that, for employers, social media sites offer an opportunity to gather information about potential staff; an inexpensive method of finding suitable employees.

4. Those same employers who are browsing social media and scrutinising sites for feedback on potential and current employees, may be disappointed to discover comments which are less than flattering about their organisation or management. Remarks placed on websites can be damning. How do browsing employers protect their organisations from loose tongues online?

5. It is important to be clear about what is happening on the net and to know when we, as managers or employees, are crossing the line. Using social media to select and reject staff could quite easily move into the realms of discrimination. Among the computer savvy, the response to the corporate lurker has been to operate under two identities: a squeaky clean version and a more reckless, perhaps honest one in which opinions are expressed more freely. The less astute may feel aggrieved to find they are overlooked for jobs or promotion on the basis of throwaway remarks on Facebook. However, some employers keen to ban use of the internet feel wronged by workplace browsing, which they believe represents a colossal theft of company time.

6. As far as managing workplace issues which do arise with respect to the internet, the responsibility lies with both employer and employee. Perhaps the most useful practice is to treat internet issues in the workplace in the same way that we would non-internet issues. At the same time, remember to keep up to date with legislation and be aware of changes made to rights and responsibilities.

7. In the end, surely common sense should prevail. If you have an interview pending, don't mock the organisation on social media and if you hate your boss, don't malign him/her online. At work, confine browsing of non-work related sites to lunch and legitimate break times. As managers, take comments posted online with a pinch of salt: we all need to let off steam from time to time. Above all, a little self-scrutiny goes a long way. Pay attention to instincts; if it feels wrong it probably is wrong!

Q3: What type of text is this?

a) Newspaper or magazine article
b) University textbook
c) Extract from workplace staff induction

....

Q4:   Match the paragraph titles below to paragraphs 1-7 above.

a. Revealing posts	
b. Sensible behaviour	
c. Mistakes on both sides	
d. Widespread appeal	
e. Adopting traditional approaches	
f. Progress outstrips guidelines	
g. Critical comments	

Find words/phrases from the text with the following meanings:

Q5:   potentially undermining (paragraph 4)

....

Q6:   confident user (paragraph 5)

....

Q7:   someone who reads messages but does not take part in the discussion (paragraph 5)

....

Q8:   ignored/not employed or promoted (paragraph 5)

....

Q9:   The text is primarily intended to:

a)   entertain.
b)   advise.
c)   warn.

4.3   Listening activity: Note taking

Listening activity: Note taking	Go online

To complete this exercise, you will need the following sound file:
n5-esl2-4-1listening.mp3

Q10:

Listen to the recording. While listening take notes on the following:

a)   What jobs the speakers do
b)   Identify the main topic of discussion

Listen again and take notes about:

a) What the speakers agree about
b) What the speakers disagree about

....

Q11: Try to complete the gaps in the summary below, using no more than **three** words.

Brian is employed as a a._____. He has written a book about collaboration. He thinks that great ideas arise from b._____. He thinks that basic c. _____is not highly regarded today. Brian thinks that being shy is different from choosing a life of d._____. He thinks that only a particular kind of person can cope with being alone a lot. Julie is a e._____ who has chosen to start f. _____because she thinks the g. _____outweigh the drawbacks. Julie thinks that working in open plan office environments is h._____. She says that to do creative work one needs _____ _____. In open plan offices she was continually _____by colleagues' chatter and by _____. Brian thinks that _____lead to great ideas while Julie believes that having good ideas is likely to happen in a _____.

4.4   Writing a formal report

Writing: Staff event

You have been asked by your line manager to give feedback on a recent staff event organised by management to encourage and enhance team building. You should write a report and consider the following aspects of the day:

- Speakers
- Activities
- Catering
- Venue

Your report should be around 220 words.

4.5   Reading comprehension: Team building

Reading comprehension: Team building   Go online

1. I am not quite sure when it all started but team building events have now become standard practice for businesses and other organisations large and small. I have been coerced into attending several such events in my working life so far, to include: half day, whole day and residential experiences. As such, I feel sufficiently qualified to proffer an opinion.

2. It seems to me that approaches to staff events tend to fall into three categories. Firstly, there are the more esoteric events. These may kick off and close with lectures which promote loyalty and corporate identity. However, before long you are likely to find that you have been drafted into a group session, probably surrounded by colleagues you have never clapped eyes on before. The activities which follow will likely have no obvious relevance or practical application in your daily working life, but will be intended to encourage you to communicate with others whom, incidentally, you are unlikely to see again till the next all-staff event.

3. The overall purpose of such events is often to promote problem solving in groups with the aim of bringing us toward greater understanding of ourselves both as individuals and as group members. Thus it is hoped we will become better employees. All well and good. However, in my view, events of this sort should be treated with caution by both the management who (no doubt in all good faith) set them up and the employees who attend.

4. At this point I shall describe by way of anecdotal evidence the experience of my dear friend Pauline when she was working in international banking. Keen to encourage employees to offer more efficient and effective service, her employers 'invited' all staff to attend a residential training programme lasting three days. Pauline discovered it was not possible to decline the invitation due to a clause in her initial contract which stated that she would agree to all ongoing training. To describe the event as intense would be a massive understatement. The process seemed to be about enabling people to reveal aspects of themselves through activities and discussion which might have hitherto have been hidden or repressed. Unfortunately the results of this process were far from positive. Sometimes we hide things for good reason. It transpired that not only Pauline failed to enjoy the experience - it was universally disliked, and the training programme was scrapped.

5. The second type of event I would suggest is the opposite of that just described, offering a straightforward opportunity to enhance our skills. This type of event might be described as a professional updating opportunity. Employers may invite a series of specialists to deliver workshops which employees pick and choose from depending on perceived need. At the end of the day, the success or otherwise of such events depends upon whether we feel we have learned something useful. I have had many positive experiences at such events and have even been called upon to present at some. In my view a day out which provides an opportunity for a free taster session on Meditation or Mindfulness is well worth the trouble of signing up!

6. The third type of event also makes little pretence. This is the type of event which is organised in celebration of Christmas, a promotion, a corporate merger, retirement, new

baby or other happy event. It offers an opportunity for employees to relax and unwind together. It usually includes food and drinks. It may also include 'fun' activities, either outdoor or indoor, such as canoeing or paintballing and it may just be about hiring a disc jockey and dancing all night. This final category is by far my favourite of all staff events. I especially enjoy an event which delivers on the promise of fun. It is also particularly pleasing to chat to whoever I choose as opposed to being randomly shuffled. I always strenuously oppose efforts to make me move when I have found a seat beside someone I want to be with.

7. I am aware that my tone may seem quite cynical at times but it masks a strange contradiction. Although I am quick to point out the drawbacks of all staff events, I would almost certainly be among the first to mourn their loss. Whether massive success or outright disaster, we bond through the experience and the event becomes part of the history we share.

Complete each sentence with no more than five words from the text.

Q12: Team building events have now become _____.

....

Q13: The more esoteric events are unlikely to have _____.

....

Q14: The main function of more esoteric events is to

_____.

....

Q15: Pauline had to attend an all-staff event due to a

_____.

....

Q16: The second type of team building event is a

_____.

Find words in the text with the meanings below:

Q17: Which word in paragraph 1 means *pressurised*?

....

Q18: Which word in paragraph 4 means *based on stories which may not be true*?

....

Q19: Which word in paragraph 4 means *reject*?

....

Q20: Which word in paragraph 4 means *cancelled*?

Give a short answer in your own words.

Q21: Explain the use of inverted commas around the word 'fun' in paragraph 6.

....

Q22: What does the writer mean by use of the phrase 'masks a strange contradiction' in paragraph 7?

Choose the correct answer.

Q23: The overall tone of this piece of writing is:

a) serious.
b) light-hearted.
c) sarcastic.

4.6 Listening comprehension: Training course

Listening comprehension: Training course	Go online

To complete this exercise, you will need the following sound file:
n5-esl2-4-2listening.mp3

Complete the sentences below using no more than **three** words:

Q24: Jane and Tina are going to attend a management _____.

....

Q25: Tina listened to a lecture which was about _____.

....

Q26: Introverts are happy to spend_____.

....

Q27: Extroverts don't necessarily _____.

....

Q28: In terms of introversion and extroversion, both Jane and Tina are a _____
of both.

Choose the **two** correct answers.

Q29: Tina thinks that she and Jane should:

A) force people to sit in groups.

B) make changes to seating arrangements in the office.

C) support different personality.

D) ask team leader to do a survey.

E) abandon staff development.

....

Decide whether the following statements are true or false.

Q30: Decide whether the following statements are true or false.

A) Jane thinks that a change in layout could improve quality of work.

B) Jane is negatively affected by noise level in the office.

C) Jane and Tina are in charge of the their team.

Unit 3: ESOL in Context : Society

Unit 3 Topic 1

Learning in context

Contents

Learning objective

By the end of this topic you will be better able to:

- participate in a conversation about business;
- recognise and produce phrases which are appropriate in the context of a formal business meeting;
- write a formal report including analysis and recommendations.

1.1   Vocabulary: Language of business

Business words (15 min)   Go online

Look at the following exercise related to the topic of Business. Can you unscramble the letters to make familiar words?

Q1:

1. CUTDROP
2. CIRPE
3. RABDN
4. KEMTAR/SECEHRAR
5. OMORPOTNI
6. LEDVOMNEPTE
7. TINASIDVEGR
8. BULCIP/LARETSONI
9. SNOMUCRE
10. STOIRTUBIDNI

Defining business terms (10 min)   Go online

Can you match the words from the previous exercise with their definitions?

Q2:

1)	product	a)	the cost at which an item is set
2)	price	b)	the delivery process of items to shops and consumers
3)	brand	c)	offers of discounts or deals
4)	market research	d)	a particular kind, or make, of an item
5)	promotion	e)	something which is made to be sold
6)	development	f)	the methods used to generate publicity for an item
7)	advertising	g)	creating and keeping a positive public image
8)	public relations	h)	a person who buys or uses an item
9)	consumer	I)	the creation of new items
10)	distribution	j)	study/survey of consumer needs

1.2   Reading: Selecting appropriate vocabulary

How I became a businessman (35 min)   Go online

Complete the text by choosing the best word from the options given below. Think about what is the most natural collocation as well as which word is best grammatically.

1) student	employee	undergraduate	job seeker
2) life	world	situation	place
3) wall	promotion	rope	ladder
4) vocation	education	employment	role
5) concerned	hopeful	sad	disappointed
6) watching	opening	seeing	scanning
7) caught	took	got	had
8) leader	boss	human	manager
9) respond	reply	responsibility	response
10) self	decision	chance	destiny
11) profit	unemployment	firm	companies
12) me	true	real	believable
13) hope	mood	expectations	motivation
14) drive	money	walk	happiness
15) plan	package	programme	way
16) group	work	businessman	company
17) employs	employ	employment	employed
18) websites	products	gifts	offers
19) clients	consumers	workers	employees
20) manager	business	entrepreneur	money maker

Q3:

Having studied for four years as an 1)_____in order to gain my degree in teaching, I soon learned that in the real 2)_____, once the day to day satisfaction starts to wean, the career prospects and opportunities for climbing the 3)_____ are limited for all but the elite few.   Teaching had been my 4)_____ for several years though, and I was 5)_____ about allowing my dissatisfaction to lead me down a different career path which may prove to be a disaster. But it was one morning around that time, when I was 6)_____ a newspaper article, something 7)_____ my eye, and I decided I had to find out more.

I had been searching for a way to be my own 8)_____. That was part of the problem. Teaching had given me a sense of 9)_____ for others, but I never really felt in control of my own 10)_____. This advertisement was calling out to me - 'How to start your own 11)_____: 3 easy steps to a new life'.

I have to admit, it sounded too good to be 12)_____, so I approached the idea with caution and low 13)_____. However, having answered the advert and signed up for the course, I realised that I had a lot more 14)_____ to succeed in business than I ever had as a teacher.

Within three months, the training 15)_____ had helped me set up my own 16)_____, doing something that I had always enjoyed but never realised I could do professionally: photography.

Four years on, I now 17)_____ two members of staff to assist me, and the company has 18)_____ and services to cover all kinds of occasions, from children's portraits to wedding packages. Thanks to the internet, we have increased our distribution network and even had a few international 19)_____ who have used our services, and this has meant travel to places such as Paris, Rome and Budapest.

Would I go back to teaching? No. I realise now that it wasn't for me. The course brought out the 20)_____ in me, and I am doing things now in my new career that I would otherwise only have been dreaming of.

1.3   Vocabulary: Language of business meetings

Language of business meetings (10 min)	Go online

Look at the following stages of a typical business meeting. What is the correct order of the stages?

Q4:

- Moving the meeting forward
- Outlining the Agenda
- Opening the meeting

- Concluding
- Welcomes/Introductions

Choosing appropriate language in business meetings (15 min)   Go online

Using the stages of a business meeting as category headings place the following expressions under the correct heading.

Opening the meeting; Welcomes/Introductions; Outlining the Agenda; Moving the meeting forward; Concluding

Q5:

- Is everyone present? Let's get underway.
- If we could go around the table and just state who we are and what department we work in. . .
- Let's quickly summarise the main points.
- Good morning, ladies and gentlemen.
- Distribution is the third topic we have to cover today. . .
- My name is Michael Lane and I'm pleased to welcome you all to Optec Computers.
- Any comments on what Jim has outlined there? No? That brings us to. . .
- Is there any other business to be discussed?
- May I begin by welcoming you all to our monthly update. . .
- The reason we are here today is to discuss. . .
- Next up is an outline of the costs. We turn to Sally for this. . .
- Let's get down to business. Point one. . .
- We're delighted to have Alex Smith with us today.
- If nobody has anything to add, that will do it for today.
- Is everyone happy with the order of the points of discussion?

1.4   Listening Activity: Vocabulary: Definitions

Pre-listening activity: Vocabulay: Definitions (10 min)   Go online

Match the vocabulary to the definitions.

Q6:

1)	response	a)	the most important people in a situation
2)	launch (noun)	b)	lack of agreement
3)	unprecedented	c)	make something better/more successful
4)	lukewarm	d)	purchase/use of a (new) product
5)	contradiction	e)	arguments used to sell a product
6)	pitch	f)	unenthusiastic response
7)	key players	g)	first time a product is made available to the public
8)	enhanced	h)	people who buy a new (technological) product before it becomes popular
9)	early adopters	l)	something which has never happened before
10)	leap	j)	increase/improvement in quality of a product
11)	uptake	k)	reaction
12)	boost (verb)	l)	a high jump

1.5   Listening: A business meeting

A business meeting (15 min)   Go online

You will need the following sound file to complete this activity:
n5-esl2-5-1listening.mp3

Q7:   While listening take notes on:

a) Which departments are represented at the meeting.
b) The main areas of discussion.

. . . .

Are the following statements true or false?

Q8: The launch attracted a lot of interest.

a) True
b) False

....

Q9: The media response to the campaign was extremely positive.

a) True
b) False

....

Q10: E-Reader 'Relax' has more features than the earlier model.

a) True
b) False

....

Q11: The response from UK Today was unexpected.

a) True
b) False

....

Q12: Sales are expected to level off in forthcoming weeks.

a) True
b) False

....

Q13: The chairman of the meeting is happy with the team.

a) True
b) False

....

Q14: What factors have affected sales? Give two answers.

....

Q15: What is included in the next stage of the campaign? Give two answers.

1.6   Writing: Report writing

Business reports (60 min)

As a business student at university, you have been asked by your lecturer to complete a report based on the introduction of new technology into the university campus.

In your writing consider the following points:

- an outline of the current technology the university has for students and staff;
- an analysis of where improvements to technology could be made;
- suggested costs, time frame and training that may be required.

Write a report to your lecturer which examines the factors above. You may use the internet to find sources of information to help you research this essay. Remember to reference any information from your sources.

Before you begin, consider the following questions:

- What is the purpose of the communication?
- Who is the intended audience?
- What level of formality and register would be appropriate?

Make some notes or a mind map to help plan your writing before you begin. Write a report of approximately 200-250 words. Ask your teacher to check your work.

1.7   Vocabulary: Business definitions

Business vocabulary (20 min)   Go online

Look at the following exercise related to the topic of Business. Can you unscramble the letters
to make familiar words?

Q16:

- S A T S E
- M E C O C E M R
- T A C T N O R
- T I D E R C O R
- D E V E H O R A
- T O P F I R
- H U C E R P A S
- T I N E R U M I C E R T
- L A S E S \ R E C O F
- G O S L A N
- C S O K T
- I N U N O

Definitions (15 min)

Match the vocabulary to the definitions.

Q17:

1)	asset	a)	a legal written agreement regarding employment or sales
2)	commerce	b)	the operating expenses of a business
3)	contract	c)	to get something by paying for it
4)	director	d)	an organisation which represents workers' rights
5)	overhead	e)	a short, memorable expression used in advertising
6)	profit	f)	buying and selling
7)	purchase	g)	a high level manager in charge of a company or activity
8)	recruitment	h)	products/merchandise which a business sells
9)	sales force	i)	property or stock owned by a company
10)	slogan	j)	the process of hiring the best candidate for a job
11)	stock	k)	the sales department - the business area which sells products
12)	union	l)	The financial difference between what is earned and what is spent

1.8   Writing: Practice: Accurate use of business terms

Creating sentences (15 min)

Write an example sentence using each of the words given here. The first one has been done for you. Work with a partner if possible.

a) asset [example sentence: The new product is going to become the company's biggest **asset** in the European market].

b) commerce

c) contract

d) director

e) overhead

f) profit

g) purchase

h) recruitment

i) sales force

j) slogan

k) stock

l) union

1.9 Pronunciation: Listen and repeat

(15 min) Go online

You will need the following sound files to complete this activity:
n5-esl2-5-2listening1.mp3 to *n5-esl2-5-2listening12.mp3*

Look again at some of the words from this topic. Listen to each word in the recording.

Q18: How many syllables does each word have, and where is the main stress in each word?

e.g. business	*Oo*
asset	
commerce	
contract	
director	
overhead	
purchase	
recruitment	
slogan	
union	
advertising	
consumer	
distribution	

1.10   Reading comprehension: Tax

A Taxing Problem

For many self-employed individuals, the process of filling out tax returns is necessary but also painstaking and laborious. Most of those who are required to complete a tax return do so because the repercussions for not complying can be severe, even a prison term is a possibility. What may surprise some people is that many of our country's largest companies appear to be cooking the books and getting away with it.

A large internet auction site and one of the world's leading social networking sites have both been found to be paying astonishingly low taxation rates. According to an investigation by the Daily News, 'Auction Giant' paid only £2 million in tax in the UK in the year 2015, while 'Social Butterfly' paid £4.2 million.

At first glance, these may seem like reasonable sums for large businesses to be paying, but when you consider that Auction Giant took in more than £900 million, and Social Butterfly had a turnover of £1.6 billion in the year 2015, you can begin to see why the man in the street, typically paying between 20-40% tax on his earnings, may feel somewhat cheated.

The response of both of these online companies has been terse. A spokesperson for Auction Giant stated that the company ". . . fully complies with all the relevant laws on taxation in the UK". A director at Social Butterfly responded merely by saying, "We have no comment to make because there is no story there to comment on."

The Daily News alleges that the discrepancies in the amount of taxes paid by these firms is due to them treating a large amount of UK business deals as 'offshore and international transactions', and therefore paying either lower rates of tax overseas, or, in some instances, no tax at all.

A representative of the auction site expanded on their comments to the news channel, CBD: "These allegations are damaging and potentially libellous. We are a transparent, honest company, and all of our financial records are filed properly, following UK, European and international law." Commentators believe that these two companies are not the only culprits of some questionable business practices. Roger Smith of the Daily News stated, "This is the tip of the iceberg. . . we're already following leads on six other large international companies with dubious tax records. They can deny it all they like, but the evidence speaks for itself and the public deserves to know."

Reading comprehension: Tax (40 min)   Go online

A Taxing Problem

For many self-employed individuals, the process of filling out tax returns is necessary but also painstaking and laborious. Most of those who are required to complete a tax return do so because the repercussions for not complying can be severe, even a prison term is a possibility. What may surprise some people is that many of our country's largest companies appear to be cooking the books and getting away with it.

A large internet auction site and one of the world's leading social networking sites have both been found to be paying astonishingly low taxation rates. According to an investigation by the Daily News, 'Auction Giant' paid only £2 million in tax in the UK in the year 2015, while 'Social Butterfly' paid £4.2 million.

At first glance, these may seem like reasonable sums for large businesses to be paying, but

---

when you consider that Auction Giant took in more than £900 million, and Social Butterfly had a turnover of £1.6 billion in the year 2015, you can begin to see why the man in the street, typically paying between 20-40% tax on his earnings, may feel somewhat cheated.

The response of both of these online companies has been terse. A spokesperson for Auction Giant stated that the company "... fully complies with all the relevant laws on taxation in the UK". A director at Social Butterfly responded merely by saying, "We have no comment to make because there is no story there to comment on."

The Daily News alleges that the discrepancies in the amount of taxes paid by these firms is due to them treating a large amount of UK business deals as 'offshore and international transactions', and therefore paying either lower rates of tax overseas, or, in some instances, no tax at all.

A representative of the auction site expanded on their comments to the news channel, CBD: "These allegations are damaging and potentially libellous. We are a transparent, honest company, and all of our financial records are filed properly, following UK, European and international law." Commentators believe that these two companies are not the only culprits of some questionable business practices. Roger Smith of the Daily News stated, "This is the tip of the iceberg... we're already following leads on six other large international companies with dubious tax records. They can deny it all they like, but the evidence speaks for itself and the public deserves to know."

Q19: What kind of text is this?

   a) A tabloid newspaper article

   b) A broadsheet newspaper article

   c) A business journal

                                     ....

Q20: Are the following statements True or False?

   a) People who are employed by large organisations do not need to fill out tax returns.

   b) The average man pays a higher tax rate than the companies mentioned in the article.

   c) The companies involved have provided the press with detailed responses to accusations.

                                     ....

Use between three and five words for each of the following answers

Q21: Find an expression which means 'changing accounting information illegally'.

                                     ....

Q22: Find an expression in the text with the same meaning as 'the average person'.

                                     ....

Q23: Find an expression which means 'only a small part of the overall problem' in the article.

                                     ....

Q24: Which answer best describes the writer's viewpoint?

a) Slightly biased against the large companies

b) In support of the large companies

c) Neutral

1.11   Listening Comprehension: Advertising

Listening comprehension: Advertising (30 min)	Go online

You will need the following sound file to complete this assessment activity:
n5-esl2-5-3listening.mp3

Listen to the recording about finding work in the Advertising industry.

Q25: What is the speaker's advice about working in London?

a) It is the only place to find advertising jobs

b) It is the main centre of commerce and advertising companies

c) It isn't important. You can find good jobs anywhere.

....

Q26: What does the speaker say is one of the most exciting parts of the job?

a) Discovering new ideas before others

b) Communicating with your competitors

c) Using the internet to advertise

....

Q27: When the speaker started his advertising career, he:

a) Never used the internet

b) Was dependent upon the internet

c) Had limited use of the internet

....

Q28: Name the two factors that the speaker says are the most important to agencies when hiring new recruits.

....

Q29: Are the following statements True or False?

a) An interview for an advertising job usually lasts thirty seconds.

b) Your first answer is rarely the most important during interview.

c) You need more than just personality to get a job in advertising.

d) The speaker says that coping with rejection is an important element in success.

....

Q30: Who is the speaker?

a) A Business Studies lecturer

b) An advertising executive

c) A journalist

....

Q31: Who is the intended audience?

a) School pupils

b) Postgraduate students

c) Undergraduate students

Unit 3 Topic 2

Further education

Contents

Learning objective

By the end of this topic you will be better able to:

- participate in a conversation about issues in education;
- make a formal written application for a job;
- write a personal statement;
- ask for clarification in formal contexts.

2.1   Vocabulary: Education

Approaches to education (10 min)   Go online

Look at the words (1-5) listed below which describe approaches to education and then talk
about the differences with a partner between these concepts.

1. Strict

2. Traditional

3. Disciplined

4. Teacher led

5. Mainstream

Q1:   Try to match these to the words (a-e) that express opposite concepts.

a) Modern
b) Student led
c) Alternative
d) Lenient
e) Undisciplined

2.2   Speaking: Discussion: Your school

Your school (15 min)

With a partner or group discuss the following questions.

1. Do you remember your first teacher? What was he / she like?

2. Who was your favourite teacher? Why did you like him / her? What did he / she teach?

3. What was your favourite subject at school?

4. Were your teachers strict?

5. Would you describe your school as traditional or modern?

6. Was the work in the classroom teacher-led or student-led?

2.3   Pre-reading: Vocabulary: Educational definitions

You are going to read a text about a school in a subsequent topic. Some of the vocabulary from the text is in the next activity. Before moving to the reading text attempt this activity.

Educational definitions (20 min)

Match the vocabulary on the left with definitions on the right.

Q2:

1)	non-denominational (adj)	a)	freedom to make decisions
2)	interdisciplinary (adj)	b)	cared for (often while in a developmental stage)
3)	nurtured (verb)	c)	young person aged around 14-18
4)	adolescent (noun)	d)	includes
5)	critical (thinking) (adj/noun)	e)	open to people of different religious groups
6)	ultimate (adj)	f)	methods/means
7)	autonomy (noun)	g)	idea/belief that soul leaves the body after death to live in a new body
8)	vehicles (noun)	h)	making careful judgements
9)	incorporates (verb)	I)	final
10)	reincarnation (noun)	j)	involving different areas of study or knowledge

---

2.4   Reading: Steiner - a very particular school

Pre-Reading: Steiner - a very particular school (25 min)

Look at the questions below then read the passage that follows to find the answers. Take notes while you read.

Q3:   Is the Steiner school traditional?

a) Yes
b) No

....

Q4:   Take note of examples which support your answer. You can use the following categories for notes.

a) Philosophy

b) Approach to learning

c) Organisation

d) Subject matter

e) Emphasis

f) Criticisms of the school

Steiner - a very particular school

Steiner schools are independent, non-denominational schools in which the curriculum is based on the educational philosophy of Rudolf Steiner (1861-1925). Steiner was an Austrian scientist, philosopher and educationalist. The first Steiner school opened in Stuttgart in Germany in 1919. This school was set up to serve the children of employees of the Waldorf-Astoria Cigarette Company. There are now over one thousand Steiner schools worldwide, thirty-five of which are in the UK.

The basic philosophy of the school is that all the needs of a child should be addressed. This means: academic, physical, emotional and spiritual needs. In order to achieve this, an interdisciplinary approach to learning is taken, which includes practical, artistic and conceptual aspects of education and emphasises the role of the imagination. Steiner identified three stages of development in children, all of which he believed should be nurtured. In the early years of childhood the focus is on play and there is an emphasis on learning through activities. The middle years around age 9-14 concentrate on the artistic imagination, while in adolescence developing intellectual understanding and critical thinking are stressed.

The organisation of Steiner schools also differs from more conventional or mainstream schools. Rather than a principal or head teacher taking ultimate responsibility for making decisions, in a Steiner school, decisions around learning and teaching are likely to be the responsibility of a group of experienced teachers. Financial and legal issues concerning the schools would be the responsibility of a group of trustees.

The Steiner philosophy aims to allow teachers to have a high level of autonomy within the classroom. The idea would be that one teacher stays with a group of pupils for as many years as possible. This maximises the opportunity for individual needs to be recognised and developed. An important feature of the Steiner approach is the idea of a main lesson of around two hours in which all academic subjects except languages would be taught. The topic of the main lesson is explored over a period of around six weeks allowing sufficient time for the learners to become completely involved in it. There would be opportunities for this to be revisited later in the year for revision.

Languages are introduced at an early stage in Steiner schools and taught by specialist teachers. This is considered a great advantage and is not generally possible in more mainstream schools. Story-telling and craft as vehicles for learning are considered very important. The potential of seasons and seasonal festivals are maximised to provide opportunities for learning and teaching.

Critics of the schools suggest that the emphasis on creativity and spirituality is at the expense of intellectual and scientific pursuits. Some are also suspicious of Steiner's belief in Anthroposophy, a spiritual path that incorporates ideas about reincarnation and which they believe influences the curriculum. Use of television and computers is discouraged and while many adults would accept that use of televisions and computers among children is too high, nevertheless total avoidance could seriously disadvantage a child.

Post Reading: Steiner - a very particular school (25 min)

Complete the sentences using no more than three words:

Q5: 1. Very young children at Steiner schools are expected to learn through _____.

....

Q6: 2. In _____, children at Steiner schools are expected to learn skills such as making careful judgements?

....

Q7: Children stay with one teacher for as long as possible so that _____ are met.

....

Q8: Children spend around six weeks on themes so as to become completely _____ in them.

Give short answers to the following questions. Use your own words.

Q9: What two ways of learning are thought valuable?

....

Q10: Why are critics suspicious of Anthroposophy?

....

Q11: Why might the lack of computers and televisions be a problem?

2.5 Speaking: Discussion: The Steiner School experience

Discussion: Your thoughts (10 min)

Discuss the following points with a partner or in a group.

1. Do you like the ideas which are promoted at the Steiner school?
2. Would you like your children to be educated at this kind of school? Explain your answer.

2.6   Writing: Applying for a course: Preparing a personal statement

Your personal statement may be the deciding factor in your acceptance to a college or university course in a situation where several students have suitable qualifications. Therefore it is important that you put relevant, interesting content into the personal statement and that it is well written. You should think carefully about what information the admissions board would expect to see.

Application forms (25 min)

You would like to apply for a course in Drama at college or university. Look at the list below and decide which of the qualities would be most interesting to an admissions officer. Put the list in order from 1-10 (where '1' is the most desirable/important).

a) You have a good sense of humour

b) You have a keen interest in the subject

c) You are good at sport

d) You meet the entrance requirements in terms of qualifications

e) You have demonstrated an ability to cope with assessment/exams

f) You are capable of looking after yourself

g) You are hard working

h) You have a wide group of friends

i) Everyone in your family is in the theatre

j) You love parties

Compare your answers with a partner, justifying your answers where necessary.

2.7   Reading and Speaking: Personal statements

Personal statements (15 min)

Read the following points and decide which of these points might be suitable for inclusion in a personal statement for a university course and why.

a) Work experience including volunteering

b) Any reading you have done around the subject of the course you are applying for

c) Reasons why you want to study this subject

---

d) Future plans

e) Humorous stories or anecdotes

f) Membership of clubs and/or societies

g) Positions you have held such as chair of societies

h) Hobbies and interests

i) Languages spoken

j) Family background

Now discuss your answers with a partner justifying your answers where necessary.

2.8   Reading: Extracts from personal statements

Read the following texts (a-e) which are extracts from personal statements and then do the activities.

a) As a child, I loved nothing more than going to the theatre with my family. I would enter into that magical world wholeheartedly, soaking up the atmosphere, throwing myself into the story, becoming one with the characters. At home I would use my imaginative and creative power to invent shows starring my brothers, sisters and friends. Now I am a member of a local amateur group and my deepest joy is the process which takes us from rehearsal to ultimate performance.

b) I have been working as a Saturday volunteer in a hospital for six months which has convinced me that this is the career I would like to have. While I know that the role may often be demanding and difficult, I also know that the rewards are great. The personal qualities which I can bring to this career are that I am dedicated, enthusiastic and hard working. I am also sympathetic, a good listener and have good interpersonal skills.

c) The process of debate fascinates me and the power of language to persuade enthrals me. Truth and justice are not always easy to defend but I am adventurous, I am not afraid of a challenge. I have spent the last few years ensuring that I have the necessary qualifications and have gained experience in a local practice. I am also chair of the school debating team. I now feel ready to embark on the course that will lead me to my chosen career.

d) I have always enjoyed taking responsibility for projects and encouraging others to succeed. As captain of the hockey team, and head prefect in my school, I have gained experience in team building and was described as motivational. This experience also taught me more about the importance of delegation and accountability. I was recently given an opportunity to become involved in a business enterprise scheme for young adults. This was a fantastic experience through which I learned more about the importance of time management and communication in business which I think will support me in the future.

e) As a young child I was very curious about everything around me. I loved finding out about how things worked, often taking things apart in order to rebuild them. At school my strengths have always been Science and Mathematics in which I have a keen interest. In my final year at school I was accepted for a work experience programme with a large aeronautical company and this has convinced me that this is the area in which I would like to work.

2.8.1   Vocabulary: Adjectives to describe character

Adjectives to describe character (30 min)

Q12: Find words in the extracts (a-e) to match the following definitions. The paragraph to look in is given with each definition.

a) Having the ability to think in new and exciting ways. (paragraph a)

b) Having the ability to produce something new. (paragraph a)

c) Someone willing to work hard at something they care about. (paragraph b)

d) Excited and interested in something. (paragraph b)

e) Someone who shows concern for another who is in emotional or physical pain. (paragraph b)

f) Willing to take risks and try new things. (paragraph c)

g) Someone who galvanises others to action. (paragraph d)

h) Someone who wants to know about things (paragraph e)

2.8.2   Selecting appropriate content

Selecting appropriate content

Read the following texts (a-e) which are extracts from personal statements.

a) As a child, I loved nothing more than going to the theatre with my family. I would enter into that magical world wholeheartedly, soaking up the atmosphere, throwing myself into the story, becoming one with the characters. At home I would use my imaginative and creative power to invent shows starring my brothers, sisters and friends. Now I am a member of a local amateur group and my deepest joy is the process which takes us from rehearsal to ultimate performance.

b) I have been working as a Saturday volunteer in a hospital for six months which has convinced me that this is the career I would like to have. While I know that the role may often be demanding and difficult, I also know that the rewards are great. The personal qualities which I can bring to this career are that I am dedicated, enthusiastic and hard working. I am also sympathetic, a good listener and have good interpersonal skills.

c) The process of debate fascinates me and the power of language to persuade enthrals me. Truth and justice are not always easy to defend but I am adventurous, I am not afraid of a challenge. I have spent the last few years ensuring that I have the necessary qualifications and have gained experience in a local practice. I am also chair of the school debating team. I now feel ready to embark on the course that will lead me to my chosen career.

d) I have always enjoyed taking responsibility for projects and encouraging others to succeed. As captain of the hockey team, and head prefect in my school, I have gained experience in team building and was described as motivational. This experience also taught me more about the importance of delegation and accountability. I was recently given an opportunity to become involved in a business enterprise scheme for young adults. This was a fantastic experience through which I learned more about the importance of time management and communication in business which I think will support me in the future.

e) As a young child I was very curious about everything around me. I loved finding out about how things worked, often taking things apart in order to rebuild them. At school my strengths have always been Science and Mathematics in which I have a keen interest. In my final year at school I was accepted for a work experience programme with a large aeronautical company and this has convinced me that this is the area in which I would like to work.

Q13: Match each of the extracts (a-e) to a course which the writers applied for from the list below (note: five are not required).

a) Fashion Design
b) Mathematics
c) Engineering
d) Management
e) Philosophy
f) Law
g) Vet Medicine
h) Drama
i) Nursing
j) Sports and Leisure

2.9 Writing: A personal statement

Personal statements (60 min)

Write a personal statement to accompany an application for a course of study. You may choose from the list given below, or select something different. Ask your teacher if your choice is acceptable. Write 200-220 words.

Fashion Design	Mathematics	Engineering	Management	Philosophy
Law	Veterinary Medicine	Drama	Nursing	Sports and Leisure

Before you begin, consider the following questions:

1. What is the purpose of the communication?
2. Who is the intended audience?
3. What level of formality and register would be appropriate?

2.10   Pre-Listening vocabulary

Pre-Listening vocabulary (15 min)   Go online

Before moving on to the next activity, try to match the words/phrases on the left with definitions on the right.

Q14:

1)	inner city (adj)	a)	something that has to be done according to rules or laws
2)	abuse (verb)	b)	to have enough money to pay for essentials
3)	policies (noun)	c)	to treat someone or something badly
4)	compulsory (adjective)	d)	achievement
5)	persistent (adjective)	e)	ban (from school for bad behaviour)
6)	exclusion (noun)	f)	spending money on goods and services /belief that this is a good thing
7)	consumerism (noun)	g)	plans for action made by organisation/business for example
8)	logo (noun)	h)	area centre of a city (often with social problems)
9)	to make ends meet (idiomatic phrase)	i)	something which continues over a period of time
10)	attainment (noun)	j)	design or symbol used by a company or organisation

2.11 Listening: Fairways School case study

Listening for main ideas (20 min)   Go online 🔊

You will need the following sound file to complete this activity:
n5-esl2-6-1listening.mp3

Take notes while listening to the recording, in order to answer the questions which follow.

Q15: What kind of school is Fairways?

....

Q16: Describe the children who attend the school.

....

Q17: What approach is taken in the school towards discipline?

....

Q18: What approach is taken in the school towards persistent problems with pupils ?

....

Q19: What approach is taken in the school towards Uniform?

....

Q20: What approach is taken in the school towards learning/attainment?

Compare your notes with your partner. You may listen again if necessary.

Listening for detail (20 min)   Go online 🔊

You will need the following sound file to complete this activity:
n5-esl2-6-1listening.mp3

Q21: Use one or a few words to complete the gaps in the following notes on the text.

a) Compared to other similar schools Fairways has _____ exclusions.

b) Parents often buy fashionable clothes for their children because _____.

c) The guidance time is _____.

2.12   Study skills: Asking for clarification

In some academic situations, such as tutorials and seminars, you may find that some of the discussion is difficult to follow. With your partner or group, think of as many ways as you can of asking a speaker to rephrase a statement or question.

Asking for clarification   Go online

Here are some possibilities, but the words are in the wrong order. Can you rearrange them?

Q22:

a) please? I'm could you sorry, say again that

b) example that please? Could give of me an you

c) clarify point please? Could that you

d) not sure I'm follow you I'm sorry, I

e) you Do . . . ? mean

2.12.1   Speaking: Discussion: Asking for clarification

Asking for clarification

Now listen to the sound files in which speaker uses his/her voice to convey the request. Note the use of rising intonation.

Listen and repeat the phrases to practise your intonation.

You will need the following sound files to complete this activity:
n5-esl2-6-2listening1.mp3 to *n5-esl2-6-2listening5.mp3*

- I'm sorry, could you say that again please?

- Could you give me an example of that please?

- Could you clarify that point please?

- I'm sorry, I'm not sure I follow you.

- Do you mean. . . ?

2.12.2 Vocabulary: Word transformation

Word transformation Go online

The verbs below were used in the topic. Can you find adjectives and nouns from the same root where possible? The first example has been done for you.

Q23:

Verb	Noun	Adjective
To compare	*Comparison*	*Comparable*
To dedicate		
To exclude		
To persist		
To approach		
To guide		
To attain		
To interfere		
To endeavour		-
To furnish	-	

2.13 Reading comprehension: Etre et avoir

Reading comprehension: Etre et avoir Go online

Être et Avoir ('To be and to have'), directed by Nicolas Philibert in 2003, is a completely captivating and entrancing documentary film. Philibert takes the viewer into the world of a one-class school in a farming community in Auvergne in rural France.

The pupils in the class range in age from four to eleven. The film, which was shot over a six month period, quietly observes their school life alongside their gentle and talented teacher George Lopez. The children are taught reading, writing and arithmetic, but we also observe them learn through baking and tobogganing in the snow, for example. Part of Lopez's job, as he understands it, is to prepare his group for the wider world. They are fortunate to be in this learning environment in the meantime, but inevitably they will move on to secondary school and the context there will be entirely different.

Within the film we watch Lopez support the children through the various problems which they encounter. This includes disagreements, withdrawal and family illness. In each of these situations Lopez treads lightly. Resolution of conflict is reached through discussion rather than confrontation, as Lopez encourages the children to explore and express their feelings. Through such methods the children learn strategies of peaceful co-existence which will support them in later life.

The success of the film is perhaps due in part to the sensitivity of the director. The children are observed with respect and the teacher with admiration. *Être et Avoir* depicts a school setting which is rare nowadays, and shows us what we have lost as a consequence.

Q24: What kind of text is this?

a) A magazine article

b) A film review

c) An journal article

....

Q25: How does the writer feel about *Être et Avoir*?

a) Positive

b) Negative

c) Neutral

....

Q26: Are these statements true or false?

a) *Être et Avoir* is a film about education.

b) The pupils in the film are in a mainstream learning environment.

c) The teacher in the film is a strict disciplinarian.

d) Problems in the school classroom are worked out through conversation.

e) The film maker was not concerned about the feelings of the people he filmed.

f) There are many schools which are similar to that depicted in the film.

....

Q27: Use your own words to explain the phrase 'peaceful co-existence'. Keep your answer short.

....

Q28: Use your own words to explain the phrase 'shows us what we have lost as a consequence'. Keep your answer short.

2.14 Listening comprehension: Supportive parents

Listening comprehension: Supportive parents Go online

You will need the following sound file to complete this assessment activity:
n5-esl2-6-1listening.mp3

Q29: What is the context of the conversation?

....

Q30: What is the main subject of discussion?

....

Q31: There are three speakers (Moira, Jenny and David) - which speaker expressed each of the opinions below?

  a) Middle class parents tend to schedule activities for their children.

  b) Good attendance is a positive indicator of performance in schools.

  c) Parents need support to know how to help their children.

....

Q32: Complete the gaps in the following notes from the recording using no more than three words.

Parents can help children in weak schools to **a)** _____ by helping with **b)** _____ and **c)** _____. Middle class parents tend to **d)** _____ for their children which helps in their development but **e)** _____, which costs nothing, also helps. It is not just exam results which show that a school is doing a good job, **f)** _____ ethos and **g)** _____ also indicate performance.

Glossary

abstract

(adjective) Existing as an idea or feeling rather than a material object

accountability

(noun) State of having responsibility for something

acquisition

(noun) act of getting something (particularly knowledge) e.g. language acquisition

additive

(noun) Substance added to food in small amounts to improve colour or flavour for example

adhere

(verb) To stick to something e.g. wallpaper paste will help the paper adhere to the wall/all members must adhere to the no smoking policy in the club

aeronautical

(adjective) Concerned with building and flying aircraft

agenda

(noun) List of items to be discussed at a meeting

allocate

(verb) Give something to someone for an official purpose

alternative therapies

(noun) Range of treatments for illnesses which can be used instead of conventional medicine

ambler

(noun) Person who walks at a leisurely pace

angler

(noun) Person who catches fish as a hobby

anticipate

(verb) To imagine that something will happen

antisocial

(adjective) Not keen to spend time with other people

appeal

(noun) Quality which makes someone or something attractive e.g. I've never understood the appeal of rock music

appreciate

(verb) To recognise the good qualities in someone/something e.g. He really appreciates good food

aspiration

(noun) Desire to have or do something e.g. He has strong political aspirations

aspiring

(adjective) Keen to have a particular job or position e.g. She was an aspiring pop star when I met her

auxiliary nurse

(noun) Person who assists the nursing staff in a hospital

bewildered

(adjective) Confused e.g. her behaviour has left me completely bewildered

birds eye

(adjective) Good view/vantage point e.g. From the top of the hill I had a bird's eye view of the town

bleak

(adjective) Not encouraging or without hope e.g. Unemployment was high and the future looked bleak

body swerve

(noun) Sudden movement to the left or right often to avoid collision. Metaphorically - to avoid someone /an uncomfortable question e.g. I had to make a swift body swerve to avoid my least favourite person

bombarded

(past tense of verb to bombard) Showered or attacked with a multitude of information (or bombs in a war zone)

borne fruit

(verb past participle/noun) Having had a successful outcome

bottle bank

(noun) Container for saving glass bottles for future use

brooding

(adjective) Dark and mysterious e.g. the characters in romantic novels are often described as brooding

buggy

(noun) Cart/chair on wheels for child

burning question

(adjective/noun) idiomatic, Question of great interest to everyone

camaraderie

(noun) Friendship which evolves through shared work or other experience

canister

(noun) Metal container for storage

capitulation

> (noun) An act of surrender to something after a struggle e.g. The defeat of the last few hundred soldiers on the ground led to a complete capitulation

captivating

> (adjective) Extremely attractive and interesting

caring

> (adjective) Describing someone who gives emotional or physical support to others

cautious

> (adjective) To be careful about choice of words or actions so as to avoid making mistakes

charitable

> (adjective) Giving food, money or shelter to the poor and/or needy

child-rearing

> (noun) Work involving taking care of children when they are young

chilly

> (adjective) Slightly cold

circadian

> (adjective) Connected with the changes in the body over a 24 hour period

circumnavigate

> (verb) To travel around the circumference of coast, park or other place

claustrophobia

> (noun) Fear of small, enclosed spaces

coastal

> (adjective) Beside the sea

co-existence

> (noun) Living together in the same place and at the same time

compensate

> (verb) To pay money in exchange for something lost or damaged

complex

> (adjective) Problematic or involving many different parts

complicit

> (adjective) Involved with others in something illegal or wrong e.g. She was complicit in her daughter's crime because she didn't report it to the police

conceptual

> (adjective) Based on ideas or principles

conducive

>   (adjective) Conditions appropriate to something happening e.g. loud music is not conducive to private conversation

conducting

>   (present participle of verb to conduct) To lead or host e.g. The police officer said he was conducting an investigation into crime in the North of Britain

conformist

>   (adjective) Person who aspires to think and behave in the same way as others e.g. she was always more conformist than her sister, whose behaviour she found strange and embarrassing

conservation

>   (noun) Process of protecting animals, plants, open spaces and buildings

constitutional

>   (noun) Walk intended to maintain health

contrast

>   (noun) Clear difference when two things are compared

convictions

>   (plural noun) Occurrences of being found guilty of crimes e.g. He was given a hard sentence of several years in prison because he had previous convictions

councillor

>   (noun) Member of a council

coverage

>   (noun) Range or quality of information included

craft

>   (noun) Activity involving a skill in making things by hand

culprit

>   (noun) Person found responsible for doing something wrong

customary

>   (adjective) Usual/general. Behaviour typical of an individual or group e.g. She dealt with the situation with customary skill

cyclical

>   (adjective) Following in a particular order and generally repeated

dapper

>   (adjective) Small neat man with nice smart clothes

decay

>   (noun) Gradual damage/destruction

decorative

(adjective) Intended to look attractive

deeds

(noun) Legal documents proving ownership of a property e.g. I have to sign the deeds for my new house tomorrow morning

delegation

(noun) Process of giving others work which might otherwise be your own

depict

(verb) Show, describe or give an impression of someone in words or pictures

destiny

(noun) A force believed by some to control the future

detrimental

(adjective) Damaging

diabetes

(noun) Medical condition affecting the body's ability to regulate sugar and insulin

dilemma

(noun) Situation which is forcing a choice between two important things e.g. The dilemma I face is whether to invest in a new smart telephone or a tablet

dimension

(noun) Aspect or way of looking at something e.g. Learning to dance has brought a new dimension to my life

disastrous

(adjective) Bad or unsuccessful

disciplined

(adjective) Able to manage and control one's life in order perhaps to achieve a goal

discontentment

(noun) State of unhappiness or dissatisfaction with a situation e.g. He was experiencing a strong sense of discontentment with his job and decided to look for something else

discourage

(verb) Make someone feel less confident

disorder

(noun) Lack of organisation

disorientation

(noun) Sense of confusion about place or purpose

disparaging

(adjective) Suggesting something is unimportant /words or actions which are designed to make someone feel small e.g. she was very disparaging when I told her I wanted to be a doctor

disregard

(verb) To fail to consider something or consider something unimportant e.g. I decided to disregard the terrible rain and just go out walking anyway

distinction

(noun) Describing a quality of excellence

diverse

(adjective) Various and different e.g. I have had a diverse range of jobs

dividends

(noun) Rewards e.g. My piano practice is now starting to pay dividends as I can play better

domain

(noun) Territory or land owned by someone e.g. the dog is very territorial and thinks the house is his domain

draughts

(noun) Cold air entering through gaps in windows and doors for example

drizzly

(adjective) Wet (weather due to light rainfall) The weather in Scotland is often wet and drizzly.

dubious

(adjective) Uncertain as to whether something is good or bad

dwindling

(continuous form of the verb to dwindle) Falling away/gradually become smaller

eccentric

(adjective) Considered strange or odd by others e.g. she started to collect animals in her old age which others found quite eccentric

eco-friendly

(noun) Concerned with the future of the environment

elated

(adjective) Very excited

embark

(verb) Begin /start something

embellish

(verb) Add details to a story which may be exaggerated or untrue e.g. She tended to embellish stories about the past in order to make herself seem more interesting

emphasis

(noun) The level of importance given to something

enchanted

(adjective) Affected by magic

encountered

(past tense of verb to encounter) Met (often by chance)

enthral

(verb) To keep all of one's attention and interest

entourage

(noun) Group who travel and work with an important person

entrancing

(adjective) Someone/something who/which is extremely beautiful or interesting

entrepreneur

(noun) Person who makes money by starting or running a business

entrusted

(adjective) Someone given responsibility for something e.g. We have entrusted our secretary with the keys to the office

erosion

(noun) Gradual rubbing away

ethos

(noun) Moral ideas /attitudes associated with a particular group

evacuate

(verb) To move people out of a dangerous area

exploit

(verb) Take advantage of someone/ a situation

extensive

(adjective) Covering a lot of ground

fall out

(noun) Consequences (of something bad)

fatigue

(noun) Tiredness

fell swoop

(idiomatic phrase) All at the same time e.g. she completed her Christmas shopping in one fell swoop

fictitious

(adjective) Untrue e.g. The stories she wrote for the magazine were usually fictitious although some were based on fact

flash floods

(noun) Short, severe episodes of flooding

flexible

(adjective) Able to adapt to change

flourishing

(adjective) Growing and developing well

fondness

(noun) Warm feelings of liking or love

foresaw

(past tense of verb to foresee) To predict something /know something is going to happen in advance

fuelled

(past tense of verb to fuel) Given power to something

fully-fledged

(adjective) Completely developed e.g. when I have finished my probationary year I will be a fully-fledged teacher

futuristic

(adjective) Modern and unusual e.g. The design of the new computer is quite futuristic

gale

(noun) Strong wind

generalising

(continuous form of verb to generalise) Drawing conclusions /making statements based on limited or basic understanding and knowledge of something

glaciers

(noun) Large mass of ice

glutton

(noun) Person who eats much more than they need

gourmand

(noun) Person who enjoys eating a lot of food

gourmet

(adjective) Describes food or drinks of the highest quality

graffiti

(noun) Writing or drawings placed (often illegally) in public places

greed

(noun) Strong need/desire for more food or money for example

gritty

(adjective) Realistic/ Showing the negative realities often in film or TV e.g. The Independent cinema is showing a new film following the gritty day to day work of Inspector Dougan

handy

(adjective) Easy to use /of great practical use

hologram

(noun) 3 dimensional image captured on a 2 dimensional surface e.g. Our local visitors' centre uses a hologram to welcome customers

hostile

(adjective) Unfriendly/aggressive e.g. We walked into private land by mistake and the owner seemed very hostile

hub

(noun) Central or main part of something

hues

(noun) Degrees of light, strength etc. of a colour

humiliation

(noun) Sense of having lost respect for oneself

iconic

(adjective) Famous or popular/ thought to be representative of a time or place

immerse

(verb) To become completely involved in something

impede

(verb) Prevent something from happening

imperative

(adjective) Urgent

implications

(noun) Suggestions which are not overtly stated

impression

(noun) Idea or feeling about a person or place

incentive

(noun) Something which encourages a person to do something

incompatible

(adjective) Unable to live or work together because of basic differences

inevitably

(adverb) Certain to happen

initially

(adverb) At the start

initiate

(verb) To start

initiative

(noun) Ability to work alone without being told what to do e.g. She got promoted to manager because she showed a great deal of initiative

innovations

(plural noun) New ways of doing things e.g. The new management are driving innovations

insecure

(adjective) Lacking in confidence

insomnia

(noun) Inability to sleep

instantaneous

(adjective) Happening immediately e.g. My promotion in that company was almost instantaneous

institution

(noun) Important or large organisation such as a school or church for example

interactive

(adjective) Involving working together and having influence on each other/computer program designed to involve the user

interfering

(adjective) One who gets involved in the affairs of others without being wanted

interwoven

(past tense of verb to interweave) Two threads, ideas, arguments etc. brought together e.g. She found that their ideas had become interwoven so she could not recognise who was responsible for each

intimately

(adverb) Closely/personally e.g. She is intimately involved with her boyfriend

introspection

(noun) Close examination of own thoughts and feelings e.g. He had a habit of introspection which was not always healthy

invent

(verb) To produce or design something which is new

invest

(verb) Put money, time or effort into something in order to make a profit

investment

(noun) Act of putting money, effort or time into something

isolation

(noun) State of being separate e.g. I didn't like living on a small island because of the sense of isolation

joystick

(noun) Vertical handle used to control a game

juvenile

(adjective) Young and immature (perhaps silly)

kelp

(noun) Brown seaweed e.g. She heard kelp was good for plants so she was using it as a fertiliser

laborious

(adjective) Taking a lot of time and effort

lagged (pipes)

(adjective) Wrapped in material which will keep heat in

latched on

(phrasal verb) Forced attachment to someone

learning curve

(noun) Process of learning a new skill e.g. Becoming a good doctor was full of steep learning curves and took a lot of hard work and dedication

leukaemia

(noun) Cancer affecting the blood

liaise

(verb) Deal with others/share information

libel

(noun) Act of printing negative comments about someone which are not true

limelight

(noun) Public attention or interest

linear

(adjective) Moving from one thing to another in stages such as for example in literature progressing in chronological order e.g. He wrote in a logical, linear fashion

literally

(adverb) Having the exact meaning expressed

load

(noun) Weight carried

loft

(noun) Area at the top of a building under the roof

logos

(noun) Signs or symbols used by a company as identification e.g. I've always liked the logo British Airways use. It looks very smart

mainstream

(noun) Conventional. Having ideas, values, beliefs which are agreed by many others

malaise

(adjective) Feeling of being ill and having no energy

manipulate

(verb) To control

material goods

(adjective/noun) Items associated with physical rather than spiritual well-being e.g. I have given away all my material goods and plan to devote my life to charity

medicinal

(adjective) Used to treat illnesses

menial

(adjective) Unskilled or unimportant e.g. Some tasks such as washing dishes are considered quite menial

metabolism

(noun) Chemical processes of the body and in particular those concerned with digestion of food

modest

(adjective) Small amount or number/quiet about personal achievements

morale

(noun) Confidence and enthusiasm

mourn

(verb) To feel sadness following the loss of someone or something e.g. He mourned the loss of friends when we moved abroad

multitude

(noun) Large number of people or things

muse

(noun) Source of inspiration for artist

nap

(noun) Short sleep

obsession

(noun) Describes when a person's mind is completely occupied with one person or thing e.g. tennis has become an obsession for her. She plays every day

obsolete

(adjective) No longer in use because something new has been invented

obstacles

(noun) Hindrance/something making progress difficult e.g. The fact that my computer is broken is a huge obstacle since I need it for work

offspring

(noun) Children

ornate

(adjective) Highly decorative

outlay

(noun) Money needed to start a new project

painstaking

(noun) Involving a great deal of care and attention to detail

panic

(verb) A strong sense of fear

partial

(adjective) Incomplete amount

penalties

(plural noun) Punishments

perceive

(verb) To notice or become aware of something e.g. I perceived a change in his behaviour, he started forgetting things

persuasive

(adjective) Able to change opinion or actions

physiotherapist

(noun) Medical practitioner who specialises in restoring movement when muscles are injured

physiotherapy

(noun) Treatment which helps someone grow stronger

pinned

(verb) Attached using a metal stick

pioneering

> (adjective) Introducing new ideas e.g. Tm Bernard-Lee was pioneering in his role in creating the world wide web

plagued

> (verb) To be worried, in pain or annoyed by something e.g. He is plagued by ill health

polarise

> (verb) To cause a sharp divide in opinion

pondered

> (past tense of verb to ponder) To think carefully about something for a period of time e.g. she pondered over the problem for some time

pool

> (verb) To share resources among a group

prerequisite

> (adjective) Condition that must exist before something can happen e.g. being fit and strong is a prerequisite of becoming a professional in sport

prescient

> (adjective) Appearing to know about things before they happen e.g. She claimed to be prescient of the growth of the computer industry

processed

> (adjective) Food which has been industrially prepared using additives

profiteering

> (noun) Taking advantage of peoples' needs in order to make money

profusely

> (adverb) In large amounts e.g. He apologised profusely for spilling his coffee over me

prominently

> (adverb) In an obvious position /easily seen

psychotherapist

> (noun) Practitioner who specialises in treating mental health problems

purchased

> (verb) Bought (formal) e.g. They purchased a replacement vehicle after the recent loss of their car in an accident

pursuit

> (noun) Something one does to pass the time/actively looking for something perhaps chasing it e.g. He enjoys football and other sporting pursuits/He is in pursuit of a new job

quivering

> (adjective) Shaking

radar

(noun) System using radio waves for location

rare

(adjective) Very unusual/difficult to find

realign

(verb) Restore to correct position

recession

(noun) Time when the economy in a country is contracting e.g. There are fewer jobs at the moment because we are in a recession

recipient

(noun) One who receives

reconcile

(verb) Bring together two opponents or two opposite ideas

recoup

(verb) Get back an amount of money spent

recruitment

(noun) Process of finding suitable people for jobs

rectified

(past tense of verb to rectify) Corrected

recycle

(verb) Use again

rehearsal

(noun) An opportunity for the actors/singers or musicians involved in a theatrical performance to practise

remuneration

(noun) Money given for work done e.g. I have not been given sufficient remuneration for the hours I have spent at work

repercussions

(noun) Indirect and generally negative result of action

resolution

(noun) Official or personal decision

resources

(noun) Supply of important materials

responsibility

(noun) Something which is your job or duty to deal with

reticent

(adjective) Person who avoids sharing thoughts and /or feelings with others

retired

(adjective) No longer in paid employment (generally due to advancing years)

revealing

(adjective) Showing something previously unseen

Rewarding

(adjective) Giving benefits which may be physical, emotional or spiritual e.g. I find my work as a doctor very rewarding

rigid

(adjective) Strict and difficult to change e.g. The school rules were rigid and old-fashioned

rollercoaster

(noun) Change in feelings or circumstances from one extreme to another

saboteur

(noun) Person who spoils something

salutary

(adjective) Having the effect of teaching an important lesson e.g. It was a salutary tale of love and loss which made her more cautious

severe

(adjective) Extremely bad

shy away

(phrasal verb) Avoid doing something because you are afraid e.g. She tended to shy away from responsibility

soak-up

(verb) To absorb

solar panels

(noun) Systems (generally panels attached to roofs) which take energy from the sun and change it into electricity

solely

(adverb) Involving only one element

spectacular

(adjective) Exciting to look at or watch

spectre

(noun) Ghost/unpleasant idea of a possible future e.g. It was a spooky film full of ghosts and spectres/the spectre of war is constant and depressing

splashing out

(phrasal verb) Act of spending a lot of money on something which is probably not essential e.g. I am splashing out on a new dress for our evening out as I am tired of the ones I already have

straddle

(verb) To sit or stand with one leg on either side of something /to combine two different activities, styles, subjects

strategies

(noun) Coping mechanisms

strict

(adjective) Describing someone such as a parent or teacher who strongly controls the behaviour of others

sufficient

(adjective) Enough of a quantity or a specific purpose

supportive

(adjective) Giving help, encouragement or sympathy e.g. She was always a very supportive friend

surreal

(adjective) Having a dream like quality

synchronised

(past tense of verb to synchronise) Arranged to happen at the same time

targets

(noun) Things one hopes to achieve

teeming

(adjective) Full of life/people

terse

(adjective) Using only a few words and thereby seeming rude/ unfriendly

thrive

(verb) To do well /be successful

traditional

(adjective) Following behaviours which have been in existence for a long time

transparent

(adjective) Enabling one to see through or grasp the truth of something

trappings

(plural noun) Wealth or goods associated with a particular job or lifestyle e.g. She had all the trappings of the film star life: big house, expensive car...

trauma

(noun) Severe emotional shock/pain following upsetting event, accident or injury

trodden

(past participle of verb to tread) To have stood/walked (on something) e.g. That was painful! I have just trodden on a nail

unassuming

(adjective) Not desiring attention/recognition for success and qualities e.g. He was very unassuming, we didn't realise he had had such an important role in developing technology

unceremoniously

(adverb) In a rude or uncaring way e.g. she dropped her coat unceremoniously on the floor

uncontested

(adjective) Without opposition

undergo

(verb) Experience something (often unpleasant)

understated

(adjective) Presented in a quiet way e.g. I think that the work of nurses is often greatly understated.

uniqueness

(noun) Quality of being different from others

unresponsive

(adjective) Failing to provide the expected response e.g. She was totally unresponsive when I asked for help

viable

(adjective) Can be done /should succeed

vicious circle

(adjective/noun) Situation in which one thing continually makes another thing worse which in turn makes the first thing worse again e.g. She's trying to lose weight through diet and exercise but when she exercises she feels hungrier and eats more. It's a vicious circle

volunteer

(noun) A person working without payment

vulnerable

(adjective) Weak or easy to hurt emotionally or physically e.g. Young people can be vulnerable to dangerous strangers when they surf the internet

waterproof

(adjective) Material which does not let water through e.g. we were going out in wet weather so we put on waterproof clothing

witty

(adjective) Clever and funny with words

Answers to questions and activities for Unit 1

Topic 1: Personal profile

Introductions/salutations (page 6)

Q1:

a) How do you do?

b) Pleased to meet you.

c) It's a pleasure to meet you.

d) How are you?

e) How are things?

Responses (page 6)

Q2:

a)	Pleased to meet you.	4)/5)	Likewise
b)	It's a pleasure to meet you.	4)/5)	Likewise
c)	How are you?	1)	Very well, thanks. And you?
d)	How are things?	2)	Everything is fine, thanks.

Introducing others (page 7)

Listening transcript

Steve:

Alright, let's go through to the lounge and you can meet some of my friends. Look, there's Michelle, oh she and I go way back to our school days. Great girl - Michelle, hi there, I'd really like you to meet my friend Jim.

Michelle:

Hi Jim, pleased to meet you.

Steve:

Shelly, I was just telling Jim how we've known each other for, well, forever it seems!

Michelle:

Well, not quite forever, but since our days back in school in Middlesborough. Steve was always the class clown... some things never change, eh?!!

Steve:

Yeah, thanks Michelle. Are you still at the university these days? Michelle's a proper science boffin, don't you know. Loves to pass her wisdom of all things Chemistry on to her pupils...

Michelle:

Yes, still there and still loving it, Steve...

Karen:
Pardon me for interrupting, but is that you Steve? Steve from Royal Post Service?

Steve:
Karen Hayworth? Wow! What a lovely surprise... Karen, it would be rude of me not to introduce my good friend Jim.

Karen:
Well, hello, Jim. It's a pleasure to meet you. What do you do?

Steve:
He's a jack of all trades, is Jim. Anyway, he'd love to hear how we met, that's always a funny story...

Karen:
You mean Steve hasn't mentioned me before?! That's okay. It's embarrassing for him, I guess. I met him when I was working for the police and he was in prison...

Steve:
Haha, Karen, how about the truth...?

Karen:
No, actually, Steve's sister introduced us. I was working with her in a hotel in Brighton for the summer, a long time ago, and she got her little brother a job as a kitchen porter. I was head chef, so I used to order Steve around. We were younger then, but he still does everything I say even today...

Steve:
You wish, Karen! Yeah, Karen is getting old, she's just turned 40...

Karen:
Steve! Don't broadcast my age to everyone please...

Mike:
Steve, mate. How on earth are you? Oh, hello, my name's Mike. You must be Jim, Steve told me you were coming. It's great to finally meet you.

Steve:
This is my sister's other half, Mike. How long have you two been married now? 10 years?

Mike:
Yes, nearly. If I ever forget, I always find that remembering the date when I got my first job on the oil rigs helps... it was the same week I married your sister...

Steve:
If you ever have any problems with your car or with the wiring in your house at any time, remember this guy - Mike's an electrical engineer. Jim, now here's the girl I'd like you to meet... Jenny, have you met Jim?

Jenny:
No, I don't believe we have met before. Lovely to meet you, Jim, and lovely to see you again, Steve.

Steve:
Likewise, Jenny, likewise. What brings you here to this shindig?

Jenny:
Oh, my father knows the host. He thought it would be good for me to get out and mix with new people. He says I spend too much time with other Australian friends and I need to meet more local

people.

Steve:
Haha, that sounds like your dad. Well, perhaps you and Jim can get better acquainted later. We're going to be...

Molly:
Steven, Steven! Is that you darling?

Steve:
Um, yeah, I'd like to introduce you to my friend, Jim. Jim, this is Mandy... er, sorry, Jenny, er, sorry... this is... oh, what's her name again...?

Molly:
My name is Molly. Pleased to meet you, Jim. You'll have to excuse us for a minute. My husband here seems to have a memory problem, and I think he has some explaining to do...

Q3:   Middlesborough

Q4:   chemistry lecturer

Q5:   in a hotel

Q6:   40

Q7:   the host

Q8:   brother-in-law

Q9:   electrical engineer

Q10: Australian

Q11: Molly

Q12: wife

Listening activity: social interaction (page 8)

Listening transcript

Chris: Hi, Steve! How are you? I haven't seen you in ages! Sal said you would be at her party.

Steve: Hi, Chris! Good to see you, too. I'm really well, thanks. How are things with you?

Chris: I'm fine, thanks. The business has really taken off, I'm selling international food like hot cakes. Everyone in Edinburgh seems to want more variety in their diet nowadays! Anyway, how's Spain?

Steve: Spain is fantastic. I love it! The lifestyle is just perfect for me. I can be outdoors most of the time and because the weather is so much better, it makes people much more sociable than here. Or perhaps just less ... reserved, you know? People include you in things more. It's easier to get to know new people. Hey, do you do sell haggis? I'd quite like a few of them to take back to Spain. I could take them in my hand luggage.

Chris: You might struggle with that these days! Anyway, I specialise in international delicacies rather than Scottish ones! You are certainly looking very well, Steve. Valencia must suit you. All that sunshine and the Mediterranean diet! Oh, here's Anna ... she's renting my spare room at the moment. Anna, this is Steve.

Anna: Hi, Steve! Nice to meet you. So, how do you two know each other?

Chris: Oh, we go way back don't we, Steve? In fact, I can remember when Steve was running around in ...

Steve: Anna! Lovely to meet you. Chris was best friends with my sister at school. Anna, do I detect a slight accent? Where are you from?

Anna: I'm originally from New Zealand, but I guess with all the travelling around I've done I've kind of lost much of the accent.

Steve: New Zealand, eh? Fantastic! I've always wanted to go there. Which part of the country are you from?

Anna: I'm from North Island. I was brought up in a really small village, hence the wanderlust! All my friends at school were determined to get out there and see the wider world.

Steve: Are you working here?

Anna: Yes. I teach languages and drama so I managed to get a job here quite quickly.

Steve: It's a great advantage to speak a few languages, isn't it? I have found it really easy to settle in Spain and I think that's mainly because I'm fluent in Spanish. How do you find Edinburgh in comparison to home?

Anna: I love Edinburgh! It's so lively and cosmopolitan. There is so much culture and history here. I had a ball in the summer at the Edinburgh festival; it's amazing to see so much talent converging in one city. Loving theatre and dance as I do, it was heaven.

Chris: Yes but there are lots of wonderful things about New Zealand too aren't there? I loved it when I was down there. Everyone seemed so friendly. I mean I think in Edinburgh it takes quite a long time to make new friends as Steve says we can be a bit reserved and standoffish. Also villages like yours Anna seem to foster community spirit.

Anna: For sure. I will probably go back one day and settle down there. I do miss some things about village life. Neighbours do just drop by to say hi without any formal invitation. If you are not at home they just leave a pressie on the doorstep! It's a bit different here or in any big city. Downside of course is everyone knows your business! I also miss the outdoor lifestyle.

Steve: Hmm yes. Thinking about it I reckon Valencia is the perfect home for me. It combines good weather with culture and friendly people.

Chris: So what brings you back then Steve?

Steve: Well there is nowhere like the UK at Christmas now is there?

Q13:

1. at a party
2. sociable
3. sunshine / (Mediterranean) diet
4. a small village
5. see the wider world
6. lively and cosmopolitan
7. community spirit
8. everyone knows your business
9. outdoor
10. reserved

Question formation (page 9)

Q14: The order you wrote the sentences in is not important, as long as you have all 10 sentences.

- Is the weather better in Spain?
- Is your business going well?
- Have you met Anna?
- Do you have a job in Scotland?
- Are people in Edinburgh reserved?
- Do you think Spanish people are friendly?
- Is your dog's name Murphy?
- Do you enjoy outdoor life?
- Is Edinburgh a cultural city?
- Do you like village life?
- Are you home for Christmas?

Biography (page 11)

Q15: This is an example answer to provide with direction on how to proceed with this activity should you need assistance. If you are still unsure, ask your teacher for advice.

Joe is thirty-eight years old and he lives in London. He currently works as a Hotel Manager in a famous large hotel in central London. He really enjoys his job and finds it much more rewarding than his previous career as a teacher. He used to teach primary school children but found this very stressful and not really what he wanted to do forever.

Joe got married a few years ago to Amanda. She's from England but they met in Athens when they were both on holiday. It is for this reason that Athens has remained Joe's favourite city, and he and Amanda like to return there for summer trips whenever it's possible.

Nowadays, Joe has three children, two sons, Josh and Malcolm, and a daughter, Gabrielle. That's not quite the whole family though, because they have a German Shepherd dog named Murphy as well, and Joe thinks of Murphy almost like another one of the kids!

In his free time, Joe has a keen interest in food, he loves cooking at home for the family and also loves eating out. He likes nothing better than gnocchi with pesto. It's a simple dish, but it's his favourite!

Where do you live? (page 12)

Q16: b) False

Q17: a) True

Q18: a) True

Q19: a) True

Q20: Kelp, fruit and vegetables

Q21: Reading the newspaper

Q22: a) Hermit

Q23: Capitulation

Q24: Isolation

Q25: Rat race

Listening activity (page 14)

Listening transcript

I was born in the west of Scotland and I still live there now. I am a commercial pilot and I absolutely love my job. I see no negative aspects to what I do. I am paid to fly planes and to travel, both of which I thoroughly enjoy. The positive aspects are endless. As I said, I fly planes, travel, meet lots of people and have a varied and interesting schedule. Every time I go to work, I work with a wide range of different people in diverse places and usually for a different number of days. For someone gregarious and flexible this is a joy. I have a part-time contract so I only work for three weeks before I have six weeks at home. I am married and my husband also works. He is a freelance editor and works from home. This makes looking after our two children very easy, because I never have to feel guilty or worried when I am in a far flung destination. I know the kids are safe with their dad. My hobbies and interests are all based outdoors. I am fanatical about sport. I go running and cycling, play tennis and go hill walking. My son is ten now and starting to show signs of following in his mother's footsteps. My daughter is just like her dad. She is into painting, reading and music. We all love travelling and walking though, so at least we can all get together on these pastimes!

Q26: West of Scotland

Q27: A commercial pilot

Q28: She loves/likes it.

Q29: None

Q30: Part-time contract/hours

Q31: Married

Q32: Two children

Q33: Cycling, tennis, walking, travelling

Reading comprehension: Language learning (page 16)

Q34: a) A magazine/newspaper article

Q35: 1 and 2

Q36: b) False

Q37: a) True

Q38: a) True

Q39: b) False

Q40: a) True

Q41: b) False

Q42: peers

Q43: applicant's profile

Q44: communicative approaches

Listening comprehension: Bilingualism (page 18)

Listening transcript

Presenter: The recent census figures suggest that the numbers of bilingual and multilingual households in the UK have increased dramatically. Paradoxically, we see a serious lack of interest in learning languages among British school children. We thought it would be instructive then to talk to people who have a career in language related fields. My first guest is Daisy. Daisy, can you tell us a bit about your career history please?

Daisy: I studied Japanese at university, and when I completed my degree I went to live and work in Japan as an English teacher. After six months in Japan, I came back to the UK where I decided to study towards a formal qualification in Teaching English as a Foreign Language, or TEFL as it's commonly known. When I had completed that course, I taught in the UK for a couple of years and then decided that I wanted to travel again. I did a short, intensive Italian course over a period of only six weeks and then set off to Italy to look for a job. I was extremely lucky because I found a teaching job, in a small town on the East coast of the country really quickly, and before long I was asked to assist in running the department.

Presenter: Was your Italian good enough to manage living and working in Italy?

Daisy: My Italian improved dramatically while living in the country. I made friends through work which helped, and also took classes in Italian. Later, I did a language exchange where I taught English to an Italian girl, and she taught me Italian in return. As a result of my greatly improved language skills, I started being asked to translate and interpret. At first this was on quite an informal basis, but as I became more experienced and started to acquire a reputation, I received formal requests to translate and interpret through our language school. This became a major part of our business.

Presenter: Which do you prefer; translating or interpreting, because they are very different jobs, aren't they?

Daisy: They are very different jobs. I found interpreting very stressful at first. Sometimes I got nervous in meetings as the subject matter might be quite obscure and I had to think about specialist vocabulary which I didn't have much familiarity with. Now my vocabulary is wider and, in any case, I know I could find ways round these problems by using other words. With translation you generally have the luxury of working at your own pace and are not having to come up with answers in the moment, but arguably you have to be more precise because we are talking about written documents rather than spoken language.

Presenter: If I could bring Tamsin in now. Tamsin, you have also taught in Europe haven't you?

Tamsin: Yes, I have. I got involved in teaching in a slightly more circuitous way. I left school with some quite good qualifications, including Spanish, but I didn't want to carry on in education. I wanted to travel, so I went to Spain where I fell in love with the culture and the climate. I got a job as a representative for a tour group. My job was to go to the airport and meet tourists who had just landed in Spain and then help make sure that their holiday went well. If there were any problems, for example with hotels, food, banks or health, I would liaise with the necessary people in Spanish and help resolve issues. It sounds like a nightmare job, but it was great fun. I gained a lot of confidence through this job and enrolled on an Advanced Spanish course in the University of Valencia.

After a few years in Spain, I was asked to teach some young children English. I taught friends' children at first, a small group of around five of them, so it wasn't pressurised. I enjoyed this so much that I decided to teach properly. I studied for a qualification while still in Spain and have now taught professionally for ten years.

Presenter: Do either of you think that learning languages at school is important?

Daisy: I learned French and Spanish at school and I think that this gave me a good grounding when it came to learning other languages later. I think that immersion in the country is really powerful because your motivation to learn is high, but I think that at some point you want formal lessons to fine tune your use of language.

Tamsin: Absolutely. I think that in many situations you can get by without having been formally taught, but it really does help you to advance within the new country if you go to formal classes. Similarly, as a teacher I could get by for a while without a qualification, but my skills grew exponentially after the course.

Presenter: Thank you both for joining us today. Later in the week we will be speaking to the Education Secretary who will be telling us about the plans for development of languages within the curriculum. . .

Q45: False

Q46: True

Q47: False

Q48: False

Q49: True

Q50: False

Q51: True

Q52: Friends / a language course / a language exchange

Q53: Working at your own pace

Q54: Motivation is high

Q55: Formal language classes

Q56: Using languages at work

Topic 2: Lifestyle

Do, play or go (page 22)

Q1:

DO	PLAY	GO
Taekwondo Zumba	Golf	Fishing
	Basketball	Diving
	Hockey	Cycling
	Volleyball	Bowling
	Badminton	Hill walking

Do, play or go: The rules (page 22)

Q2:

We use DO with...	Sports which do not end in the letters '-ing'
We use PLAY with...	Many sports which involve the use of a ball
We use GO with...	Sports which end in the letters '-ing'

Phrasal verbs: Sport (1) (page 23)

Q3:

a) Jones repeatedly fouled players in the other team and argued with the referee all the way through the first half. I'm amazed that he hasn't been **sent off**.

b) Sports physiotherapists think that a lot of injuries are caused by people not **warming up** correctly or for long enough before they start exercising.

c) Kirsty's never believed that sport is just about **taking part** . She always wants to win in everything she does!

d) Alonso tried his best, but with the car seriously underpowered he wasn't able to **catch up** on the McLarens and Ferraris ahead of him.

e) Gail keeps herself in shape by going to the gym three times a week to **work out**.

f) Because he wasn't getting any younger and he had a recurring problem with his knees, Jenas reluctantly **gave up** professional football three years ago.

g) Everyone in the tennis world was shocked when Nadal was **knocked out** of Wimbledon in the early rounds last year.

h) The surprising thing about the winning athlete was that he didn't even **take up** running until he was eleven years old. Before that he played rugby.

i) Chelsea vs. Barcelona in the Champions League final will **kick off** at 7.45pm on Saturday.

j) The great thing about amateur sport is that more or less anyone can get down to their local sports centre and **join in** the activities.

Phrasal verbs: Sport (2) (page 23)

Q4:   1-j, 2-f, 3-e, 4-c, 5-g, 6-b, 7-d, 8-i, 9-a, 10-h

Sports crossword (page 24)

Q5:

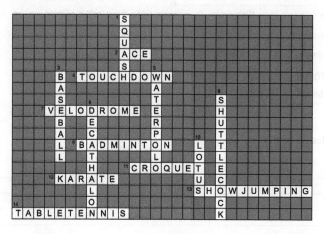

Hobbies and pastimes (page 26)

Q6:

a) Jackie was never the best at painting when she was young, but she always maintained an interest in art. Recently she decided to take a course in **life drawing**.

b) The map of the world took her about two years to complete, and a lot of material! Now, Linda is working on a new **cross-stitch** pattern for her friend's grandchildren. . . pictures of farm animals!

c) It can take a few months to become familiar with using the equipment and trying to keep all the clay off your clothes when you're learning **pottery** .

d) Shannon's grandmother has a fascinating **scrapbook** collection; hundreds of newspaper articles and cuttings of the royal family from the 1940s to 1980s.

e) People often laughed at Peter when he was young because he enjoyed **stamp collecting**, but he's made a successful career out of it, and earned himself a lot of money selling some of the rarest ones available at auction.

f) The difficulty with **coin collecting** is that there are so many variants of the same one, perhaps with a slightly different picture for heads or tails, that it can actually end up being quite expensive to collect all of the different versions!

g) Lucy was really disappointed that a window box was all she could have in her new flat. She had been so used to all that space for **gardening** when she lived with her parents in the detached house.

h) Every month, about fifty like-minded fans of Middle Earth meet together and take on the personas of Elves, Goblins and Werewolves, as they enjoy **role playing games**.

i) In spite of the often overcast weather which means a good waterproof jacket and boots are a necessity, **rambling** remains one of the most popular pastimes in Scotland.

j) There is a misperception that only elderly people are interested in **genealogy** and that it is some kind of dull, isolated pastime for those who love the inside of libraries.

My favourite hobby (page 27)

Model answer

It all began in a nightclub in Barcelona. I had gone there with my girlfriend to a salsa dancing night. I was uncertain about it initially, but then thought, "Why not?". However, when we arrived at the club, she instantly took off dancing and I barely saw her again all evening. I meanwhile, was glued to the bar, wishing I had taken dancing lessons, literally the only person in the club who could not dance!

Fast forward three months, and I was taking regular lessons back home. Learning the basic steps took me about a month. After six months, I was able to perform a multitude of turns and lifts with confidence in Latin dancing club nights all over the country. The great thing about dance is, you don't really need to buy anything to do it, apart from classes, and maybe a pair of dancing shoes.

Soon the club scene wasn't enough for me, so I took qualifications to become a dance teacher. I had to prepare for the examination for about a year, but I achieved my certificate and started teaching salsa only three years after I had first learned the basics! I also performed on stage in front of a crowd of 1500 people. How things have changed since that first night in Barcelona!

With the new dancing club having opened near our university, I suggest you give it a try. Dancing is great fun, great exercise and has a really good social dimension too. You might think you have two left feet, but that's nonsense, everyone can dance... I'm living proof!

Emotive language (1) (page 28)

Q7: 1-i, 2-d, 3-g, 4-c, 5-a, 6-e, 7-j, 8-b, 9-f, 10-h

Emotive language (2) (page 28)

Q8: The answers given here are for guidance only, you may have come up with different examples.

NEUTRAL	EMOTIVE 1	EMOTIVE 2	EMOTIVE 3
Opponent	Rival	Enemy	Nemesis
Defeat	Capitulation	Submission	Surrender
Winner	Champion	Victor	Conqueror
Rise	Soar	Ascend	Rocket
Fall	Slump	Crash	Plummet
Important match	Defining moment	Critical moment	Turning point
Unfortunate behaviour	Disgrace	Shame	Humiliation
Successful	Glittering	Glowing	Brilliant
Difficult	Adverse	Hostile	Antagonistic
Win	Success	Triumph	Victory

Identifying emotive language (page 29)

Q9: The Swedish ice hockey team had a **disastrous collapse** in their **heroic** effort to secure the **ultimate** prize of the Olympic gold medal. The **fall out** of the **humiliation** was **plastered** all over the front covers of **shameless** tabloid newspapers all week.

Q10: Model answer:

The Swedish ice hockey team had a sad defeat in their good effort to win the top prize of the Olympic gold medal. The consequences of the loss were written all over the front covers of tabloid newspapers all week.

Syllables and word stress (page 29)

Q11:

	Syllables and word stress
e.g. Leisure	*Oo*
Opponent	*oOo*
Rival	*Oo*
Capitulation	*oooOo*
Champion	*Ooo*
Eliminate	*oOoo*
Badminton	*Ooo*
Croquet	*Oo*
Shuttlecock	*Ooo*
Zumba	*Oo*
Genealogy	*ooOoo*
Participant	*oOoo*
Velodrome	*Ooo*

Reading comprehension: Olympic parents (page 30)

Q12: c. tabloid

Q13: Informal language, direct speech, long sentences, idiomatic phrases.

Q14: Technology

Q15:

    a) rollercoaster of emotion

    b) take the rough with the smooth

Q16: Emotional highs and lows; financial difficulties.

Q17:

1. Broken legs
2. Leukaemia
3. Lack of height

Q18: They have sold their house.

Listening comprehension: Video games (page 32)

Listening transcript

Terence Connors, professor of child psychology, has spent the last twelve years researching the effects that video games have on the minds of children and young people. Professor Connors is at pains to point out that much of the research that makes its way through to the public at large tends to polarise the findings as having either a uniformly 'good' or 'bad' effect.

"It has been the case that the press gets hold of the research that people such as I have been carrying out, oversimplify it, and then inform the general population that Grand Theft Auto is making their children into criminals, or the Nintendo Wii is creating a positive family environment which had not been seen since the days of Scrabble and Monopoly... Positive hand and eye co-ordination is another lazy journalistic effort at reporting the effects of video games, and that might be true about the latest interactive sports games, but it barely scratches the surfaces of the positive mental effect that playing a strategy game online with like-minded individuals can have."

In his investigative experience, Connors thinks that it is about time people stopped generalising the studies around video games in such simplistically positive and negative ways. He argues that much of what influences young people from the world of video games often falls somewhere in the middle, or straddles the two camps.

Through years of research, Connors has isolated the main ways in which video games can affect players as being dependent upon: time spent on the game, the content of the game and the physical mechanics of the actual gameplay.

"The reasoning behind the identification of these categories was to find out all the different effects on game players. Too often I had read reports which pinned everything on the fact that the child played the game for X number of hours, which led to addiction and antisocial behaviour and so on. Equally, I had also encountered numerous studies which seemed biased from the outset, basically assuming that only the content of the game would determine whether or not it had a negative influence on children."

With regard to the link between gameplay hours and negative effects on children, Connors believes that:

"It is a classic cyclical argument. "Maybe children who have social problems or don't fit in at school, or get poor grades, maybe they use video games as escapism, or to make them feel powerful, like a soldier or a king in this other world"... "It is entirely possible that spending long amounts of time playing video games is a direct effect of feeling unhappy at school or not having any friends, rather than being the cause of that problem."

Studies on game content also provide interesting food for thought. Most research has focussed on the scripts of the games, the dialogue and themes involved within them, and the likelihood of children to copy the behaviour or language of the video game character. Such studies have concluded that there is a definite link between game content and future behaviour, including problem solving and aggression. Again though, Connors believes that looking at this single factor without considering the others is something of a pointless exercise.

"Can we say for sure that a child playing a game which involves murdering other characters or has sexual or drug related content is influenced by that alone? Should we not examine what the child's state of mind before gameplay is, or family and social factors surrounding that child? Equally, if the child only plays once a week for half an hour, will the content of the game have the same effect if they play for ten hours every day?"

Finally, Connors is pioneering new research into the effects of physical game mechanics, meaning the type of controls that are used in different video games.

"We have seen a lot more technology such as the Wii and Xbox Kinect which use full body control, instead of the old fashioned joystick or control pad, and the makers of games for these systems claim that they make video games lively and full of exercise, but there has not yet been any real study into the depth of these claims"

"And once again, the game content and time spent playing are surely also key factors in such claims - if I spend five minutes a day playing a tennis game and moving my arms and legs around, is it likely to be the same as spending five hours a day doing this? And what if I am using my body as a gun or other weapon? Does that have a positive effect on my fitness but damage my mental health?"

These ideas need a lot more research, and Professor Connors is under no illusions that he has a long way to go before he can offer any concrete conclusions.

Q19: psychology

Q20: 12

Q21: False

Q22: True

Q23: True

Q24: 1, 3, 5

Q25: Radio broadcast

Q26: True

Q27: False

Q28: True

Topic 3: Physical environment

Vocabulary: Parks (page 37)

Q1:

1. Pond
2. Grass
3. Trees
4. Flowers
5. Swings
6. Children
7. Ice cream van
8. Putting green
9. Bowling green
10. Dogs

Post listening activity: Answer the questions (page 38)

Listening transcript

Presenter: As regular listeners will know, we are doing a special series on leisure in Scotland for the whole of this month. We aim to find out more about what people are getting up to in their spare time. From the modest amblers and anglers to the more ambitious bikers and bungee jumpers, we hope to inspire you to get out there and get active, whatever your circumstances might be. Well, to start off we sent our reporter June down to her local park to find out what was happening there.

June: Good morning all. I am standing in front of the very fine Victorian gates which open into my local park. It is a beautiful day, a refreshing cool breeze, and although it is only nine o'clock, I can see that there is already quite a lot going on here. So I will approach my first victim, a rather dapper gentleman wearing a tweed jacket and hat and see if he will talk to us. 'Excuse me, I am from Channel Two Radio - could I possibly have a quick chat with you and your friends?'

Elderly man: Yes of course, my dear. How can we help you?

June: Well firstly, can I ask how often you use the park and what you like to do here?

Elderly man: Certainly. I am here every morning, come rain or shine, with my friend Charlie. We circumnavigate the park. Do you think your listeners will understand that? I love my big words. We stroll around the park making sure we go past the pond. The pond is teeming with life - we have swans, ducks, birds and even a heron from time to time. Not bad for a city centre park. There are a couple of people with dogs who join us when they can, but it's not always the same group. We just chew over the issues of the day, look at the trees and flowers and then head home. It is our daily constitutional.

June: How long have you been doing this?

Elderly man: Oh, years now. We used to come with John, he's another chum but sadly he's not really up to it now. It was John who got us into this. You see when you are retired like we are, life can be a little uneventful and you may feel a little bit over the hill. When you start each morning with a walk and a chat though, it really sets you up. I'd say I am probably addicted. We're a bit of an institution here now, lots of people know us and greet us with a wave or a smile each day.

© HERIOT-WATT UNIVERSITY

June: Thank you so much for talking to us. 'Oh hello, who do we have here?' - a busy looking young man with lots of papers and lots of children. 'Hi, sorry to disturb you. Could I ask you some questions for our listeners?'

Younger man: Eh, why not? I suppose. . .

June: Can I ask you how often you come to the park and why?

Younger man: Okay. To be honest, I don't come here that often as it's not really that handy for me, but I really am a fan of the place. I'm a teacher and I bring the kids down here towards the end of each term for a fun day out. We go to the activities area. There are several different games that you can play. My only rule on the day out is that all the kids have to play every game. There is a putting area, a bowling green, tennis courts and croquet. It's all free of charge, even the hire of the equipment. After we have finished, we all have an ice cream from the ice cream van. The kids all enjoy getting out and about, even the really 'cool' kids who might act like a park is too juvenile for them end up letting their hair down and really enjoying it too.

June: That sounds great fun, thanks for your time. I'll let you get on. I must dash; I must get to the other side of the park where I can see something that looks very interesting happening. Let me describe the scene. I can see a group of about ten women - no, not quite all women, there is one man there as well. They are all dressed in fitness gear and they have prams. What they seem to be doing is a kind of synchronised exercise regime while babies sleep or watch presumably. I'll just approach the trainer who looks very energetic and see if she will talk to us. Hello, June from Channel 2 Radio - can you tell us what you are doing?

Instructor: Hello. Yes of course this is called 'buggy training', and as you can see it's a way of exercising with a new baby. You don't really need to buy anything special - it's just the usual exercise clothes, and of course you need a buggy, not to mention a baby!

June: What a fantastic idea! How did you get involved in this?

Instructor: The idea came about when I was struggling to get back into my favourite jeans post-delivery! I realised how difficult it can be as a new mum to get back into fitness and exercise, even with the best will in the world. I said to my friends, "I have to do something". I had always been very active but this situation was a real challenge. Anyway, I went online and discovered this amazing website about exercising while you take the baby out, and that's how it all started for me. First new mum, then fitness trainee and now part-time trainer! I love it! Any new mum who enjoys exercise and meeting people should definitely try it.

June: What a story! Thank you very much for talking to us this morning. Enjoy the class... and thanks to all who have chatted with us this morning. It seems that you really have no excuse whether you are retired, busy with work or a new baby or even just a bit hard up, there are cheap and cheerful ways to get out, get active, and at the same time meet up with others. Back to the studio. . .

Q2: Putting, tennis, croquet and bowling green

Q3: Walks, chats/brings school groups to do activities/ trains new mums

Post-listening activity: Match words and phrases to the correct speaker (page 38)

Listening transcript

Presenter: As regular listeners will know, we are doing a special series on leisure in Scotland for the whole of this month. We aim to find out more about what people are getting up to in their spare time. From the modest amblers and anglers to the more ambitious bikers and bungee jumpers, we hope to inspire you to get out there and get active, whatever your circumstances might be. Well, to start off we sent our reporter June down to her local park to find out what was happening there.

June: Good morning all. I am standing in front of the very fine Victorian gates which open into my local park. It is a beautiful day, a refreshing cool breeze, and although it is only nine o'clock, I can see that there is already quite a lot going on here. So I will approach my first victim, a rather dapper gentleman wearing a tweed jacket and hat and see if he will talk to us. 'Excuse me, I am from Channel Two Radio - could I possibly have a quick chat with you and your friends?'

Elderly man: Yes of course, my dear. How can we help you?

June: Well firstly, can I ask how often you use the park and what you like to do here?

Elderly man: Certainly. I am here every morning, come rain or shine, with my friend Charlie. We circumnavigate the park. Do you think your listeners will understand that? I love my big words. We stroll around the park making sure we go past the pond. The pond is teeming with life - we have swans, ducks, birds and even a heron from time to time. Not bad for a city centre park. There are a couple of people with dogs who join us when they can, but it's not always the same group. We just chew over the issues of the day, look at the trees and flowers and then head home. It is our daily constitutional.

June: How long have you been doing this?

Elderly man: Oh, years now. We used to come with John, he's another chum but sadly he's not really up to it now. It was John who got us into this. You see when you are retired like we are, life can be a little uneventful and you may feel a little bit over the hill. When you start each morning with a walk and a chat though, it really sets you up. I'd say I am probably addicted. We're a bit of an institution here now, lots of people know us and greet us with a wave or a smile each day.

June: Thank you so much for talking to us. 'Oh hello, who do we have here?' - a busy looking young man with lots of papers and lots of children. 'Hi, sorry to disturb you. Could I ask you some questions for our listeners?'

Younger man: Eh, why not? I suppose...

June: Can I ask you how often you come to the park and why?

Younger man: Okay. To be honest, I don't come here that often as it's not really that handy for me, but I really am a fan of the place. I'm a teacher and I bring the kids down here towards the end of each term for a fun day out. We go to the activities area. There are several different games that you can play. My only rule on the day out is that all the kids have to play every game. There is a putting area, a bowling green, tennis courts and croquet. It's all free of charge, even the hire of the equipment. After we have finished, we all have an ice cream from the ice cream van. The kids all enjoy getting out and about, even the really 'cool' kids who might act like a park is too juvenile for them end up letting their hair down and really enjoying it too.

June: That sounds great fun, thanks for your time. I'll let you get on. I must dash; I must get to the other side of the park where I can see something that looks very interesting happening. Let me describe the scene. I can see a group of about ten women - no, not quite all women, there is one man there as well. They are all dressed in fitness gear and they have prams. What they seem to be doing is a kind of synchronised exercise regime while babies sleep or watch presumably. I'll just approach the trainer who looks very energetic and see if she will talk to us. Hello, June from Channel 2 Radio - can you tell us what you are doing?

Instructor: Hello. Yes of course this is called 'buggy training', and as you can see it's a way of exercising with a new baby. You don't really need to buy anything special - it's just the usual exercise clothes, and of course you need a buggy, not to mention a baby!

June: What a fantastic idea! How did you get involved in this?

Instructor: The idea came about when I was struggling to get back into my favourite jeans post-delivery! I realised how difficult it can be as a new mum to get back into fitness and exercise, even with the best will in the world. I said to my friends, "I have to do something". I had always been very active but this situation was a real challenge. Anyway, I went online and discovered this amazing website about exercising while you take the baby out, and that's how it all started for me. First new mum, then fitness trainee and now part-time trainer! I love it! Any new mum who enjoys exercise and meeting people should definitely try it.

June: What a story! Thank you very much for talking to us this morning. Enjoy the class... and thanks to all who have chatted with us this morning. It seems that you really have no excuse whether you are retired, busy with work or a new baby or even just a bit hard up, there are cheap and cheerful ways to get out, get active, and at the same time meet up with others. Back to the studio...

Q4:

Speaker 1:	Dapper, tweed jacket, hat, retired
Speaker 2:	Young, busy, carrying papers, teacher
Speaker 3:	Fitness gear, energetic, trainer, mum

Q5: (To) get out there

Q6: Have a quick chat

Q7: Teeming (with life)

Q8: Chew over (something)

Q9: Daily constitutional

Q10: Over the hill

Q11: An institution

Q12: Let (your) hair down

Q13: Get a kick out of (something)

Q14: Fitness gear

Post-listening activity: Which speaker? (page 39)

Q15:

a) Speaker 1

b) Speaker 3

c) Speaker 2

d) Speaker 1

e) Speaker 3

f) Speaker 2

g) Speaker 3

h) Speaker 1

i) Speaker 2

Modal auxiliary verbs (page 40)

Q16:

a) I **must** dash

b) You **may** feel a little over the hill

c) I **can** see

d) (they) **should** try it

Q17:

Recommendation/advice	(they) **should** try it
Necessity	I **must** dash
Possibility	You **may** feel a little over the hill
Ability	I **can** see

Positive or negative form (page 41)

Q18:

1. I **must** stop smoking as the doctor has told me it is contributing to my high blood pressure.

2. She does not enjoy walking in the park as she **can't** see the point in it.

3. I think my husband **should** try jogging. He really wants to lose weight.

4. If you pick up a local newspaper you **may** (or **should**) be able to find out about activities available in your area.

5. You **should** take your dog out for a walk if you want to meet people.

6. There are lots of amazing films on this month. We really **should/must** go to the cinema.

7. I **can** understand why he is lonely, after all his wife has only just passed away.

8. I think you **may** be surprised at how many people pass through the park, even on rainy days.

9. She really **shouldn't** spend so much time on her own. I think it's bad for her.

10. I have been told by my family that I **mustn't/shouldn't** overdo it, but I can't resist going to fitness classes.

Modal verbs: Referring to the past (page 43)

Q19:

a) You **could** see the whole of the city from my window.

b) I **had to** lose weight before the summer holidays.

c) I **should have tried** to meet new people and changed my lifestyle a bit.

d) I **might have** enjoyed life more if I had made more effort.

e) She **was able** to get her results yesterday.

f) He **might have been** late because of traffic.

g) He **shouldn't have** smoked but he was addicted.

h) You **shouldn't have** got worked up - it's bad for your blood pressure.

i) They **couldn't** understand the questions.

j) We **needed** to do more exercise.

Listening comprehension: Three mysteries (page 45)

Listening transcript

Speaker1: I left home as usual very early in the morning. I have to catch a bus at around seven thirty if I want to get to work on time. I left food and water out for Sooty and went off to work without a backward glance. I was meeting my friend in town after work for a quick bite to eat but I never worry about the cat because cats are so independent. Anyway when I got home at about ten o'clock he didn't appear as he usually does to say hello. I thought that was a bit odd but anyway just started looking around calling him. I checked all his usual hiding places but he wasn't in any of them. I actually started to panic a bit and thought someone must have broken in or that maybe he'd sneaked out when I left that morning without my noticing. An hour passed and finally I sat down feeling quite despondent. At that moment, I heard a faint little crying sound and yes, you guessed it... it was Sooty. He had climbed up my curtains and had got himself tangled in the cord which opens and closes the blinds... I was terrified in case I hurt him trying to rescue him but I managed. I was so relieved when I got him down. That's why the blind was open! Can you imagine? He could have been strangled!

Speaker2: Sharon and I met as usual for our Spanish conversation class. It's funny because we usually talk non-stop but we don't say much in Spanish! Anyway we often go for dinner afterwards to catch up. I remember we had a bit of trouble parking because it was really busy but we found a space eventually beside a little church near the restaurant. After about two hours we settled the bill and set off. We got outside and walked over to the church where we had parked the car, and kind of looked at each other stupidly. The car was nowhere to be seen. It was quite a surreal experience because we couldn't really understand what was going on. We were really confused. Our brains couldn't rationalise the information. Anyway it turned out the car had been stolen! We were shocked. From beside a church! Isn't that dreadful?!

Speaker3: I fell in love with the house at first sight. I went to see it at least three times and drove past several more. Whenever I passed the property, because it was summer, I would see the lady of the house sitting on a bench reading a book in the evening sun. Well, of course I imagined myself sitting there in future evenings; book in hand or maybe a glass of wine. I couldn't wait. When we moved in that autumn, I was horrified because it seemed that the bench had disappeared. I knew it belonged to the previous owners, but it had just seemed so much a part of the house and of my dream. To make matters worse the neighbours had a similar bench which made me really envious and even a little suspicious if I'm honest. To fast forward, about a year after I had moved in, as I was coming home one evening and approaching the house I started to feel a bit strange. Something seemed to be different. What was it? Ah! There was a bench sitting in the same spot. Lots of ideas ran through my head; the previous owners wanted me to have it, someone else had borrowed it and had now decided to bring it back. As it turned out, my husband had got me it as a surprise and was hiding behind the curtains in our house watching my face as I discovered it. I was really touched. That's one of the nicest things he's ever done for me.

Q20: panicky/terrified/relieved

Q21: confused/shocked

Q22: horrified/envious/suspicious/strange/touched

Features of connected speech: Elision (page 46)

Listening transcript

1. He **must**'ve escaped
2. He **can't** have escaped
3. He **must** be **hiding**
4. We **can't** have parked here
5. It **may** have been towed away
6. It **must**'ve been stolen
7. It **may** have been the previous owners
8. It **can't** have just appeared
9. It **must**'ve been a friend who put it there

Q23:
1. He **must**'ve escaped
2. He **can't** have escaped
3. He **must** be **hiding**
4. We **can't** have parked here
5. It **may** have been towed away
6. It **must**'ve been stolen

7. It **may** have been the previous owners
8. It **can't** have just appeared
9. It **must've** been a friend who put it there

Reading comprehension: Letters of complaint (page 47)

Q24: Litter

Q25:

1. Unsightly
2. A hazard
3. Gives a bad impression to visitors

Q26: Local government /a councillor

Q27:

1. A campaign
2. Stricter penalties

Q28:

1. Introduction
2. Description of the problem and why it is a hazard
3. Discussion of why litter creates a bad impression
4. Possible solutions
5. Conclusion

Formal language (page 48)

Q29:

Informal/Neutral	Formal
1. Building up	Amassing
2. Fixed/sorted	Rectified
3. Rubbish	Debris
4. Ugly	Unsightly
5. Sure	Convinced
6. Go/leave	Depart
7. Idea	Impression
8. Vital	Imperative
9. Start	Initiate
10. Disobey	Contravene
11. Crime	Misdemeanour
12. Immediately	Forthwith

Note taking in study situations (page 50)

Q30:
There are many reasons why it is really important to learn how to take notes effectively, regardless of the 1. **subject** which we are studying. In the first place taking notes helps us to 2. **focus** more effectively on the context. This prevents us from allowing our minds to wander in different directions; thinking about our plans for later or what we are going to have for lunch.

It has been found that the 3. **process** of doing more than one thing at a time such as listening or reading as well as taking notes, is more stimulating and, as a result, more conducive to 4. **learning**. When we take notes we are processing information as we 5. **receive** it, organising ideas in our heads as we do so. Therefore the process of note taking is 6. **active** rather than 7. **passive** which we also know is a more effective approach to learning. Finally, the notes which we take can be revisited at a later date and can be the basis of 8. **revision** for exams or assignments later which can take a lot of pressure off!

There are a number of different ways in which our notes may be organised in order to support our study. We should 9. **distinguish** between fact and opinion in our minds and summarise what we read or hear accordingly. Summaries are more useful than noting down the words of the reader or 10. **speaker** exactly since this process engages our mind. Different people have different 11. **approaches** to taking notes such as drawing maps, pictures or tables or using coloured pens. It is important to find a method that you are 12. **comfortable** with and that works for you and then stick to this.

When you have taken notes it is important not to put them away and forget about them. Revisit your notes as soon as 13. **possible** after you have written them. At this stage you should also 14. **rewrite** the notes if possible and then organise them so that you can easily find them again. Don't forget to review your notes as often as possible to keep the ideas fresh in your mind. Good luck!!

Reading comprehension: The National Trust (page 51)

Q31: c. In a leaflet promoting the park

Q32: False

Q33: True

Q34: The Maxwell family

Q35: enabled

Q36: established

Q37: it is fitting

Listening comprehension: Recycling (page 53)

Listening transcript

Simon: Hi, Magnus. I haven't seen much of you recently. How are things?

Magnus: Good, thanks. . . but this torrential rain over the last couple of months has kept me indoors. That's probably why you haven't seen me around. How are you doing yourself, Simon?

Simon: Not bad, thanks. What are you up to with that bin you are carrying? Is it for compost?

Magnus: Yes it is. Well spotted. I got it from the local council. . . it seems they are keen to encourage environmentally friendly projects, so they just handed it over.

Simon: Oh yeah? So how do you make compost?

Magnus: It really depends on whether you reckon you have enough waste to fill it up. At the moment I don't, so I am just making a layer of about 30 cm of garden waste and rubbish from the kitchen bin. I'll keep adding to it, as and when I can, until it's full, but it could take up to a year to compost this way. It's known as the 'cold heap route'.

Simon: Does it matter what you put in there?

Magnus: You should use a mixture of green stuff and brown stuff. Green stuff is material such as grass cuttings, weeds, raw vegetable peelings, tea bags and coffee granules. The brown stuff is slow to rot and could be cardboard cereal packets and egg boxes, waste mail and such like.

Simon: What about magazines? I've got stacks of these I'd like to get rid of.

Magnus: Newspapers and magazines are better sent to recycling depots. You should also avoid meat, fish or cooked food as these attract vermin. Anyway if you mix green and brown it's more efficient and if you do the hot heap route , which means fill the bin up totally and keep turning and moving the rubbish inside, then it can be really fast to make good compost.

Simon: Do you use it as fertiliser?

Magnus: Well, compost feeds the soil while fertiliser feeds the plants so it is different. Compost makes a really rich soil for growing. We just thought it's a cheap way to nourish the soil, cut down on landfill waste and at the same time it's a new hobby that gets me out from under Victoria's feet.

Simon: Good thinking. Perhaps it's time I got a compost bin for Sarah!

Q38: They are neighbours.

Q39: The local council.

Q40: Cold and hot heap routes.

Q41: Cold

Q42: He does not have enough waste at the moment.

Q43: Brown and Green.

Q44: Brown

Q45: It attracts vermin.

Q46: Fertiliser feeds plants (while) compost feeds soil.

Q47: To nourish soil, cut down on waste and keep out of Victoria's way.

Q48: The speakers' wives/partners.

Topic 4: Goods and services

Reading activity: Shopping (page 56)

Q1: in steady decline

Q2: expand and refine

Q3: charity shops

Q4: a multitude of shoppers

Q5: chance encounter

Q6: in line with

Q7: surpass

Q8: addressed

Q9: c) the experience is isolating.

Q10: b) She opts for a method that suits her purpose.

Pre-listening: Vocabulary (page 59)

Q11: 1-g, 2-j, 3-i, 4-b, 5-d, 6-c, 7-e, 8-f, 9-h, 10-a

Listening comprehension: Food shopping (page 59)

Listening transcript

Kim: That looks really healthy, Mandy! You always seem to find something really nice for lunch. I, on the other hand, have the usual canteen sandwich; not very tasty and probably not that nutritious either. What kind of bread is that? It looks really good.

Mandy: This is pumpkin seed and olive. Try it! I got it in that specialist bakery in Alison Street.

Kim: It's really lovely . . . you can tell it's good for you. I've never heard you talk about things you've got from the supermarket, Mandy. Don't you use them?

Mandy: Well, I have to use them sometimes but I try to go to the small independent shops whenever I can. If I need the basics I go to a supermarket, you know, cleaning materials, cereal and so on. For other things, I do try to support the local businesses. There are some amazing little shops around, doing some fantastic foods and I am a bit of a foodie to say the least!

Kim: Not to mention politically correct! If I didn't have a Tesco round the corner I would have to move house! I am totally dependent on it. I know it's not great for small businesses though.

Mandy: I wouldn't say the big stores are all bad, Kim. They do seem to try and meet demand. At the moment, most are stocking little packets of seeds which are good for us and wholewheat breads, which are trendy. My local supermarket has a whole aisle devoted to international foods as well, because we live in quite a multicultural area.

Kim: I suppose I eat to live really. It suits my lifestyle to grab something ready-made because I am always out, as you know. I suppose I should perhaps be more health-conscious, but there is only me to consider and I don't want to spend hours preparing food from scratch. Whenever I buy ingredients for a home-cooked meal I find the food just goes off because I am too busy to cook anything.

Mandy: I'm just the opposite. I like to buy a lot of fresh ingredients and then I know I will definitely cook something healthy. It breaks my heart to see lovely fresh food wasted.

Kim: I expect it's also cheaper to cook homemade meals for a family? Microwave dishes and takeaways don't come cheap, do they?

Mandy: No, they don't! That's certainly true. We really try to get as much fresh food into the kids as possible. Oh Kim, I have just thought of something that might suit you. There's a fantastic new place which has just opened, and it's selling homemade food to take away. Actually, it's not that far from your flat. If you go there on your way home I am sure you'll find something delicious for dinner.

Kim: That sounds great! If I had known about it, I would have gone last week when I had my mother staying with me. I could have passed the food off as my own! What's it called?

Mandy: It's called 'Homemade' and it's on Forth Street. Not the most imaginative name, really, <laughs> but you won't forget it, will you?

Kim: No, I won't. Only two more hours' slog here, then I can go and investigate!

Q12: totally dependent on

Q13: devoted to international food

Q14: more health-conscious

Q15: fresh food wasted

Q16: a) Kim

Q17: a) Kim

Q18: b) Mandy

Q19: a) Kim

Q20: b) Mandy

Q21: a) Kim

Q22: b) Affectionate and tolerant

Pre-listening activity: Speaking: Health related employment (page 61)

Q23:

a) To try something before making a firm commitment.

b) A feeling of friendship or trust among people who work /spend time together.

c) To work and socialise with equal enthusiasm.

d) Said when something has happened later than might be expected.

e) Meaning that things are not problem free.

f) My work brings me a lot of satisfaction/gives me a sense of fulfilment and achievement.

g) In my opinion.

Listening comprehension: Health care professionals (page 61)

Listening transcript

Alison:

I am an auxiliary nurse and I work for the National Health Service or NHS. I haven't done this job for very long. I worked in financial services for seven years and then decided that I wanted to do something more directly involved in helping people. I realised that I am naturally quite a caring type of person. I started as an auxiliary nurse a few months ago and thought I'd see how I got on. The idea was to test the water and later perhaps enrol on a graduate nursing course. As it turns out, I am enjoying the job very much and, if I get a place, I will definitely go on and do the nursing course. What don't I like about the job? If you are an auxiliary nurse you have to work shifts. Night shift can be tough, as can working with serious illnesses, but in spite of being very hard work and sad at times, it's a job that is a lot of fun. A hospital is a very special place. There is often a strong sense of camaraderie. We work hard and play hard too. The only regret I have is not finding this type of work sooner. If I had known how much I would enjoy it, I would have trained a long time ago... but as my grandmother would say, 'better late than never'.

Campbell:

I am a psychotherapist and I have been doing this job for about seven years. I enjoy my job very much. I love working with people and I find that the job gives me a great deal back. Of course it's not all plain sailing. Sometimes I have to deal with situations which are very complex and very painful for the individuals concerned. More recently I have been working with victims of trauma and I have found this challenging but that is why I chose this path in the first place. I am the sort of person who thrives on challenging work. I don't have any regrets about my choice of career. I did think about becoming a surveyor for a while but if I had become a surveyor I wouldn't have experienced the same sense of satisfaction over the years. My job is very rewarding; the knowledge that you are helping people live happier lives is very fulfilling. It is definitely the right niche for me.

Delia:

I'm a physiotherapist and I have been doing this job for about ten years. I like being a physiotherapist because I am really interested in the body and in movement. I have always been very keen on sport and dance. When I was at school I was in the netball and hockey teams; in fact I still play hockey. I would say that the advantages of my job are that I am not stuck in an office all day. I get to move around and work with lots of very different people. I love the process of restoring function to limbs, by which I mean if someone has lost full power and range of a leg for example following an accident, there is often a lot of work involved in getting that back. A person needs to be strong mentally and physically. They have to be motivated and disciplined and work hard. Part of my job is to get people feeling this way. To my mind there are no real disadvantages. If I could trade places with anyone though I would probably be a sports coach for an international athlete... but we can all dream can't we?

Q24:

a) What do you do?

b) How long have you been doing this job?

c) Do you enjoy your job?

d) What are the positive and negative features of this kind of employment?

e) Do you have any regrets about your choice of career?

Q25:

a) Auxiliary Nurse

b) Few months

c) Yes

d) Negatives: shifts/sad/hard work; Positives: camaraderie /play hard /special place

e) Not finding the job sooner

Q26:

a) Psychotherapist

b) Yes

c) 7 years

d) Negatives: hard / challenging; Positives: job satisfaction / helping people

e) No

Q27:

a) Physiotherapist

b) Yes

c) 10 years

d) Negatives: none; Positives: not stuck in an office / can move around

e) Would be a sports coach if this were possible

Conditional sentences: Focus on meaning (page 62)

Q28: a-2, b-4, c-1, d-3

Conditional sentences: Practice (page 64)

Q29:

a) If I **wasn't** so tired I would help you with your work.

b) I wouldn't have fallen asleep if I **hadn't been / wasn't** so tired.

c) If I **am** tired but can't sleep, I drink hot milk.

d) If you **are** sufficiently tired, you will fall asleep.

e) I wouldn't have had such a terrible nightmare if I **had not / hadn't been** unnerved by that film I watched.

f) Provided I do enough exercise in the day I **am** sleepy in the evening.

g) If I **was** a less agitated person I am sure I would sleep better.

h) Unless he **is** in bed and asleep by eight I can't get him up for school in the morning

i) Should you **be** home late please **be** quiet and don't waken us all up.

j) If I **wasn't / weren't** a doctor I would like to **be** a vet.

Grammar practice (1) (page 65)

Q30:

1a. She was in pain in the past, so she went to the hospital.

1b. She may still be in pain (she went to the hospital in the past).

2a. In the future if her head is still sore, her mother will give her painkillers .

2b. The headaches did not continue, so her mother did not give her painkillers.

3a. Lauren's mother was worried and took her to hospital.

3b. Lauren's mother took her to the hospital earlier, but she is still worried now.

Grammar practice (2) (page 66)

Q31:

1. e) If you are unable to sleep, you might benefit from meditation.
2. j) If you wanted to sleep well, you shouldn't have used your computer late at night.
3. a) If you hadn't been so stressed, you wouldn't have had a problem dropping off.
4. i) Should the doctor offer you sleeping tablets, you will be tempted to take them.
5. b) If you had a problem with headaches, you could have been suffering migraine.
6. h) If your backache continues, you will have to stop working.
7. d) Unless the pain subsides, you would be advised to continue taking painkillers.
8. g) If you hadn't gone to the doctor, you wouldn't have been referred to a specialist.
9. c) If I thought I had a serious medical problem, I would go to the doctor.
10. f) If I had a healthier lifestyle, I would probably have fewer problems.

Writing: An informal email (page 66)

Model answer

Hi Claire

I am really glad that you are going to make it over to Scotland. I am only sorry that I will not be around to entertain you but I will look forward to seeing you in Spain next month.

Let me give you a few practical tips for your visit. There is a large supermarket situated about five minutes walk from the flat. This is the best place to find basic supplies. There are also smaller shops at the end of the road which you will see as you walk from the train station to the flat. You can buy nice bread, coffee and cakes in these if you feel like something special. There are bars and restaurants within walking distance. I have put a list of my favourites along with a map on the notice board in the kitchen so you can explore these if you feel like it. There are also lots of nice little shops selling gifts and clothes on Anderson Road which is not far away. There is a sports centre with a large pool in the area and again I have left details on the board.

Hopefully you will not have any problems while you are visiting but just in case you can find a list of important numbers in a black notebook beside the telephone. This includes numbers of doctors and emergency services. My internet password is also in this book. Barbara, who lives next door, is really kind. You can ask her for help if necessary.

Make yourself at home.

Love

Jenny

Reading comprehension: Headaches (page 67)

Q32: b. Education

Q33: Cluster, migraine

Q34: Cluster

Q35: Migraine

Q36: False

Q37: True

Q38: True

Q39: False

Q40: Incapacitating

Q41: Responsive

Listening Comprehension: Food nowadays (page 69)

Listening transcript

Laura: Paul, do you remember when we were young? Were our parents as obsessed with food as people are now? I mean food's a hobby, its entertainment, we watch advertisements for food and cooking programmes on TV and then we go out for meals. "What did you do at the weekend?" we say... "Went out for lunch, had a few drinks, grabbed a takeaway", is the reply. No wonder we have such a massive problem with obesity (pardon the pun). As for kids today, do you know I heard on the radio that one in five kids in the UK are obese? I think this is an issue of bad diet and lack of exercise. The NHS simply cannot continue to support all the diet related health problems like diabetes and heart disease.

Paul: Laura, you know that our parents liked to eat just as much as anyone else, but I have been reading a bit about this subject and I don't think we have the full picture yet. We all blame the individual for a lack of discipline and for greed, but we may have been missing out on something very important, and that is the type of food that we are eating. It seems that the content of our food may be at the heart of what is wrong with us.

Laura: It's not the quality of our food that is the problem, it's the quantity. We are eating too much... that's what is wrong! And then we are sitting around too much as well, watching TV and playing computer games.

Paul: Well according to the report I read, the opposite is the case. It says that in fact kids are not less physically active than they were in the past. It seems that what we are eating is making us fat because we eat more processed food and because of the way processed food works on our metabolism. It seems that low fat food is a bit of a con. The fat has been replaced with sugar, and sugar is addictive.

Laura: No kidding... you don't mean to say that low fat yoghurts are going to make me fatter than regular yogurts?

Paul: This could be the case. I think that the scientists are still trying to work it all out, but it seems that eating sugar makes us crave more sugar. They did an experiment on rats and found that they put on lots of weight when they were fed processed foods. It has something to do with a hormone that doesn't work if bombarded with sugar and therefore we never realise if we are full.

Laura: I can't believe it! Do you have a copy of this article? I'd really like to read it. This could change everything... I mean, why isn't anyone doing anything about this?

Paul: Well, it could be because the research is quite new or it could be because the food industry is so powerful that no-one can do anything. Whatever the reason, I think we can let ourselves off the hook just a little. I think we are obsessed with food because eating is enjoyable, and maybe the so-called gluttons among us are poor addicts who have become victims of the secret added ingredients!

Q42: c. siblings (brother and sister)

Q43: b, e and f

Q44:

Laura thinks that we have a 1. **massive** problem with obesity. She thinks that the nation is 2. **obsessed** with food, that children eat too much and don't 3. **exercise** Paul doesn't think we have 4. **enough information/the full picture** .

He thinks that 5. **sugar** is the biggest problem we face. He suggests two possible reasons for lack of information on this topic which are 6. the **powerful food industry** and **the newness of research** .

Topic 5: Entertainment and leisure

Pre-reading activity: Vocabulary quiz: Art (page 72)

Q1:

1. Sculpture
2. Palette
3. Impressionism
4. Pablo
5. Michelangelo
6. Andy Warhol
7. Edvard Munch
8. Frida Kahlo
9. Wassily Kandinsky
10. Vincent Van Gogh

Reading activity: Text and questions: Art (page 72)

Q2:

1. excludes	includes
2. rejected	accepted
3. flexible	rigid
4. seldom	frequently
5. vivid	muted
6. lifeless	dynamic
7. dull	exciting
8. failing	flourishing
9. conventional	independent
10. foreground	background

Q3: b) False

Q4: a) True

Q5: a) True

Q6: a) True

Q7: In France, J.D. Fergusson enjoyed the company of post-impressionist painters. They painted objects in unexpected ways using bold **a) colour** and vivid **b) brushstrokes**. Their paintings give a sense of **c) movement** and **d) rhythm** . Fergusson and Morris who met in 1913 had much in common. They were both **e) independent** thinkers, had a connection with France and a fascination with the **f) physical** form.

Q8: central

Q9: muse

Q10: collaborated

Q11: idyllic

Pronunciation: Strong and weak forms (page 75)

Listening Transcript

a) I'm a fan of the theatre (weak form of)

b) She was a big star in Hollywood (weak form was)

c) I know you don't think theatre is worthwhile but this was (strong form was)

d) Has he done much acting? (weak form has) Yes he has. (strong form has)

e) You can't have a new guitar Tom (weak form can't)

f) He can't sing! (weak form) Yes he can! (strong form)

g) At last! (strong form at) I thought that film was never going end. (weak form was)

Q12: The number of words and form of each sentence is given here.

a) 6; weak form **of**
b) 7; weak form **was**
c) 11; strong form **was**
d) 5 / 3; weak form **has** / strong form **has**
e) 6; weak form **can't**
f) 3 / 3; weak form / strong form
g) 2 / 9; strong form **at** / weak form **was**

Sources of 'Authentic English' (page 76)

Q13: Compare your list with these ideas,

- Listening to your teacher (who may be a native or near native speaker of English)
- Listening to the radio
- Using a computer to read or listen to news and broadcasts
- Watching films in English (with or without subtitles)
- Reading books
- Speaking to people whose first language is English e.g. through computer technology
- Reading English language newspapers
- Writing/emailing someone who is an English speaker
- Social Networking sites such as Facebook
- Travelling to an English language speaking country

Pre-listening activity: Vocabulary: Films (page 77)

Q14:

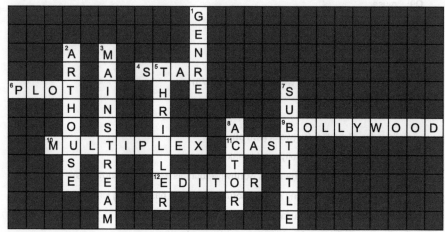

Listening activities: Note taking: Films (page 78)

Listening transcript

Greg: Hi Nicola. How are you? What have you been up to today?

Nicola: Oh, I stayed at home and watched a movie. A really old one from the fifties called 'All about Eve'. It was great; perfect for a cold winter day.

Greg: I've never heard of that. What's it about?

Nicola: It was directed by Joseph Mankiewicz. It was about a great actress called Margo Channing, played by Bette Davis who allows a fan, the Eve of the title played by Anne Baxter, to get a bit too involved in her life. Although Margo is huge star, she is a bit insecure about her age as she has just turned forty and knows this is not good for her acting career. She is also insecure about her lover, a director called Bill Simpson who is much younger than she is. She is never truly convinced he loves her, although he really does. Eve charms her way into their lives and nearly manages to destroy all that Margo has. The dialogue is brilliant; Bette Davis has some fantastic lines. She is really sharp at times. In the end, they all see through Eve, but this takes a long time and Eve manages to become a successful actress herself simply by manipulating everyone around her.

Greg: Wow! That doesn't sound like an old-fashioned script really, does it?!

Nicola: No, like most of the true classics of cinema I still think this film has a lot to offer audiences today. The themes are still relevant: the fear of aging, age gaps in relationships, success, power, insecurity, jealousy... you name it and it's in this movie!

Greg: Was it a success at the time it was released?

Nicola: Oh, yes! I've been reading up on it and it seems that it was nominated for fourteen Academy Awards. No other film matched that until Titanic, four decades later!

Greg: I'm intrigued! I think I have to see this film. Can I borrow the DVD from you?

Q15:

Plot	Eve wants Margo's life and all that is in it. She manipulates all around her and almost destroys Margo's life in her attempt to get to the top.
Characters	Margo Channing, Eve, Bill Simpson
Director	Joseph Mankiewicz
Cast	Bette Davis, Ann Baxter
Star	Bette Davis
Genre	Drama
Why the film was good/bad	Great actors, great scripts, issues are contemporary although the film is quite old

Q16: All about Eve is a film starring Betty **1. Davis** as Margo Channing. Eve played by Ann Baxter wants Margot's life and all that is in it. She **2. manipulates** all around her and almost **3. destroys** Margot's life in her attempt to get to the top. Margot is **4. insecure** about her age and her relationship, she realises that parts are often given to **5. younger** actresses. The film has great actors and scripts and although the film is quite old, many of the issues explored are **6. contemporary**.

Writing: Informal email (page 78)

Model answer

Hi Samia

Thanks for your email. It was great to hear from you. I am so glad that you are well

I am really sorry but I can't go to the cinema this weekend as I have my sister and her boyfriend coming to stay with me. I haven't seen them for about six months. They have no car so I will be busy driving them around all weekend!

Do you use 'Film Fanatics', the internet movie service? I saw a fantastic old film on that last week called 'All about Eve'. You should check it out. I think you would enjoy it.

Maybe we can get together later in the month and catch up?

Love

Alicia

(117 words)

Pre-listening activity: Vocabulary: Technology (page 79)

Q17:

1. Network
2. Database
3. Screen
4. Hypertext
5. Search
6. Memory
7. Software
8. Mouse
9. Tablet
10. Processor

Pre-Listening activity: Vocabulary: Collocations: Technology (page 80)

Q18: 1-n, 2-h, 3-l, 4-a, 5-d, 6-j, 7-c, 8-b, 9-m, 10-k, 11-f, 12-i, 13-e, 14-g

Listening activity: Note taking: Technology (page 80)

Listening transcript

Presenter: Good morning. In 1969 the very first internet message was sent between UCLA and the Stanford Research unit. Since those early days of the internet, further technological innovations followed this which completely transformed the way that we do things. In the studio today I have guest Gus Trimble of London College of Media Studies to talk about the closely interwoven worlds of literature, cinema and technology. Welcome Gus, so, just what technological advancements do you see happening in the next 40-50 years?

Gus: Delighted to be here. Well, firstly, I think that if we want to know what the future is going to be like, we should read the work of some of the good science fiction writers. Often what they show in books or films is curiously accurate when we consider the ways things do in fact develop. For example, a film which proved to be enormously prescient about the future is Minority Report, which is based on the work of science fiction writer Philip K. Dick. The film was directed by Stephen Spielberg and is set in the future, in 2054 to be exact. The technology in this film is amazing and although it was only released in 2002, much of what we see in that movie is either with us now or is something I think we will definitely see very soon.

Presenter: Can you give us some examples?

Gus: One example is the 3D hologram computer which Anderton, a futuristic police officer played by Tom Cruise, controls through gestures. A company has already marketed a similar computer in which the software responds to hand movements. It's likely that we will all be using similar technology soon. Also featured in the film were flexible electronic displays replacing newspapers which are continually updated, another technology which we will almost certainly see very soon. One of my favourite scenes in the film is where cameras scan Anderton's eyeballs as he is walking around and then holograms jump out at him, offering uniquely targeted products. Targeted advertising is already here, albeit in a simpler form, but before long we will probably all be experiencing it holographically.

Presenter: It seems Philip K. Dick was a very discerning writer, and when you consider he was writing in the sixties, it's all the more impressive.

Gus: Yes, very much so. Consider the classic movie, Blade Runner, which was based on one of his other novels and released in 1982. At the time it was very high-tech and futuristic, but in fact not that different from present day Japan or Hong Kong really, apart from the flying cars of course! If you remember, Deckard, played by Harrison Ford, is employed to get rid of genetically engineered creatures called replicants. The trouble is it's quite difficult to establish whether they are replicants or not, so Deckard has questions which he asks them to find out if they can experience empathy or not. In fact, Deckard falls in love with a replicant, and we're never quite sure if he is a replicant himself! What is interesting is that the film raises moral dilemmas which we have encountered and which we'll continue to encounter as scientists make further progress in genetic engineering techniques. The movie questions what it means to be human. Deckard discovers that, at the most fundamental level, he and the so-called replicants are not that different. Famously, Deckard highlights this point when talking about a replicant. "All he'd wanted was the same answers the rest of us want. Where do I come from? Where am I going? How long have I got?"

Presenter: So what are the writers and film makers presenting now?

Gus: There must be fierce competition at times among innovators to produce the next great thing. "The Social Network" is an example where Mark Zuckerberg is shown developing the social networking site that became Facebook, and is then sued by twin brothers who say he stole their idea. I think that in the future there will be more examples of creative young people making headline news as they become inspired by direct access to information sources. "We Live in Public" deals with a future where we have a complete lack of privacy, where all that we do is in the public domain. This is a salutary tale which explores the potentially destructive power of the internet and of the erosion of our mental health when we make what should be our private lives public. Many believe this is going to happen to us very soon if it hasn't already.

Presenter: Be warned! Gus, thank you so much for coming in today and talking to us.

Q19: Either: A radio talk show or radio broadcast

Q20: Minority Report, Blade Runner, The Social Network, We Live in Public (the work of Philip K. Dick)

Post-listening activity: Responding to questions: Technology (page 81)

Listening transcript

Presenter: Good morning. In 1969 the very first internet message was sent between UCLA and the Stanford Research unit. Since those early days of the internet, further technological innovations followed this which completely transformed the way that we do things. In the studio today I have guest Gus Trimble of London College of Media Studies to talk about the closely interwoven worlds of literature, cinema and technology. Welcome Gus, so, just what technological advancements do you see happening in the next 40-50 years?

Gus: Delighted to be here. Well, firstly, I think that if we want to know what the future is going to be like, we should read the work of some of the good science fiction writers. Often what they show in books or films is curiously accurate when we consider the ways things do in fact develop. For example, a film which proved to be enormously prescient about the future is Minority Report, which is based on the work of science fiction writer Philip K. Dick. The film was directed by Stephen Spielberg and is set in the future, in 2054 to be exact. The technology in this film is amazing and although it was only released in 2002, much of what we see in that movie is either with us now or is something I think we will definitely see very soon.

Presenter: Can you give us some examples?

Gus: One example is the 3D hologram computer which Anderton, a futuristic police officer played by Tom Cruise, controls through gestures. A company has already marketed a similar computer in which the software responds to hand movements. It's likely that we will all be using similar technology soon. Also featured in the film were flexible electronic displays replacing newspapers which are continually updated, another technology which we will almost certainly see very soon. One of my favourite scenes in the film is where cameras scan Anderton's eyeballs as he is walking around and then holograms jump out at him, offering uniquely targeted products. Targeted advertising is already here, albeit in a simpler form, but before long we will probably all be experiencing it holographically.

Presenter: It seems Philip K. Dick was a very discerning writer, and when you consider he was writing in the sixties, it's all the more impressive.

Gus: Yes, very much so. Consider the classic movie, Blade Runner, which was based on one of his other novels and released in 1982. At the time it was very high-tech and futuristic, but in fact not that different from present day Japan or Hong Kong really, apart from the flying cars of course! If you remember, Deckard, played by Harrison Ford, is employed to get rid of genetically engineered creatures called replicants. The trouble is it's quite difficult to establish whether they are replicants or not, so Deckard has questions which he asks them to find out if they can experience empathy or not. In fact, Deckard falls in love with a replicant, and we're never quite sure if he is a replicant himself! What is interesting is that the film raises moral dilemmas which we have encountered and which we'll continue to encounter as scientists make further progress in genetic engineering techniques. The movie questions what it means to be human. Deckard discovers that, at the most fundamental level, he and the so-called replicants are not that different. Famously, Deckard highlights this point when talking about a replicant. "All he'd wanted was the same answers the rest of us want. Where do I come from? Where am I going? How long have I got?"

Presenter: So what are the writers and film makers presenting now?

Gus: There must be fierce competition at times among innovators to produce the next great thing. "The Social Network" is an example where Mark Zuckerberg is shown developing the social networking site that became Facebook, and is then sued by twin brothers who say he stole their idea. I think that in the future there will be more examples of creative young people making headline news as they become inspired by direct access to information sources. "We Live in Public" deals with a future where we have a complete lack of privacy, where all that we do is in the public domain. This is a salutary tale which explores the potentially destructive power of the internet and of the erosion of our mental health when we make what should be our private lives public. Many believe this is going to happen to us very soon if it hasn't already.

Presenter: Be warned! Gus, thank you so much for coming in today and talking to us.

Q21: through gestures

Q22: flexible electronic displays

Q23: targeted

Q24: futuristic

Q25: genetically engineered

Q26: not (that) different

Q27: a) True

Q28: b) False

Q29: a) True

Pronunciation: The phonemic script (page 82)

1.	/ teknə'lɒdʒɪkl /	n.	/ əd'vɑːnsmənt /
2.	/ ɪˌlek'trɒnɪk /	h.	/ dɪ'spleɪs /
3.	/ dʒə'netɪk /	l.	/ endʒɪ'nɪərɪŋ /
4.	/ mɒrəl /	a.	/ dɪ'leməs /
5.	/ ˌfʌndə'mentl /	d.	/ levl /
6.	/ fɪəs /	j.	/ kɒmpə'tɪʃn /
Q30: 7.	/ səʊʃl /	c.	/ netwɜːkɪŋ /
8.	/ pʌblɪk /	b.	/ də'meɪn /
9.	/ hedlaɪn /	m.	/ njuːz /
10.	/ də'rekt /	k.	/ ækses /
11.	/ ɪnfə'meɪʃn /	f.	/ sɔːrsɪz /
12.	/ sæljətri /	i.	/ lesn /
13.	/ mentl /	e.	/ helθ /
14.	/ praɪvət /	g.	/ laɪvz /

Pronunciation: Phonemic collocations (page 83)

Q31:

1.	Technological Advancements	h.	/tɛknəˈlɒdʒɪkəl ədˈvɑːnsmənts/
2.	Electronic Display	m.	/ɛlɛkˈtrɒnɪk dɪˈspleɪ/
3.	Genetic Engineering	e.	/dʒəˈnɛtɪk ɛndʒɪˈnɪərɪŋ/
4.	Moral Dilemmas	g.	/ˈmɒrəl dɪˈlɛməs/
5.	Fundamental Level	d.	/fʌndəˈmɛntəl ˈlɛvəl/
6.	Fierce Competition	a.	/fɪərs kɒmpɪˈtɪʃən/
7.	Social Networking	b.	/ˈsəʊʃəl ˈnɛtwɜːkɪŋ/
8.	Public Domain	f.	/ˈpʌblɪk dəʊˈmeɪn/
9.	Headline News	j.	/ˈhɛdlaɪn njuːz/
10.	Direct Access	i.	/daɪˈrɛkt ˈaksɛs/
11.	Information Sources	n.	/ɪnfəˈmeɪʃən sɔːrsɛs/
12.	Salutary Lesson	k.	/ˈsaljʊtəri ˈlɛsən/
13.	Mental Health	l.	/ˈmɛntəl hɛlθ/
14.	Private Lives	c.	/ˈpraɪvət laɪvz/

Pronunciation: Syllables and word stress (page 84)

Q32:

Word	Syllables and word stress
e.g. Computer	*oOo*
Technological	*ooOoo*
Electronic	*ooOo*
Genetic	*oOo*
Moral	*Oo*
Fundamental	*ooOo*
Fierce	*o*
Social	*Oo*
Public	*Oo*
Headline	*Oo*
Direct	*oO*
Information	*ooOo*
Salutary	*Oooo*
Mental	*Oo*
Private	*Oo*

Pre-Reading: Questions (page 84)

Q33: Bill Gates

Q34: Steve Jobs

Reading: Tim Berners-Lee (page 85)

Q35:

  a) Paragraph 5
  b) Paragraph 4
  c) Paragraph 3
  d) Paragraph 6
  e) Paragraph 1
  f) Paragraph 2

Q36: modest

Q37: Vague

Q38: Vulnerable

Q39: streamline

Q40: Pioneering

Q41: b) False

Q42: a) True

Q43: a) True

Q44: b) False

Q45: b) False

Answers from page 87.

Q46: The first phrase is not based on evidence while the second sentence is based on present evidence.

Grammar: Future forms: Meaning (page 88)

Q47: 1-h, 2-a, 3-g, 4-c, 5-f, 6-d, 7-e, 8-b

Grammar: Future Forms: Choosing the correct form (page 90)

Q48:
Good afternoon ladies and gentlemen. I am here today to show you around the university. Firstly I **1. am going to show** you around the academic departments. We **2. are taking** a tour of the library at 10 a.m. You **3. will be able to get** library cards and have a look around. After this we **4. are going to have** a look around a laboratory, a typical lecture theatre and seminar room. All lectures **5. finish** at twelve noon for lunch and the canteen **6. will be** very busy. That is not a problem however as we **7. are eating** in a specially reserved section which I**8. will direct** you to on arrival. We **9. are meeting** with the principal at one thirty and after the principal has spoken to you we **10. are going to take** you to the residential area of campus where you **11. will receive** keys and information on our social programme. We **12. will have finished** the tour by around three thirty and at that stage you **13. will be** free to wander as you wish. Our more established students **14. will be handing** out tickets for various fresher's week activities later on today at the halls of residence and I believe they **15. are giving** away free drinks vouchers so look out for that. On the subject of drinks, you **16. are invited/will be invited** all to our first cocktail party of the season tonight. Cocktail parties **17. Are held/will be held** on the first Friday of every month. Just think by the time **18. you attend / you have attended** the second party you **19. will have been studying** at this university for four whole weeks. Believe me the next three to four years **20. will roll** by at a tremendous speed and before you know it you **21. will have finished** your degree and **22. will be looking** for a job.

Reading comprehension: Technology (page 90)

Q49: b. An article from a newspaper or magazine

Q50:

a) True

b) True

c) True

d) False

e) False

f) False

Q51: paraphernalia

Q52: functionality

Q53: No

Q54: The tone is ironic/use of exclamation mark suggests irony.

Listening comprehension: Keeping fit (page 93)

Listening transcript

Q55:

The presenter suggests that the use of technology in diet and exercise programmes is **1. a gimmick**. Lisa is positive about technology and **2. runs through /gives** a few examples of what is available. The presenter describes **3. the wristband** as a more expensive version of a pedometer. Lisa says that some of the devices available are **4. Fun** while some give **5. valuable information** . Lisa is **6. positive** about the value of technology in assisting exercise and fitness regimes.

Q56:

a) True

b) False

Q57: a. A university lecture

Q58: b. To educate/inform

Topic 6: Planning a trip

Pre-listening activity: Vocabulary: Song: Air travel (page 96)

Q1: Bombay, Peru and Acapulco Bay.

Answers from page 96.

Q2:

1. exotic
2. one man band
3. glide
4. words
5. glide
6. words

Pre-listening activity: Vocabulary: Collocations: Air travel (page 97)

Q3: 1-g, 2-e, 3-a, 4-j, 5-h, 6-i, 7-b, 8-c, 9-f, 10-d

Speaking: Discussion: Air travel (page 97)

Q4:

a) What attracted you to airline work?
b) Can you tell us about the selection process?
c) Did you have any training?
d) Would you say it is a glamorous job? If so, why?
e) Have you ever had any incidents or emergencies in your flying career?

Listening comprehension: Note taking: Air travel (page 98)

Listening transcript

1. Probably the main thing was travel. I had always been attracted to the idea of travel and finding out about different countries and cultures. Being in airports is fun for me; some people don't like it; but I really love the atmosphere of an airport. Working on an aircraft was also something I liked the idea of. Another thing was the fact that it wasn't 9-5... I really liked that idea!

2. The job was advertised in the press and in job centres. That is unusual, but there was an urgent recruitment drive at the time, so I applied. There was a mass interview to start with, and if you got through that then you had a smaller group interview.

3. Training is generally six weeks long. During that time you are trained on all aspects of flying such as accident and emergency procedures. You have to show that you can evacuate an

aircraft using a mock up. Inflating slides and jumping out in the safest way possible is an important part of this, as is crowd control. We also had first aid and customer service and language training.

4. Yes, I would. Of course there are aspects of the job that are not so wonderful and at times it can be very hard work, but eating in restaurants in Singapore, shopping in New York, visiting the most famous landmarks in the world... now I think that's quite glamorous!

5. I had an incident on a flight from Munich to Birmingham. We were over Cologne when we came over the top of a thunderstorm and hit clear air turbulence. We had no warning; it didn't show up on radars. The plane dropped about 2,000 feet and most passengers didn't have seatbelts on. Everyone was screaming. Overhead lockers flew down and contents spilled out, canisters fell out of their stowage as well. I hit the ceiling and cut my head. It was completely surreal. For moments I felt like I was watching a film. Then the training kicked in really quickly. I started shouting at people to sit down and keep their heads down. We were really lucky and didn't need to prepare for a full evacuation. We were driven from Birmingham to our London base later that day as the airline didn't want to risk putting us on a plane again so soon after the incident. The aircraft had a twisted tail and there were some cuts and bruises. I found it very frightening, but I am grateful we were so fortunate; it could've been a lot worse.

Q5: 1, 3 and 6

Q6: job centres

Q7: accident and emergency procedures

Q8: hard work

Q9: Birmingham

Q10: clear air turbulence

Q11: a) She hit her head

Q12: b) There was no warning

Q13: a) watching a film

Q14: a) watching a film

Q15: c) there were no serious injuries.

Q16: b) she was lucky to have survived this experience.

Grammar: Activity: Gerunds: Identifying structure (page 100)

Q17: 1-d, 2-b, 3-f, 4-b, 5-e, 6-e, 7-a, 8-d, 9-c, 10-a

Grammar: Activities: Verb patterns: Gerund or infinitive (page 102)

Q18:

a) enjoy - gerund

b) decide - infinitive

c) expect - infinitive

d) risk - gerund

e) mention - gerund

f) wish - infinitive

g) imagine - gerund

h) want - infinitive

i) consider - gerund

j) promise - infinitive

k) involve - gerund

l) refuse - infinitive

m) fail - infinitive

n) dislike - gerund

Answers from page 102.

Q19:

a) She refuses **to apply** for a position as ground staff at the airport, only a flying job will please her.

b) She really dislikes **eating** the food on planes.

c) His application has been accepted but he has been asked if he will consider **relocating** to London.

d) He enjoys **being** a pilot but he hates **leaving** his family.

e) I have decided **to take** a year out of work and do some travelling.

f) 'I wish **flying** wasn't so boring, I never enjoy being on a plane.'

g) She encouraged me **to apply** for a job in the travel industry because she enjoys it so much.

h) He said he didn't mind **giving** me a lift to the airport because my car had broken down.

i) I would like **to travel** all over the world before I reach fifty.

j) I hate **working** shifts - nine to five is much better for me.

Answers from page 104.

Q20: 1 - a, 2 - d, 3 - e, 4 - b, 5 - c

Answers from page 104.

Q21:

  a) quivering

  b) restricting

  c) zone

  d) claustrophobia

  e) viable

  f) abusive

  g) illusion

  h) pace

  i) unrelated

  j) anticipate

Reading activity: Fear of flying: Transport (page 104)

Q22: a) True

Q23: b) False

Q24: b) False

Q25: b) False

Q26: a) True

Q27: a) True

Q28: a) True

Q29: a) Fact

Q30: b) Opinion

Q31: b) Opinion

Writing: Informal email: Arranging a trip (page 107)

Q32:

  a) An email

  b) Informal

  c) To confirm travel arrangements

  d) A friend

Q33:

Hi Sue

It's great to hear from you. I am so glad that you are coming down at last! You have made the right decision to book a seat on that train. It can get very busy.

Unfortunately I have a small problem with picking you up in Windsor. We have a meeting at work on the day you arrive and I will have to stay later than usual. I won't be able to get to the station in time. Don't worry though, I have an alternative plan. Dave, my brother, is free that afternoon. He is happy to collect you. The two of you can go to the flat and have a coffee until I get home.

What do you think? Is that okay?

See you soon

Joanne x

Grammar and listening: Idiomatic phrases (page 108)

Listening transcript

My daughter Michelle has been trying to get a job with an airline for a while now. Her brother Jacob is very mean to her because when she announces "I'm going to be an international air hostess", he says, "yeah right and pigs might fly". This generally leads to an argument. Temperamentally they are so different that sparks fly all the time no matter what we are talking about, but when he laughs at her airline dreams she really flies off the handle. Anyway, she finally got an interview for a job with a good company - not one of those fly by night outfits you hear about. We were all delighted and really hoped she would do well. First she had a group interview and test and apparently she got off to a flying start because there was quite a bit of Maths and Geography in the test and she loves both of these subjects. She had a small group interview after that and again seemed to pass with flying colours because they offered her a job! We just can't believe it and neither can she. We are all delighted. There is just one worry; she has to fly the nest to be closer to London's Heathrow airport. I have to accept it though. Jacob's attitude has been interesting and flies in the face of all he has said in the past. One of the first things he said was, "Who am I going to fight with now?" - that's his little joke. He thinks she'll have a fantastic time in London. I can tell he's proud of her. "She'll soon be flying high" he says "living a glamorous life, forgetting all about us, up here in the frozen north!" He probably has a point but I hope she doesn't forget her old mum when she goes away. To let you into a secret, I wish it was me. Anyway, must fly. Washing up and cleaning to do!

Q34:

My daughter Michelle has been trying to get a job with an airline for a while now. Her brother Jacob is very mean to her because when she announces "I'm going to be an international air hostess", he says, "yeah right and **(1) pigs might fly**." This generally leads to an argument. Temperamentally they are so different that **(2) sparks fly** all the time no matter what we are talking about, but when he laughs at her airline dreams she really **(3) flies off the handle**. Anyway, she finally got an interview for a job with a good company - not one of those **(4) fly by night** outfits you hear about. We were all delighted and really hoped she would do well. First she had a group interview and test and apparently she **(5) got off to a flying start** because there was quite a bit of Maths and Geography in the test and she loves both of these subjects. She had a small group interview after that and again seemed to **(6) pass with flying colours** because they offered her a job! We just can't believe it and neither can she. We are all delighted. There is just one worry; she has to **(7) fly the nest** to be closer to London's Heathrow airport. I have to accept it though. Jacob's attitude has been interesting and **(8) flies in the face** of all he has said in the past. One of the first things he said was, "Who am I going to fight with now?" - that's his little joke. He thinks she'll have a fantastic time in London. I can tell he's proud of her. **(9) "She'll soon be flying high"** he says "living a glamorous life, forgetting all about us, up here in the frozen north!" He probably has a point but I hope she doesn't forget her old mum when she goes away. To let you into a secret, I wish it was me. Anyway, **(10) must fly**. Washing up and cleaning to do!

Grammar and listening: Definitions: Idiomatic phrases around flying (page 109)

Q35: 1-j, 2-a, 3-f, 4-h, 5-c, 6-e, 7-l, 8-g, 9-d, 10-b

Grammar and listening: Idiomatic phrases (page 109)

Q36:

a) My mother thinks that the reason we haven't **flown the nest** is that she has made our home too comfortable.

b) We opened the travel agency on Monday and have been enormously busy all week. We really **got off to a flying start**.

c) My son has just got all his standard grades. He **passed with flying colours**.

d) I warned my husband not to invest in the new airline. I had heard they were just a **fly by night** company and wouldn't last.

e) I think I can become an aircraft engineer if I work hard, but my sister says "**pigs might fly**."

f) Whenever I see my sister's boyfriend **sparks fly**. I just do not like him!

Pronunciation: Use of polite intonation (page 110)

Q37:

a) **Can** I **help** you sir/madam? Rise/fall/rise

b) **Can** I see your boarding card please? Rise/fall/rise

c) Do you want an **aisle** or **window** seat? Rising on window seat

d) Would you like something to **drink**? Rising on drink

Reading comprehension: Travel and work abroad (page 110)

Q38: b. Varied and interesting

Q39: c. tense

Q40:

a) True

b) True

c) False

Q41: Generic

Q42: Placate

Q43: Egotistical

Q44: Redundant/made redundant

Q45: a. Appreciative

Listening comprehension: Healthy Living Show (page 112)

Listening transcript

Presenter: In our Healthy Living show today we talk to experts in the fields of Anger Management and Hypnotherapy. We also have a feature on Health and Travel and will be talking to experts on issues such as food and drink abroad, vaccinations and jet lag. Victoria McKinley - you not only worked as a nurse for an international travel company but you are also a seasoned traveller yourself. Can you tell us about jet lag, first of all?

Victoria: Yes, jet lag can be an annoying feature of travel. Whether you are a holidaymaker or business traveller, the effects can be very troublesome to say the least. The symptoms, as many will know, range from confusion and disorientation to fatigue, insomnia and general feeling of malaise.

Presenter:
What actually causes this problem?

Victoria: The problem is caused by travelling on aeroplanes across a number of time zones. When we cross time zones our natural body rhythms are upset, and on arrival in far flung places we often find that the body clock which regulates our sleeping, eating, digestive and other systems has simply not caught up with the changes.

Presenter: Are some people more susceptible to jet lag than others?

Victoria: Not really. We are all equally likely to suffer, though it seems to have a greater impact on the over sixties.

Presenter: It does seem to be worse in some countries than others...

Victoria: Yes, it is likely to be much worse if we have crossed several time zones, if we go from the UK to Australia, for example, rather than just across Europe. It is also understood that travelling east to west is easier than west to east. If for example you travel west to east you will in effect move forward in time or gain hours, which makes for a shorter day. The body finds this much more difficult to deal with.

Presenter: What can we do to minimise the effects of jet lag?

Victoria: The advice which I would give all travellers is to drink lots of fluid before and during a flight, avoid alcohol and rest as much as possible in flight. When you arrive at your destination, try to establish a routine which matches the new time zone... that means eating and sleeping at the appropriate local time. You should avoid a nap though, however tempting on arrival. It is far better to wait until a normal bed time as this will help you adapt more speedily to local time. Finally, get out and get fresh air, exercise and, above all, natural light. This will help the circadian rhythms to become realigned.

Presenter: Thank you very much, Victoria. That was extremely interesting and informative. I am sure we all feel far more confident about dealing with jet lag now. Moving on, I'd like to introduce our next guest...

Q46: nurse / traveller

Q47: a, b and f: confusion, disorientation, fatigue

Q48: crossing time zones

Q49: (to the) west

Q50: False

Q51: True

Q52: False

Q53: True

Q54: A radio broadcast.

Topic 7: Current affairs

Pre-reading activity: Speaking: Discussion: Homes (page 116)

Q1:

1. An attic is space at the top of a house while a cellar is space below the ground floor of a house.
2. A front door is one which leads in and out of the house.
3. A roof is outside and a ceiling is inside.
4. A lamp gives additional lighting to a room and often sits on a table while a light provides the main source of lighting in a room
5. A heater is a machine which makes a room warmer and may use gas or electricity to do so. A fire is the flames, light and heat produced when something burns. Traditional homes would have had a fireplace and this would have been the main source of heat.

Environmentally friendly homes (page 116)

Q2:   1-f, 2-a, 3-h, 4-c, 5-d, 6-b, 7-e, 8-g

Post-reading activity: Matching paragraph headings: Environmentally friendly homes (page 118)

Q3:   1-f, 2-c, 3-d, 4-b, 5-a (e is not required.)

Post-reading activity: Identifying informal language (page 118)

Q4:

Use of active rather than passive constructions e.g. 'many people already use energy efficient light bulbs' rather than 'energy efficient light bulbs are already used by many people'.

Post-reading activity: informal to formal language: Environmentally friendly homes (page 119)

Q5:

1. Chilly (par.1)	Cool/cold
2. Check out (par.1)	consider
3. (It) doesn't matter (par.2)	(It is) of no consequence
4. Cut down on (par.2)	reduce
5. Enough (par.2)	sufficient
6. Stop (par.2)	prevent
7. Around (par.4)	approximately
8. Want (par.4)	desire
9. Investment of Cash (par.5)	Financial investment
10. Turn off (par.5)	disconnect

Answers from page 119.

Q6: a) True

Q7: b) False

Q8: a) True

Q9: b) False

Q10: The phrase *cost the earth* has literal and metaphorical meaning suggesting certain behaviour will cause less damage to the planet and at the same time will not cost too much money.

Pre-listening activity: Vocabulary: Environmental issues (page 120)

Q11:

a) Flash floods
b) Coastal erosion
c) Rising tides
d) Melting glaciers
e) Freak weather
f) Violent storms
g) Warmer climate
h) Heat wave

Listening activity: Note taking: Environmental issues (page 121)

Listening transcript

Jeff: Perhaps we should just have a chat about the issues around global warming and then see if that helps us to prepare for writing the essay. What do you think, Samantha? Louise?

Samantha: Yes good idea. Okay with you, Louise?

Louise: Absolutely!

Samantha: Shall I start then? I think that the most frightening thing about global warming is freak weather conditions. Flash floods are absolutely terrifying, aren't they? When you see the amount of damage which can be done to people's homes in such a short space of time it really strikes a chord. It's the lack of any real warning I find particularly frightening. One minute there is a road and the next it has become a river; homes and cars are destroyed in a couple of hours.

Louise: Yes, it's difficult to know if this is just something which the media have latched on to... you know, if they are making us panic more about things that have always happened but have maybe gone unreported. In spite of that, I do have concerns which I think are realistic and based on what I see around me. I live near the seaside and find the idea of coastal erosion and rising tides really alarming. I mean, in the future, coastal homes may be totally unthinkable. The idea of land disappearing, that kind of thing keeps me awake at night. What do you think, Jeff?

Jeff: I know what you mean about the media, but I think there are definitely more problems with freak weather now than in the past and we are all much more aware of that. That's why weather stories get reported all the time. I think the crisis facing the planet is all too real. I saw some pictures on a website just the other day and they showed comparisons between places in the world today and the way they looked some years ago. That was really disturbing. They showed the extent to which glaciers in South America have melted and the thick layers of pollution over the Taj Mahal in India. Those examples made it very clear to me that the world we live in is changing dramatically, and we just can't hide our heads in the sand any more, can we?

Samantha: Have either of you have been affected by global warming directly?

Louise: That's an interesting question, Sam. I was in the USA on a skiing holiday a couple of years ago and half the resorts were closed due to lack of snow... and that was supposed to be peak season! It was a rubbish holiday, but more seriously... if that isn't direct evidence of global warming, I don't know what is! What about you guys?

Jeff: I've been affected by floods. My house is close to the river bank and the rain was so intense a couple of months ago that we were told to expect severe flooding.

Louise: You live in a flood zone, do you? How worrying! What happened?

Jeff: We were issued with sand bags and asked if we wanted to be evacuated. It's difficult to decide in these circumstances whether to sit tight or jump ship. Anyway, I stayed and watched the water gradually taking over the garden and moving up to my front door. I was on the point of bailing out when it stopped raining and things calmed down a bit, but it was pretty hair-raising.

Samantha: That sounds awful! I've never had these kind of problems where I live. Just lucky, maybe! I think you should both move house!

Q12:

1. Strike a chord	d. something which reminds one of something and/ or makes one feel sympathy
2. Latch on to	a. become attached to something or someone
3. Peak season	e. time of the year when most tourists visit
4. Sit tight	f. wait where you are
5. Jump ship	c. escape from a situation in which you no longer wish to be involved
6. Bail out	b. abandon a situation

Q13: Frightening, Terrifying, alarming, panic, disturbing, keeps me awake at night, worrying, hair-raising.

Q14: c) Samantha

Q15: b) Louise

Q16: b) Louise

Q17: a) Jeff

Q18: b) Louise

Q19: a) Jeff

Q20: c) Samantha

Q21: thick layers of pollution

Q22: resorts were closed

Q23: to be evacuated

Q24: c) fellow students.

Grammar: Discuss types of question tags (page 123)

Q25: c) You live in a flood zone, **do you**?

Q26: a) a and b

Q27:

- The tag takes the form of auxiliary (+ n't) + pronoun
- Positive statements are generally followed by negative tags or negative statements are followed by positive tag where we expect agreement (even if tentative)(examples a & b)
- Positive statements are followed by positive tag where we are surprised by new information or have just remembered something (example c)

Grammar: Choose the correct (page 124)

Q28:

a) Climate change is affecting all of us now, **isn't it**?

b) The planet isn't likely to survive if we don't make changes, **is it**?

c) We should all try to recycle our rubbish, **shouldn't we**?

d) Some countries are more eco-friendly than others, **aren't they**?

e) You live in a very eco-friendly way, **don't you**?

f) The changes in climate have affected wildlife too, **haven't they**?

g) These old fashioned houses certainly eat up energy, **don't they**?

h) The new boiler we have installed wasn't very expensive, **was it**?

i) You've just installed solar panels, **haven't you**?

j) Mr Smith, you have been employed as an energy specialist for ten years, **have you not**?

k) So you have never been to a bottle bank before, **have you**?

l) Madam, your party has only considered environmental issues worthwhile in the lead up to the election, **has it not**?

Pronunciation: Question tags: Patterns of intonation (page 126)

Q29:

a) I don't think you give much thought to the future of the planet, **do you** ↗? (tentative suggestion) **Rising**

b) I don't think you give much thought to the future of the planet, **do you** ↘?(expecting agreement) **Falling**

c) She has given her heart and soul to designing sustainable homes, **hasn't she** ↘? (expecting agreement) **Falling**

d) She has given her heart and soul to designing sustainable homes, **hasn't she** ↗? (tentatively) **Rising**

e) So you think you are eco-friendly, **do you** →? (sarcastically) **Flat intonation**

f) You are very eco-friendly, **aren't you** ↘? (expecting agreement) **Falling**

g) So you're saying I can't install solar panels on my roof, **are you** ↗? (surprised) **Rising**

h) So you're saying I can't install solar panels on my roof, **are you** ↘? (expecting agreement) **Falling**

i) The future of our wildlife is under threat if we don't take radical steps to reduce pollution, **isn't it** ↗? (tentatively) **Rising**

j) The future of our wildlife is under threat if we don't take radical steps to reduce pollution, **isn't it** ↘? (expecting agreement) **Falling**

k) You don't think my giving up driving a sports car will save the planet, **do you** ↗? (expressing disbelief) **Rising**

l) You don't think my giving up driving a sports car will save the planet, **do you** ↘? (expecting agreement) **Falling**

m) The state of the planet is our responsibility, **isn't it** ⟍? (expecting agreement) **Falling**

n) The state of the planet is our responsibility, **isn't it** ⟋? (tentatively) **Rising**

o) You are an eco-warrior, **are you** ⟋? (surprised) **Rising**

p) You are an eco-warrior, **are you** →? (sarcastic/disbelieving) **Flat intonation**

Formal and informal language (page 127)

Q30:

1. For	On behalf of
2. Worried	Concerned
3. Things we do	Actions
4. Lots	Many
5. Like	Such as
6. Started	Commenced
7. To get people to see	To raise awareness
8. To work together	To collaborate
9. To pool	To share
10. To come up with (something)	To produce
11. To start off	Firstly/in the first place
12. The last thing	Finally
13. About	Regarding
14. Giving (people) encouragement to do something	Incentives
15. Facts and figures	Statistics/data
16. Urge	Encourage
17. Get (attention)	Attract
18. Think	Consider

Use of formal language (page 128)

Model answer

Dear Mr Robinson

I am writing on behalf of the Go Green Society at Western College's Student Union. We have grave concerns about global warming, climate change and the future of the planet. We are also aware that many of our actions, such as frequent use of cars as opposed to use of public transport waste energy resources.

We have embarked on a project in attempt to raise awareness of this problem among students and staff and at the same time to try to change behaviour. We have collaborated with another college in order to share resources and have thereby developed a plan of action.

In the first place we intend to survey a sample of students and lecturers about their travel habits. Secondly we intend to analyse the results in order to develop ideas. Finally, we intend to make decisions about how to be environmentally friendly when we travel to college. We have had some thoughts regarding developing car share schemes and cycle incentive schemes.

We should be very pleased if you could provide us with some statistics about environmental issues that would attract attention and encourage people to consider their actions more carefully.

Thank you for your attention to this matter
Yours sincerely

Focus on writing formal letters (page 128)

Model answer

Dear Mr Robinson

Thank you very much for your help in providing the Go Green group at Western College with statistics on pollution in Glasgow. This information has really helped in our campaign to change behaviour among staff and students.

We have set up a car sharing system in our college which is administered by students for students and staff. It has been a great success so far. We are also running a weekend cycle club offering group excursions and support with cycle maintenance.

We would be delighted if you were able to visit our college for afternoon tea. This would allow you to see some of our projects first hand.

Please advise us of a suitable date.

Yours sincerely

Rebecca James

Reading comprehension: Green fashion (page 129)

Q31: b. A magazine

Q32: c. To entertain and educate

Q33:

- a) True
- b) True
- c) False
- d) False
- e) True
- f) True

Q34:

- Charity and vintage shops
- Recycle banks

Q35:

- Wastes water
- Use of pesticide

Q36: Label shows supplier has a commitment to ethical and sustainable production.

Q37:

- Trendy
- Chic
- In vogue

Q38: b. Ethical shopping and recycling can help to protect the environment.

Listening comprehension: Compost (page 131)

Listening transcript

Simon: Hi, Magnus. I haven't seen much of you recently. How are things?

Magnus: Good, thanks. . . but this torrential rain over the last couple of months has kept me indoors. That's probably why you haven't seen me around. How are you doing yourself, Simon?

Simon: Not bad, thanks. What are you up to with that bin you are carrying? Is it for compost?

Magnus: Yes it is. Well spotted. I got it from the local council. . . it seems they are keen to encourage environmentally friendly projects, so they just handed it over.

Simon: Oh yeah? So how do you make compost?

Magnus: It really depends on whether you reckon you have enough waste to fill it up. At the moment I don't, so I am just making a layer of about 30 cm of garden waste and rubbish from the kitchen bin. I'll keep adding to it, as and when I can, until it's full, but it could take up to a year to compost this way. It's known as the 'cold heap route'.

Simon: Does it matter what you put in there?

Magnus: You should use a mixture of green stuff and brown stuff. Green stuff is material such as grass cuttings, weeds, raw vegetable peelings, tea bags and coffee granules. The brown stuff is slow to rot and could be cardboard cereal packets and egg boxes, waste mail and such like.

Simon: What about magazines? I've got stacks of these I'd like to get rid of.

Magnus: Newspapers and magazines are better sent to recycling depots. You should also avoid meat, fish or cooked food as these attract vermin. Anyway if you mix green and brown it's more efficient and if you do the hot heap route , which means fill the bin up totally and keep turning and moving the rubbish inside, then it can be really fast to make good compost.

Simon: Do you use it as fertiliser?

Magnus: Well, compost feeds the soil while fertiliser feeds the plants so it is different. Compost makes a really rich soil for growing. We just thought it's a cheap way to nourish the soil, cut down on landfill waste and at the same time it's a new hobby that gets me out from under Victoria's feet.

Simon: Good thinking. Perhaps it's time I got a compost bin for Sarah!

Q39: (the local) council

Q40: hot and cold

Q41: enough waste

Q42: green (stuff) / brown (stuff)

Q43: attracts vermin

Q44: b. Compost feeds the soil while fertiliser feeds the plants.

Q45: a, c, e

Q46: b, colleagues

Topic 8: Cultural awareness

Stereotypes (page 134)

Q1:

These are possible answers you may have arrived at, compare your answers to the ones provided here.

	Clothes	Food/Drink	Home/transport	Others
Japan	Kimono	Rice, noodles Sake Green Tea	Enormous city Bicycle or train	Advanced technology Travel in large groups Quiet/polite
England	Bowler hat Suit	Bacon and eggs Tea Toast	House with a garden Double decker bus Mini's	Read Financial Times Reserved
France	Beret	Baguettes and cheese Wine	Country villas Citroën/Renault cars Bicycles	Nationalistic feeling
Italy	Designer clothes Sunglasses	Pizza Pasta Coffee	Busy flats Fiat cars	Careless driving Hot tempered

Cross cultural quiz (page 135)

Q2: c) You have forgotten to remove your shoes before entering the home which is customary in Iranian homes.

Q3: b) British people believe it is rude to discuss salaries.

Q4: a) In Poland it is considered unlucky when someone wishes you luck.

Q5: c) The removal of your jacket is an inappropriate lack of formality.

Q6: b) The applicant is showing respect to you and your position.

Q7: c) It is not usual to make enquiries about the personal life of a French person if you do not know them well.

Q8: b) A selection of cakes.

Q9: c) Spanish people are less rigid about punctuality than others and would not have thought this was insulting.

Q10: a) She is being friendly. This is normal behaviour in Scotland.

Q11: c) She is offended by your lack of punctuality. This is a big issue in Germany and she perceives your lateness as extremely rude.

Living in Scotland (1) (page 137)

Listening transcript

Speaker 1: Brigida I came to Scotland to study English. I planned to stay for a couple of years but I met my husband here, so now I will be here indefinitely. I have to tell you at first I found the weather extremely difficult to deal with. The darkness and the rain were quite hard for me to bear as I was used to lots of sunshine in Tenerife. I think that the sunshine in my country also makes people live very different kinds of lives. I think we spend far more time outdoors - for me this is a much healthier way to live. I think it raises your spirits. Also, little things can take some time to adjust to when you are trying to adapt to a new culture. For example, my husband is quite traditional in many ways. He really likes to eat dinner at about six but this is something unheard of in my hometown!

Speaker 2: Claudia I am German and I came to Scotland to work because of my husband's job. He was offered a really good position in Glasgow and I came with him in the hope that I would also find a job. At first we found it quite difficult to get used to the culture and climate but I think we are quite settled now. My husband has a solution which overcomes the lack of sunshine and vitamin D; he walks to work and rarely uses a car or bus at the weekend. He actually looks as though he has a Mediterranean suntan. It took me some time to find a job but doing so helped me make friends and find out more about Scottish people. At first I thought that most people stayed in their homes in winter. I realise now that a lot of people rely on activities to get them outside in the winter. Hill walking for example is extremely popular and since Scotland has an amazing landscape with fabulous scenery this is a fantastic hobby. One just has to disregard the weather and join in.

Speaker 3: Justyna I came from Poland to Scotland because I was offered a job in a major international bank. I live in Edinburgh and have felt quite comfortable here from the start, although I have found some aspects of Scottish manners and language a little difficult. I am from Krakow, which is a very cultured city, and in Edinburgh I have found people here also enjoy culture such as cinema and theatre. We Polish are not offended by alcohol so the fact that Scottish people go to pubs does not matter to me - I go with them. However, at work I sometimes have some small communication problems; occasionally people don't understand me. Apparently my intonation is rather flat I have been told, whereas British people really use intonation in their voices to sound happy, angry or surprised. This is something I have had to practise.

Speaker 4: Nazhin I am Iranian and I have lived here in the UK for about four years. I love living here but at first I was very homesick and I found it quite difficult to get used to many things. I came to join my husband; he's a lecturer here. In Iran, women do not have the same freedom as women in the UK. We have our own ways of doing things but this is quite different from the ways in which Scottish women do things! Just now in Iran we would have to cover our heads in public places and our social life would tend to be in the home. We have guests to our homes more often than we go out to restaurants. We love to have parties, but we would not usually dance with men the way women here do. In my country, men dance with other men and women also dance together. I think that Scottish men find this strange.

Q12: Tenerife

Q13: Germany

Q14: Poland

Q15: Iran

Q16: To study English

Q17: She was offered a job

Q18: Work

Q19: To join her husband

Living in Scotland (2) (page 138)

Listening transcript

Speaker 1: Brigida I came to Scotland to study English. I planned to stay for a couple of years but I met my husband here, so now I will be here indefinitely. I have to tell you at first I found the weather extremely difficult to deal with. The darkness and the rain were quite hard for me to bear as I was used to lots of sunshine in Tenerife. I think that the sunshine in my country also makes people live very different kinds of lives. I think we spend far more time outdoors - for me this is a much healthier way to live. I think it raises your spirits. Also, little things can take some time to adjust to when you are trying to adapt to a new culture. For example, my husband is quite traditional in many ways. He really likes to eat dinner at about six but this is something unheard of in my hometown!

Speaker 2: Claudia I am German and I came to Scotland to work because of my husband's job. He was offered a really good position in Glasgow and I came with him in the hope that I would also find a job. At first we found it quite difficult to get used to the culture and climate but I think we are quite settled now. My husband has a solution which overcomes the lack of sunshine and vitamin D; he walks to work and rarely uses a car or bus at the weekend. He actually looks as though he has a Mediterranean suntan. It took me some time to find a job but doing so helped me make friends and find out more about Scottish people. At first I thought that most people stayed in their homes in winter. I realise now that a lot of people rely on activities to get them outside in the winter. Hill walking for example is extremely popular and since Scotland has an amazing landscape with fabulous scenery this is a fantastic hobby. One just has to disregard the weather and join in.

Speaker 3: Justyna I came from Poland to Scotland because I was offered a job in a major international bank. I live in Edinburgh and have felt quite comfortable here from the start, although I have found some aspects of Scottish manners and language a little difficult. I am from Krakow, which is a very cultured city, and in Edinburgh I have found people here also enjoy culture such as cinema and theatre. We Polish are not offended by alcohol so the fact that Scottish people go to pubs does not matter to me - I go with them. However, at work I sometimes have some small communication problems; occasionally people don't understand me. Apparently my intonation is rather flat I have been told, whereas British people really use intonation in their voices to sound happy, angry or surprised. This is something I have had to practise.

Speaker 4: Nazhin I am Iranian and I have lived here in the UK for about four years. I love living here but at first I was very homesick and I found it quite difficult to get used to many things. I came to join my husband; he's a lecturer here. In Iran, women do not have the same freedom as women in the UK. We have our own ways of doing things but this is quite different from the ways in which Scottish women do things! Just now in Iran we would have to cover our heads in public places and our social life would tend to be in the home. We have guests to our homes more often than we go out to restaurants. We love to have parties, but we would not usually dance with men the way women here do. In my country, men dance with other men and women also dance together. I think that Scottish men find this strange.

Q20: The weather

Q21: Quite traditional

Q22: Vitamin D

Q23: Join in

Q24: Cultural activities and alcohol

Q25: Flat intonation

Q26: Cover their heads and socialise at home.

Q27: They dance together

Grammar: Present simple and continuous (page 139)

Q28: The *a)* sentences are in the present simple tense and the *b)* sentences present continuous. The use of present simple in the *a)* sentences indicates that these are general truths. The use of the present continuous in the *b)* sentences conveys the sense that the action is taking place as we speak and *2b)* is not necessarily permanent.

Grammar: State verbs (page 139)

Q29: The verbs in these sentences are *state* verbs and are rarely used in a continuous form.

Grammar: Present perfect simple and continuous (page 139)

Q30:

The *a)* sentences are in the present perfect simple and the *b)* sentences are present perfect continuous.

The use of present perfect simple in the *a)* sentences emphasises the duration of time i.e. in sentence *1a)* how long the speaker has lived in Scotland from a point in the past.

In *2a)* there is a sense of completion, the idea that the action, that is the cooking is probably finished.

The use of the present perfect continuous in the *b)* sentences conveys the sense that the action (in *2b)* cooking) is likely to continue.

Grammar: Activity: Identifying errors (page 140)

Q31: The mistakes have been scored out.

I am living in Scotland for two years and I am very happy here. When I first arrived in the UK, I found the culture a little strange and I was a bit homesick. However, now I am relaxed and comfortable here as I am knowing a lot of people and have a lot of friends.

First I will telling you about the little problems because nowhere is perfect. A lot of people is complaining about the food in Scotland. This is really not a big problem. I find that although some Scottish people eating fried foods a lot, there are lots of very good shops and restaurants for buy or eat other foods. You don't have to eating chips. Also some people drink a lot of beer but not everyone drinks.

The weather in Scotland is not the best. If you are coming to Scotland there is something that it is very important to ~~be bringing~~ with you and that is waterproof clothes. I ~~am buying~~ lots of waterproof clothes now so I do not have a problem with the rain any more. It ~~is raining~~ here a lot. Last month it rained every day. The local people are used to rain but even they were upset because this is supposed to be summer.

Something that you should know about Scotland is that people in Scotland are very friendly. People in Glasgow ~~are talking~~ to you all the time, at bus stops, in shops and in the street. They ~~are often talking~~ about the bad weather. I ~~am making~~ lots of friends because the Scots like people from different countries and often want to help you.

Another really good thing about Scotland is the scenery. It is really important to visit the north of the country. I ~~am visiting~~ many towns and villages in the north of Scotland already and I ~~visit~~ three islands, Mull, Islay and Skye. The scenery is fantastic! I recommend you ~~visiting~~ them too.

Finally, I would like to say that I ~~am not regretting~~ the chance to be here and experience the Scottish culture. I think I ~~am going~~ back to Spain one day but for now I am glad to be here.

Grammar: Correcting grammatical errors (page 140)

Q32: The correct answers have been emboldened and the mistakes scored out.

I **have been living** in Scotland for two years and I am very happy here. When I first arrived in the UK, I found the culture a little strange and I was a bit homesick. But, now I am relaxed and comfortable here as **I know** a lot of people and have a lot of friends.

First I **will tell** you about the little problems because nowhere is perfect. A lot of people **complain** about the food in Scotland. This is really not a big problem. I find that although some Scottish people **eat** fried foods a lot, there are lots of very good shops and restaurants for **buying** or ~~eat~~ **eating** other foods. You don't have to **eat** chips. Also some people drink a lot of beer but not everyone drinks.

The weather in Scotland is not the best. If you are coming to Scotland there is something that it is very important to **bring** with you and that is waterproof clothes. I **have bought** lots of waterproof clothes now so I do not have a problem with the rain any more. It **rains** here a lot. Last month it rained every day. The local people are used to rain but even they were upset because this is supposed to be summer.

Something that you should know about Scotland is that people in Scotland are very friendly. People in Glasgow **talk** to you all the time, at bus stops, in shops and in the street. They **often talk** about the bad weather. I **have made** lots of friends because the Scots like people from different countries and often want to help you.

Another really good thing about Scotland is the scenery. It is really important to visit the north of the country. I **have visited** many towns and villages in the north of Scotland already and I **have visited** three islands, Mull, Islay and Skye. The scenery is fantastic! I recommend you **visit** them too.

Finally, I would like to say that I **do not regret** the chance to be here and experience the Scottish culture. I think I **will go** back to Spain one day but for now I am glad to be here.

Grammar: Select the correct tense (page 141)

Q33:

a) I **have lived** in Aberdeen since 1999.

b) I **am meeting** some new friends at the university bar tonight.

c) Today I **have been working** on an essay but I **haven't finished** it yet.

d) I **enjoy** meeting new people but I am a little shy.

e) My family **have visited** a few times since I moved to this city.

f) I **walk** into the city centre every day to buy food or have a coffee.

g) My friend Isabel **is studying** Psychology as well, so we work on projects together.

h) I **love** being a student but sometimes I **worry** in case I don't pass my exams.

i) The principal of the university **gives** a lecture at the start of every term.

j) I have no idea about my future career but I know I **want** to work with people.

Writing: Genre analysis (page 142)

Q34:

- Introduction
- Purpose for organisation of the event
- Travel arrangements
- The venue and entertainment
- Conclusion

Q35: a) A student magazine

Q36: b) Light-hearted

Q37: b) Other students

Q38: c) Informal

Writing: Article for student publication (page 143)

Model answer

Model answer: You may remember last month an exciting advertisement appeared on the intranet, inviting all students to attend an International Food Night? If you were among the hundred or so guests who made it, then what I am going to describe will be very familiar. The event finally took place last Saturday. For those who did not make it, for whatever reason, I hope that by the time you have finished reading this you will be signing up for the next event organised by your student union committee.

The choice of a venue was easy; where else but the canteen? A bit of furniture re-organisation, some decorations and music and we were all set to go. We had recruited six additional events planners from students to join the six of us in the committee. Together we drew up a plan of action to include:

Food and drinks, Entertainment, Fire prevention and safety measures, Charity collection, Media coverage.

We sought expert help to provide knowledge and experience on issues we had questions about, such as food hygiene and service, fire drills and charity donations. However while it seemed like an enormous task at the start, before long we started to feel sure that things would go well.

The event was a huge success by all accounts. We all had a wonderful time. The food represented cuisine from eighteen different countries. The music and dancing originated from areas across Europe, Asia, Africa, the far and Middle East. We also raised an amazing £600 for charity. To all who supported the event we would like to say an enormous thank you. Let's do something else soon!

Learner training (page 144)

Q39: The correct answers are B, H and J.
Grammar is important but practice in the skills of reading, writing, speaking and listening are equally important. It is very useful to do homework but sometimes watching/listening to a film with subtitles or speaking in English at home is also helpful. It is important to contribute as much as possible in class and to get involved in group activities as these are opportunities to practise use of language and learn from others. Mistakes are inevitable so do not worry about saying the wrong thing! Working out grammar rules is a useful cognitive process which can enhance learning. The teacher can help you, but ultimately the student must take responsibility for his/her own learning.

Reading comprehension: Scandinavian drama (page 144)

Q40: TV Review

Q41: Nordic noir

Q42: Subject matter, plot, characters, roles for women, social commentary

Q43: "Landscapes conducive to brooding introspection"

Q44: Dumped

Q45: "... are not what they once were"

Q46: Morality and social policy

Q47: Hooked

Listening comprehension: Marion and Sandy (page 146)

Listening transcript

Marion: Hi Sandy. How are you? How have you been? Fancy a coffee?

Sandy: Hi Marion. I'm fine. It's great to see you. Yes, coffee sounds good! We could just go to the café across the road. I often go there when I drop the kids off in the morning, though later on you've got no chance of a table because the sixth year pupils all come in for snacks.

Marion: Okay, I'll grab the coffees if you get a table.

Pause

Marion: Here we are.

Sandy: Thanks, Marion... so have you had a good summer?

Marion: Yeah, it was really good; we went down to Cornwall and had a month in a cottage. Have you been down there? It really is beautiful.

Sandy: Well, we just went over to Spain to see Carlos's family. We tend to do that most holidays now.

Marion: 'Just went to Spain!' Really Sandy! That sounds fantastic to me!

Sandy: Oh, I know. I'm not knocking it. It is a beautiful country, but sometimes staying with the in-laws and socialising with Carlos's friends can be a bit exhausting. Don't misunderstand me - they are all extremely nice, but it is another language and culture and sometimes I get really tired.

Marion: Hmm, yes I can imagine that could be a bit of a strain, regardless of how lovely the people are!

Sandy: Yes, and there are cultural differences that can be a little problematic at times. For example, Spanish people eat very late at night and I'm afraid I am an old bore in that respect. After a full day in the heat with the kids, I am shattered by ten, which is exactly the hour I am expected to eat dinner! Apart from that I am so used to my own routine that my digestive system just can't cope. I just can't sleep if I eat late.

Marion: Gosh, yes I can imagine that would be difficult, and of course you don't want to offend anyone.

Sandy: Yes, and another little thing is sense of humour. Even as a couple, Carlos and I often find very different things funny, but this becomes magnified when I am with his family. They will often collapse in heaps on the floor about something while I am poker faced and vice versa!

Marion: Oh dear

Sandy: I know, but really I mustn't complain. There are many positives. I knew Carlos was not Scottish when we got together and I wouldn't swap him for anyone else. We agree on most things and we are able to go to Spain all the time. His family are really warm and welcoming and they dote on the kids. It could be a lot worse.

Marion: Absolutely! Tell you what, why don't you get them all to come to Cornwall next year? That'd be great! We could get neighbouring cottages and introduce a two tier system for meals... seven o'clock for the bores and ten for the party animals.

Sandy: Sounds like you might have a good idea there Marion. I shall see what I can do for next

---

summer! Seriously though, maybe we should alternate visits between the two countries in the future.

Q48: a) Happy

Q49: c) Mixed

Q50: (a bit of) a strain

Q51: warm and welcoming

Q52: neighbouring cottages

Q53: Alternating between Spain and UK for holidays

Q54: At their children's school

Q55: In a café

Answers to questions and activities for Unit 2

Topic 1: Jobs

A to Z of jobs (page 152)

Q1: Sample answers are given here, but other jobs exist. Show your work to your teacher if possible.

Artist	Builder	Cleaner	Doctor
Engineer	Farmer	Gardener	Hairdresser
Interpreter	Journalist	K	Lawyer
Mechanic	Nurse	Optician	Policeman
Q	Receptionist	Soldier	Teacher
Undertaker	Vet	Welder	X
Youth worker	Z		

Careers (page 153)

Listening transcript

Speaker 1

Jonathan Varsen is the life and soul of his workplace. That may be due to the fact that those with whom he spends most of his working day are corpses.

"If you dwell on that for too long, it does seem slightly disturbing, I suppose. But I'm used to it by now".

Jonathan's job is perhaps not the most glamorous, but he prides himself on providing an essential service for his local community.

"There is a lot of skill in this profession. I've had to learn how to use various tools and instruments in this job. I have undertaken, pardon the pun, professional training to do this job, but I also learned a lot from my uncle - I worked for him in his business before opening my own. I couldn't say that I 'enjoy' being around death as much as I am, but embalming and dressing the bodies is an important task to maintain the respect and dignity of the deceased and for the family's sake, and it gives me a sense of purpose and satisfaction when the grieving relatives can see their loved one looking at peace and in comfort for their final voyage."

Speaker 2

Melissa Olson is a paramedic. She considers the job to be an altruistic one.

"You don't get a lot of time to yourself in this profession. It's all about helping others."

Melissa has had to train in various areas of emergency medicine, as well as take courses in radio operating and advanced driving techniques.

"There are many facets to my job. People often think we are like mobile nurses, but, and I mean no disrespect by this, apart from helping sick people, there aren't many parallels between the two jobs. We perhaps don't possess as much medical knowledge in some areas as nurses, and certainly most of us are so rushed off our feet it's difficult to have as calm and soothing a bedside manner with patients as they do, but what we offer is first aid, fast transport and professional advice to hospital staff. We also liaise closely with the police force as we regularly get called out to the same situations as they do"

Melissa wouldn't change her job for anything.

"Despite some of the grizzly episodes I've witnessed, I feel like I'm making a difference, doing something worthwhile. I could study for years and be a lawyer or something and earn big bucks, but frankly, this job is so rewarding that I wouldn't trade it for any kind of salary hike".

Speaker 3

David 'Huckle' Berry isn't happy unless he is hovering high above the bustle of the commuters below.

"After I left high school, I enrolled in the Air Force and, after a few months of working in various posts on the ground, I embarked on my pilot training. I learned how to fly fighter jets, but I was never deployed overseas, and to be honest, the armed forces just wasn't my cup of tea".

David found it too competitive in the world of commercial airlines to continue being an airline pilot in the 'real world', so he re-trained to fly helicopters, initially working as a private pilot for hire.

"I used to ferry the celebs around to their parties and mansions and whatnot. It was enjoyable for a while, but I quickly became nothing more than a glorified taxi driver. That's when the CBA News offer came along. They needed a pilot-come-roving reporter for news stories and weather bulletins, and, as luck would have it, I had learned a lot about meteorology through my airline work, so I was ideally placed to take up that role. I've been doing it for a decade now, and something new and fascinating occurs every day on the streets below. It's great to have a bird's eye view of it all."

Q2: service

Q3: corpses

Q4: uncle

Q5: dignity

Q6: A, C, E

Q7: b) False

Q8: a) True

Q9: b) False

Q10: a) True

Q11: a) True

Volunteering (1) (page 155)

Q12: 1-c, 2-f, 3-b, 4-e, 5-a, 6-d

Volunteering (2) (page 156)

Q13: b) Advice

Q14: c) helps both the organisation and the individual recruited.

Q15: skills (and ambitions)

Q16: a (paid) career

Q17: (the) time involved

Q18: love for animals, desire to learn

Q19: in close proximity

Q20: prerequisite

Q21: filtered out

Q22: a) Recommend volunteering

Q23: c) A magazine article

A job application with a difference (page 159)

Model answer

Dear Sir /Madam

I would like to apply for the position of astronaut in the team required to man the International Space Station. I believe I have the qualifications, skills and personal qualities necessary to succeed in this role.

I have always had a keen interest in science and studied Mathematics, Chemistry and Physics at the University of Exeter. On completion of my undergraduate degree, I continued my studies and gained an MSc in Physics. I therefore have the qualifications required for the post.

In the second year of my undergraduate programme, I spent one year in the United States through Exeter University's study abroad scheme. During this year I pursued my interest in flight and took private flying lessons. I now have a significant number of flying hours.

Following my graduation I travelled extensively and became interested in languages. I studied Russian while continuing full-time employment as a nuclear physicist for British Aerospace.

As well as having an interest in flying and languages, I am also an enthusiastic mountaineer with regular involvement as a volunteer in mountain rescue services. I have a high level of fitness, good eyesight and I am of suitable height and weight for the role.

I believe I am a strong candidate with excellent interpersonal and intrapersonal skills. I should therefore be pleased if you would consider my application.

Yours faithfully

Reading comprehension: Ronan Abbey (page 160)

Q24: b) talk about the work of Fiona Kelly.

Q25: the historical background

Q26: the massive response

Q27: interests and experience

Q28: ensure maintenance

Q29: upsurge

Q30: generated

Q31: afterglow

Q32: 1-E, 2-C, 3-F, 4-D, 5-B, 6-A

Listening comprehension: Small businesses (page 162)

Listening transcript

Julian (presenter in TV studio): The last six years have had a profoundly negative effect on the retail market. Unemployment is high and money is tight. There has been a fall in consumer confidence and a lack of affordable credit which makes investment in small business as difficult as buying a house. A walk down any local high street will show that many giants of the retail world have fallen as the impact of the credit crunch has taken hold, and at the same time many small shops lie empty. Our reporter, Val Kennedy, has taken a walk along her local high street to see which businesses have survived the troubles so far.

Val: I'm standing in Alexander Street which is in the east end of my home town of Middlesfield, where like many towns the credit crunch has had an impact. There are many boarded up shop fronts which are sadly quite a common sight these days. However, there are also a few shops here which seem to be flourishing at the moment, so let's have a chat with the owners and see if we can find out how they are managing to cope. First, let me introduce Jon, a local businessman. Jon, can you tell us about your shop and how, if at all, the financial crisis has affected you?

Jon: I have been running a business in this spot for over 20 years. I inherited the shop from my father and have done very little to change the business since I took over. My father had the right idea as far as I can see, believing that the most important element in survival was offering good service at affordable prices. One thing I do to keep prices down is keep staffing levels down. I employ one assistant to help serve customers while I concentrate on the repairs which I do by myself on site at the back of the shop. We sell some other products associated with shoes such as laces, polish and dye. We also sell bags and purses and engraved nameplates for front doors. I keep the extras to a minimum though because it's just not the way we make most money. Lots of others stores sell bags and such like so we focus on what we can do that they can't. I feel a little guilty when I see other businesses close by struggling, many neighbours have closed down; I have had my moments too. Ironically though the recession has affected us in quite a positive way because of the emphasis on restoration. The trend is to mend rather than buy new, and we have certainly benefitted from that.

Val: Thanks, Jon. I now turn to one of Jon's neighbours, Ken, who has the shop two doors down. Hello, Ken... can you tell us about your work?

Ken: Hi, Val. As you can see, I have a bicycle shop. We sell new and reconditioned bikes and also do repairs on location. The business is doing quite well in spite of the financial downturn. I have recently taken over the premises next door which had been lying empty for some time. It is indirectly because of the financial crisis that I have been able to do that. At the moment there is significantly less demand for premises because of the lack of affordable credit and also because of a lack of consumer confidence. The balance in what I do has changed over the last few years. Now I am doing lots of business in the repair side of things, and in cycle accessories. People are not so keen to splash out on new bikes, but they do want to keep the bikes they have in good working order and to treat themselves to small things like panniers and lamps. While I am never going to make huge amounts of money, I do reasonably well. I am an enthusiast myself so it's a joy to deal with like-minded people.

Val: Thanks very much Ken. Now, let's just walk across the street where a lady is waiting to talk to us about her work. Hi, Geraldine, can we come in?

Geraldine: Hi, Val. Yes, of course, please do. It's a bit of a tight squeeze... sorry!

Val: Well, as you can see I am in a veritable treasure chest of a shop. This is what I would describe as heaven for girls who love dressing up, and as you can see the shop is stuffed full of dresses, coats, bags and jewellery. Geraldine, how did you get started?

Geraldine: We opened five years ago and fortunately have been making steady profits ever since. It seemed quite logical to me that with the credit crunch and the more widespread consequences of that, that there was likely to be a surge in interest in second hand clothing. It makes sense. I think women in particular love to shop for clothes, and if you can offer the buzz that shopping gives at a reasonable price then you are on to a winner. We buy clothes from a range of different sources. My business partner and I journey around the country, visiting other retailers, fairs, markets, car boot sales and so on... looking for the kind of products we think will sell in this area. We also buy from individuals who come in from the street with good quality clothing. We are really careful about what we accept. We have come to know our customer type very well. In this area we have a big university so a lot of students and academics come in looking for something different. We also find a lot of professionals in this area buying into the current fashion for vintage clothes. So far, it's all going well.

Val: So I see Geraldine! I shall probably pop back later!

Geraldine: Absolutely!

Val: Finally, we shall walk up to the top of the street and meet Isabella for lunch. Hi, Isabella! Tell us about your business.

Isabella Hi, Val! Well, we celebrated our first anniversary last week and I am delighted to say that things are going well. My husband and I run the business and even the kids get roped in at weekends when necessary. It was my husband's dream to open a place like this. When he was offered a severance package at work, in spite of the recession, he decided to take the risk. We have benefitted from the lack of consumer demand for shop premises.

Val: Why and how do you think you are managing to keep going?

Isabella We think that our careful planning may have made the difference. We decided that we would make the environment relaxed and friendly and that we would never sacrifice quality for economy. We use almost entirely fresh ingredients, and homemade soups and cakes are a speciality. We thought a lot about details, for example about what made us as consumers return to a café. We decided that repeat business was contingent on good food of course, but that comfort, ambience and staff all had an important part to play. We invested in comfort as much as style. I think we have found the most comfortable bar stools in the world. Bill is good with people, which is another great bonus. He talks to customers and is friendly but he doesn't push anyone to chat when they clearly want peace and quiet. We already have a strong core of regulars and lots of passing trade as well. We feel very lucky, business is steady and we are really enjoying the new lifestyle.

Val: What an interesting morning! For all aspiring businessmen and women it seems the message is clear, don't let fear stand in the way of your dreams. Do your homework and assess the market realistically, then get out there and give it a go! Now back to the studio...

Q33:

  a) True

  b) False

  c) False

  d) True

  e) False

  f) True

  g) False

Q34:

  a) Jon

  b) Isabella

  c) Ken

  d) Geraldine

  e) Isabella

Q35: c. Be sensible, plan carefully and then try it.

Q36: b. To analyse the success of local business in a financially difficult time.

Topic 2: Preparing for work

Pre-listening activity: Speaking (page 166)

Sample answers

* Job centres, newspapers, online sources including websites.

* Email / letter of application including CV, interviews (possibly including presentation).

* Full-time, part-time, shift work, zero-hour contract, seasonal work, voluntary work

Pre-listening activity: Vocabulary (page 166)

Q1: 1-h, 2-f, 3-d, 4-j, 5-g, 6-b, 7-i, 8-c, 9-a, 10-e.

Listening Activity: Finding a job (page 166)

Listening transcript

Sam: Hi, Amir. How are you doing? Are you still coming to Jamie's house tonight?

Amir: Hi, Sam. Sorry, but I don't think I am going to make it after all.

Sam: Oh, that's a shame. Are you okay? You don't sound too good.

Amir: I'm all right, but to be honest the job searching is starting to get me down a bit. It's been about a month now and still no joy.

Sam: I know how you feel. It's horrible when you're searching. I was absolutely miserable when I was looking for my job. It's hard, but you only need one lucky break and everything changes.

Amir: Yes, but it's so slow... I'm starting to doubt I'll ever get anything.

Sam: Where are you looking?

Amir: I'm registered on all the generic employment websites so they should send me an alert when any new library-related post comes up. I also look on local government and university websites and social networking sites too. I just don't know where else I can look!

Sam: Yes, I know what you mean, but do you remember when Jamie and I finished the course? He got a job really quickly because he sent his CV to every library within a twenty mile radius!

Amir: Did he really? Did that work?

Sam: It certainly did! Actually, it was incredible! His own local library needed someone to do a few hours a week and they had just been about to advertise. He had to submit a formal application and go for an interview with other applicants. I think he got the job in the end though because he had impressed them early on by seeming so keen and enterprising.

Amir: That's made me think, Sam. In the long-term I would obviously prefer a permanent, full-time post, but anything would be great right now: temporary, part-time, seasonal, whatever. I just need to get some experience before I forget all I have learned.

Sam: Yes, it's such a tricky situation, isn't it? You can't get a job because you have no experience and you can't get experience because you have no job!

Amir: That's about the sum of it!

Sam: What you learned from the course work will stay with you Amir, so don't panic about that. Another thing to bear in mind is that they are not going to put you in charge of anything at the start, so you can ask questions and take a bit of time to find your feet. Jamie and I can help you too.

Amir: That's true, but I am not at that stage yet. I think I will make a list of suitable organisations and send out speculative applications right now.

Sam: Good idea! Oh, and if you feel any brighter and decide to come tonight, Jamie has another friend coming too, Katy. She has a fantastic job as an information officer for a newspaper in Newcastle. They met at a conference. This would be a chance for you to do a bit of networking!

Amir: Thanks, Sam! I really should come, shouldn't I? Isn't it strange that we have all ended up going into the same field in the end?

Sam: Well, I suppose it's not that strange since we all studied Arts degrees in the first place... but I know what you mean.

Amir: We kind of already have a network, don't we?

Sam: Yes, Jamie is definitely the most skilled at networking though! He's a natural, a real people person.

Amir: He sure is, but watch and learn is what I say! See you tonight!

Sam: Great! Bye now!

Q2: (about) a month

Q3: (one / a) lucky break

Q4: a, b, e

Q5: b) False

Q6: a) True

Q7: a) True

Q8: c) both studied arts at university.

Q9: a) Kind and supportive

Reading activity: Job interviews (page 168)

Q10: a) True

Q11: b) False

Q12: b) False

Q13: b) False

Q14: a) True

Q15: a) True

Q16: c/d/e

Q17: b) Answering too quickly and without judgement

Q18: b) well prepared.

Q19: c) both inform and entertain.

Post-reading activity: Vocabulary: Definitions (page 170)

Q20:

a) Fierce

b) Laid off

c) Stage fright

d) Disclosing

e) Instantaneous

f) Disparaging

g) Embellish

h) Remuneration

i) Tactful

j) Body swerves

Syllables and word stress (page 172)

Q21:

Word	Syllables and word stress
e.g. Career	oO
Disclosing	oOo
Instantaneous	ooOoo
Disparaging	oOoo
Embellish	oOo
Remuneration	oooOo

Listening comprehension: Interview feedback (page 172)

Listening transcript

a) *Roseanne:* Hi, Tim. Thank you so much for coming in to see me today. I was hoping that I would have a chance to talk to you before the end of the week. I think it's important to have feedback while the interview is still fresh in our minds. How are you?

b) *Tim:* I am fine thanks, a little disappointed of course, not to have been selected for the permanent position, but that goes without saying.

c) *Roseanne:* Yes, of course. Can I just say that I was delighted you applied for the post? However, as you know, we had a lot of applicants and I'm afraid that the position was finally offered to someone with more experience than you have at the moment. Well, we can discuss the interview and try to work out if there are any areas which could be improved upon for future applications and interviews.

d) *Tim:* Okay

e) *Roseanne:* Which aspects of the interview do you think seemed to go well, Tim?

f) *Tim:* I think it got better as I went on. I was a little nervous and I think that I got muddled up at the start of my presentation.

g) *Roseanne:* You did a bit, but that is perfectly understandable in the circumstances. Nerves can get the better of us.

h) *Tim:* Yes, but I was annoyed with myself because I am generally good in presentations and that hiccup got me off to a bad start. I think I probably messed up a couple of questions as a result.

i) *Roseanne:* Did you get a chance to prepare much for the interview?

j) *Tim:* Well, that's just it. My brother and his girlfriend arrived to stay with me last week. They have been staying in my flat, which is tiny, and I have had no time or privacy at all. It's not their fault, just one of those things.

k) *Roseanne:* Well, that is unfortunate, Tim.

l) *Tim:* Yes, and there were a couple of questions about the company that I couldn't answer. I just wasn't expecting that kind of question at all. I thought it would just be about me and my background and experience.

m) *Roseanne:* Hmm... So what do you feel you can take away from this experience?

n) *Tim:* For one thing, I will discourage my brother from visiting me when I have an interview pending...

o) *Roseanne:* Yes, quite.

p) *Tim:* ... and I have learned that I should do a bit more research so that I can answer questions about the organisation as well as about my own potential contribution.

q) *Roseanne:* I would like to say at this point that I think you show a lot of promise, Tim. With more experience, you could make a strong contribution to our team. I also hope that you will continue to work for us for the foreseeable future. However, I would suggest that you engage in some professional development. Firstly, do some shadowing of other employees in the company. You could take advantage of the shadowing scheme we have, which is open to temporary staff as well as those on permanent contracts. This will give you an overview and that will help ensure that you are not thrown by questions aimed at establishing organisational knowledge.

r) *Tim:* Okay. I thought you had to be a permanent staff member for that.

s) *Roseanne:* Not at all. I suggest you get a shadow placement or two in the diary as soon as possible. I will meet with you as part of our professional development programme in 12 weeks and see how you are getting on.

t) *Tim:* Thanks, Roseanne. That sounds good.

u) *Roseanne*: Do you have any other questions, Tim?

v) *Tim:* I would just like to ask if there are likely to be any vacancies coming up for permanent staff in the near future. It would be great to feel that I have some security and that I really am part of the team.

w) *Roseanne*: Things change all the time and we can't tell how the business will look in six months' time. That's why I am suggesting that you make sure you utilise your time now in the most effective way, so that you are really well prepared should anything else arise unexpectedly.

x) *Tim*: Okay, yes… that sounds like a good idea.

y) *Roseanne:* Good. So, to sum up, we have identified a need for wider knowledge of the organisation to be achieved in the first instance through shadowing. We also recognised a need for more thorough planning and preparation prior to interview. Finally, we have arranged to meet again in 12 weeks. Good to see you Tim. I look forward to our next appointment.

z) *Tim:* Thanks very much for your time and your feedback. I feel much more positive now!

Q22:

1. give feedback
2. (a little) disappointed
3. more experience

Q23: a) True

Q24: b) False

Q25: a) True

Q26: b) False

Q27: b) False

Q28: C. Underprepared and inexperienced

Q29: A. offers Tim support

Reading comprehension: Volunteering and internships (page 174)

Q30:

1. qualifications and experience
2. negotiate
3. beneficial
4. (an element of) structure
5. (sufficiently) well-organised

Q31: competitive

Q32: induction

Q33: dividends

Q34: underused

Q35: C

Topic 3: Communication

Listening activity (page 178)

Listening transcript

a) I couldn't go to work this morning, I had an absolutely blinding headache - it was so bad I had to lie down in a darkened room. I haven't had a migraine for months.

b) Sasha and I were both really sick after eating out on Saturday. It was awful, the pain was a nasty cramping type of pain which came in waves. We would feel better for a bit but then it would come back again. I'm never eating in Toni's again!

c) Amir suffers chronic neck and shoulder pain. It seems to go with the territory, you know, working with a computer all day, not taking enough breaks and so on. The doctor says it is repetitive strain injury. Today he says his entire upper body is aching.

d) We had such a drama at the weekend. I was with Laura when all of a sudden she started complaining about a sharp pain in her side. She said it was excruciating! We had to rush her into the Accident and Emergency ward at the hospital. The doctor said she had a kidney stone. Apparently that can cause these acute symptoms.

e) We had a really good holiday but unfortunately I had to make an unplanned trip to the dentist. I had been having an occasional, mild twinge in one of my teeth but I just ignored it thinking it would go away. My goodness! Did I suffer when the aircraft took off?! The tooth started pounding... it was really quite severe. Luckily I was given some painkillers by the cabin crew.

f) Hi, mum! I'm a bit worried, I have been getting shooting pains in my stomach all afternoon but because it's intermittent I keep thinking I've recovered. I think I've got that bug all the other students have had. I have an essay to write today. What do you think I should do?

g) I was just chatting to Denise in the garden when suddenly I felt a sharp, stinging pain in my hand and then it seemed to radiate up my arm. The actual area felt quite numb after that and I felt faint. I think it was a bee sting.

h) My boss has been unable to use the computer all week because she managed to jam her index finger in the door. She says it is absolutely throbbing!

i) My brother has perforated his ear drum. He said it was really horrible at the start with a piercing pain that lasted until he got some strong pain relief. He said that later it subsided and became more of a dull ache.

Post listening activity: Vocabulary (page 178)

Q1:

Word	Category	Word	Category
Aching	Quality	Numbness	Quality
Acute	Duration	Piercing	Quality
Blinding	Quality	Pounding	Quality
Chronic	Duration	Severe	Intensity
Cramping	Quality	Sharp	Quality
Dull	Intensity	Shooting	Quality
Excruciating	Intensity	Stinging	Quality
Intermittent	Duration	Throbbing	Quality
Mild	Intensity	Twinge	Quality

Reading comprehension: RSI (page 179)

Q2: desk-bound

Q3: symptoms may escalate

Q4: minimise the impact

Q5: Precautionary

Q6: Implemented

Q7: Ergonomics

Q8: Paramount

Q9: adjustments to equipment / changes in behaviour

Q10: a and c

Q11: a) an article form a newspaper or magazine.

Tense review (page 181)

Listening transcript

Theresa: Hi Jack. Good to see you. How are you?

Jack: I am really well, thanks. How are you?

Theresa: Great! I'm so happy now that I have started working for myself. It has been an amazing, positive change in my life.

Jack: I can imagine! Let's order some coffee and you can tell me all about it... So, how's it going?

Theresa: I absolutely love it. Obviously it is early days, but at the moment I am treating about five patients regularly and I have had thirty additional appointments so far this month. I am over the moon.

Jack: So do you have to pay someone for the use of the room?

Theresa: Yes, the salon has a couple of therapists doing reflexology and nail treatments so I have the room three days a week and they have a couple of days each. It's fantastic because the landlord of the property has asked me to pay a flat rate, as opposed to charging a percentage on each patient. As soon as I have covered his charge, I am earning a profit. It's so exciting!

Jack: That's wonderful! And, it's been what... about four months now?

Theresa: Yes, exactly. It hasn't all been plain sailing. The first month was really frightening. I was worrying constantly because I just couldn't be sure it would take off. Already though, through word of mouth, I have been getting more customers and repeat business is also keeping me going. It seems callous to say it, but we massage therapists are really benefitting from workplace stress. If I had known then what I know now, I wouldn't have been so worried.

Jack: Hindsight is a wonderful thing.

Theresa: But I am not going to become complacent. After all, you never know what's around the corner. I think I'll allow myself to relax a little if I get through a couple of years like this, but not before! Anyway enough about me, how are you?

Jack: Well, I am planning a small adventure of my own at the moment.

Theresa: Really? What are you up to?

Jack: I am taking a year out of work to go travelling in South America. I leave in three weeks. How does that sound?

Theresa: Seriously, Jack?! That's just amazing! Good for you!

Q12:

a. I **have started** working	4. Present perfect simple
b. I **am treating**	5. Present continuous
c. The first month **was** really frightening	9. Past simple
d. I **was worrying**	7. Past continuous
e. I **have been getting**	8. Present perfect continuous
f. If I **had known** then	3. Past perfect
g. I **am not going to be** complacent	2. Going to future (plan)
h. I'**ll allow** myself	1. Will future (spontaneous utterance)
i. I **leave** in three weeks	6. Present simple for future arrangement

Writing: Health and safety (page 182)

Model answer

Dear Ms Shanks

I am writing to you in the hope that you might be able to assist me in finding a solution to a problem which has become more pressing over the last couple of months.

I have become aware of some unpleasant symptoms which I think are associated with the need to use a computer at work more often than in the past. The main symptoms are muscle pain in my back, neck and shoulders. The symptoms are worse in the right shoulder which probably reflects the fact that I am right-handed and use the mouse with my right hand. At times I experience quite severe pain which often includes a blinding headache as well. The location of my workstation is perhaps an issue. As you know, my desk and computer are located at the back of the office. I therefore suffer from a lack of light which might be contributing to my headaches as I often have to strain to see my computer screen.

I should be pleased if you would instruct a health and safety inspection of my working area together with an analysis of my computer use. In this way it might be possible to pinpoint the cause of my pain and perhaps make the changes necessary to alleviate the symptoms.

Kind regards

Julie Adam

221 words

Listening comprehension: Healthy Working Lives (page 183)

Listening transcript

Marie: Good afternoon. This is Marie Evans, with you this afternoon from two until four, during which time we will be continuing with our Healthy Working Lives series. My guest today is Parvin Abbasi, lecturer in Health and Safety at East College, who will be talking to us about legislation around abnormal working patterns. Welcome to the show, Parvin.

Parvin: Thank you, Marie. Marie: To start with, I wonder if we could ask you to define the term, 'abnormal', with respect to working hours, if you would?

Parvin: Yes, of course. Perhaps we should think about what constitutes normal working hours first of all. We understand normal working hours as hours which include a time for work and a defined rest period, which essentially means working in the daytime and resting at night. Abnormal hours, on the other hand, would be understood as hours which vary from this basic pattern. This would include night shifts or an extension of normal hours, like overtime.

Marie: How many of us work abnormal hours, Parvin?

Parvin: According to a report published by the British Medical Journal, one in five workers in Europe is a shift worker, while one in twenty Europeans has extended working hours which involve doing more than 48 hours of work in a given week.

Marie: We hear a lot of discussion about technology and the increase in consumer demand. Is the demand for goods and services having an impact on the number of people required to work abnormal hours?

Parvin: Consumer demand is part of the problem, but working abnormal hours is by no means a new phenomenon. If we consider the medical service for example, and other areas often described as essential, these organisations have been obliged to provide a 24 hour service for a long time now. We have also become used to the provision of nonessential services outside normal hours. Supplies of bread and milk have traditionally arrived at our local shops and at our doors in the early hours of the morning. In terms of current demands however, with our more sophisticated technology there is a greater need to provide a twenty-four hour service in areas which have historically been nine to five.

Marie: What are the issues around variable working patterns and abnormal hours? Are we more likely to suffer health problems?

Parvin: There has been a great deal of research into this issue but unfortunately it can sometimes be difficult to draw conclusions. The reasons for this are that shift workers have often chosen their pattern rather than having it forced upon them, so they are perhaps biased in favour of variable hours. At the same time, those who are available for study are what the BMJ refers to as 'survivors' of the varied shift pattern, so when looking at the data collected from them, one has to take that factor into account.

Marie: What kind of issues have emerged?

Parvin: Well, perhaps the most obvious and well documented problem is the disruption of circadian rhythms. This is a consequence of swapping night for day when people do nightshift. The circadian rhythms are related to our sleeping and eating patterns as well as bodily maintenance and repair. They influence hormones and cell repair. We do not know exactly how the disruption of circadian rhythms affects us. What we do know is that sleep patterns are one area negatively affected by changes in working patterns. Shift workers sleep fewer hours and their sleep is of poorer quality.

Marie: Could this be a cause of accidents at work?

Parvin: It could affect concentration and lead to errors, that's a real possibility.

Marie: And, I am sure there are other problems too?

Parvin: Yes, indeed. Many shift workers complain about feeling tired and report feeling isolated, depressed and stressed. However, we cannot necessarily take this at face value. We have to consider that those who are drawn to certain patterns of work may be the type of people who are prone to symptoms such as depression and stress already. Furthermore, stress is very difficult to measure.

Marie: Do employees have any rights in this area?

Parvin: The 1993 European Directive on Working Hours has clear guidelines showing what employers are legally obliged to offer in terms of minimum rest periods, time off, leave and also health checks. Employees affected should acquaint themselves with this literature. Employers nowadays are generally well aware of their responsibilities in this respect and many do try to shape rotas in order to support staff. Nevertheless, it is important for staff to really look into what hours they are working and the effects these hours are having on them. It is vital as well to seek help where necessary.

Marie: Thank you so much for talking to us today, Parvin.

Parvin: Thank you.

Q13: night shift / extension of normal

Q14: one in five / one in twenty

Q15: nonessential services

Q16: True

Q17: False

Q18: True

Q19: True

Q20: C

Reading comprehension: Accident and incident report form (page 185)

Q21: incident / accident

Q22: take matters forward

Q23: ignore this instruction

Q24: feedback

Q25: stooped

Q26: radiating

Q27: self-preservation

Q28: A

Q29: B

Q30: C

Topic 4: Working with others

Pre-reading activity: Collocations (page 190)

Q1: a-7, b-3, c-6, d-8, e-10, f-9, g-5, h-1, i-4, j-2

Pre-reading activity: Definitions (page 191)

Q2: a-6, b-10, c-4, d-7, e-3, f-9, g-1, h-5, i-8, j-2

Reading activity: Internet politics (page 191)

Q3: a) Newspaper or magazine article

Q4: 1-f, 2-d, 3-a, 4-g, 5-c, 6-e, 7-b

Q5: can be damning

Q6: computer savvy

Q7: lurker

Q8: overlooked for jobs or promotion

Q9: b) advise.

Listening activity: Note taking (page 193)

Listening transcript

Presenter: Good morning and welcome to this afternoon's Work Life Balance. Our guests today are Brian Jonas, management consultant, whom we welcome all the way from Philadelphia following the publication of his new book: *Open the door, free the mind and connect.* We also welcome Julie Allan, freelance graphic designer for Pronto, a company who publish educational materials. We will be considering the isolation of private offices and working from home versus the open plan workplace and how this affects employees today. If I can turn to you first Brian, born and brought up in Scotland you find yourself living, working and lately, writing in Philadelphia. Can you tell us about your new book?

Brian: Good morning. Well, as the title of my book suggests, I am a great believer in collaboration. I believe that some of our best ideas, in fields as disparate as science and art emerge through conversations with others. My own experience as a senior manager has led me to the view that sitting alone in an office is one of the most stultifying experiences one can have. It can also be a disabling experience in my opinion. Managers and others in lonely offices fall out of step with fellow staff and as a result miss out on much of the necessary social stimulation which leads to creative thought. While researching my book, I spoke to hundreds of office workers and found that even just leaving the house to go to work is one of the most uplifting parts of the day for many people. The social contact which starts when we say 'good morning' to fellow human beings is incredibly undervalued in society today.

Presenter: Brian, do you think that this is a cultural phenomenon? Was your research carried out exclusively in the United States? I am thinking now about the archetypal grumpy British workman versus the American wishing everyone 'Have a nice day!'

Brian: My research was carried out in both in the US and in the UK. As a Scotsman myself I understand the British reserve but I think that being shy and retiring is quite different from choosing a life of isolation. Technology, remote access and working from home all sound great in theory. In my view though, only a particular type of person can cope with this kind of work.

Presenter: Let me bring in Julie Allan at this point. Julie you have been involved in publishing for over fifteen years and you have recently opted to set up an office at home. Is this a choice you made to fit in with family or do you feel you are more creative at home?

Julie: Very much the latter, Amy. In terms of family I don't have children to support so I have no childcare issues. I think having young children sometimes encourages people to try to work from home. My situation, on the other hand, is that I have tried both working in an office and working at home and in my experience the benefits of home working far outweigh the drawbacks. I do agree with Brian to a certain extent insofar as I accept that people can very easily become isolated at home, but I think there are ways to counter this. The workplaces which I have most experience in have tended to be open plan with open door policies. I simply find this environment counterproductive. I think if you do creative work which involves thinking quite deeply about something then you need peace and quiet. It becomes quite impossible to achieve anything at all in an open plan office. There are endless interruptions, not just from colleagues chatting but also from managers and meetings. Some people like to collaborate constantly and this means a lot of discussion about projects. I accept that discussion is useful but I think this has to be formalised and happen at specific times and places.

Brian: I hear what you are saying Julie, but creative thought cannot be scheduled into a planned meeting. I would argue that it's the spontaneous exchange which often leads to great ideas.

Julie: Sorry Brian, I have to disagree. The endless chatter in workrooms is totally disruptive and makes concentrating impossible. Even if someone did have a breakthrough as a consequence of casual conversation, this would be quite rare. To my mind, having good ideas and executing them is far more likely to happen in a quiet place.

Presenter: We'll take a break now for some music. If you have any thoughts on this issue please get in touch on our phone lines or by email. In the meantime, I would like to thank my guests Brian and Julie for starting such an interesting debate.

Q10:

a. Management consultant / graphic consultant, b. Main topic of discussion: Working at home or alone in an office vs. working in an open plan office

a. They agree that those working at home or alone in an office can become isolated, b. Brian thinks that open plan offices and collaboration is the best way to generate ideas while Julie thinks that ideas evolve in peaceful moments.

Q11: a. management consultant, b. conversations with others, c. social contact, d. isolation, e. graphic designer, f. working from home, g. benefits, h. counterproductive, i. peace and quiet, j. interrupted, k. managers and meetings, l. spontaneous exchanges, m. quiet place

Writing: Staff event (page 194)

Model answer

Introduction

The purpose of this report is to present feedback on the staff event held on February 20th. The event was attended by 350 people in total. Forty staff from our section were present. The findings presented here are based on discussion and feedback forms.

Speakers

The day began with a whole staff event. Guest lecturer, Lindsay Davis, this year's leader of the year in the category of Business Communications at the UK Business awards, is an accomplished speaker. She gave a very inspiring presentation on team building in the age of technology, focusing on virtual communication. A motivational closing speech was given by our deputy director of Sales and Marketing.

Activities

In the afternoon we attended workshops and events chosen in advance from a range of twenty options. Informal discussion suggested that some of these were considered more useful than others. Staff members felt that there should have been more emphasis on practical skills.

Catering

The catering was a resounding success. It was felt that the lunch and array of snacks were first class. This was supported by comments in feedback forms.

Venue

People liked the hotel but some thought it was rather inaccessible and that parking facilities were quite limited.

Conclusion

Overall, staff found the event useful and enjoyable. Lindsay Davis was particularly well received and staff enjoyed meeting other team members.

226 words

Reading comprehension: Team building (page 195)

Q12: standard practice

Q13: obvious relevance or practical application

Q14: promote problem solving in groups

Q15: clause in her (initial) contract

Q16: professional updating opportunity

Q17: coerced

Q18: anecdotal

Q19: decline

Q20: scrapped

Q21: Fun is a subjective/personal experience

Q22: The writer has both positive and negative feelings about team building events

Q23: b) light-hearted.

Listening comprehension: Training course (page 197)

Listening transcript

Tina: Hi Jane! How are you doing? How was your weekend?

Jane: Very lazy indeed! How are you? What did you get up to?

Tina: I saw some friends on Saturday but yesterday I stayed home all afternoon cleaning and tidying. It all looks much better now thankfully.

Jane: Oh dear. I hate housework, don't you? Tina: Yes, but I was listening to some things on my computer at the same time so the time passed really quickly. I had some music on and then I found some really interesting lectures. They were about work and I thought they might help when I start the new management training course. In fact, I'll give you the links so you can listen too before you start your course. Anyway there was one lecture I particularly enjoyed which was called, "How we interact in groups". Actually I had a tea break to listen to this one!

Jane: What was it about?

Tina: Well, it was about introversion and extroversion. The speaker was talking about the idea that in our culture and society today, the extrovert is more highly valued than the introvert. The speaker was saying that it is almost embarrassing to admit to introverted behaviour, you know, like being happy to spend time alone. She said the culture of personality, which is widespread today, probably reflects the movement away from agriculture to big business. I'm kind of simplifying what she said, but basically she said that we now focus highly on group work in schools and workplaces and that this emphasis suits the extrovert rather than the introvert. The introvert needs time alone to think. The speaker also said that the extrovert makes the most noise and talks a lot but doesn't necessarily have good ideas. The extrovert is just very good at getting people to listen to their thoughts.

Jane: Okay. So what do you think you are Tina, introverted or extroverted?

Tina: Well, I think I am a mixture of both but I think it's important as a manager to consider the makeup of your staff.

Jane: Hmm, yes, that's really interesting. I think I am quite introverted. I have always liked spells of solitude but on the other hand I like company too. I am probably mixed like you.

Tina: I think we are quite alike in that respect. I like a balance. I have been thinking about our team. We have quite a range of different personality types among us. I was wondering if there might be benefits in changing the way we do staff development so that we can bring out the best in everyone. We should also think about our office space, in terms of layout. I feel we are forcing people to sit in groups all the time and I think this could be undermining. We would have to run things past Alison, of course, as she is team leader, but I am sure she would be supportive.

Jane: Maybe we should do some research on this first? I mean, it wouldn't cost anything to change the furniture and it could dramatically change how people feel about work as well as what they achieve. I do think that we need to work on managing the noise level. It can be quite unbearable sometimes. Would you like me to get a questionnaire written up and distributed, to find out how people feel about the layout?

Tina: Yes that would be great, Jane. I would appreciate it.

Jane: I'll get started on that this morning then and let you know what feedback I get. I think if we can get some individual workstations in place we could revolutionise the office.

Tina: Yes, although it'll be a disaster if everyone wants to sit alone though, won't it?

Jane: Not necessarily... mind you, if we have to resort to rows it could start to feel like school!

Q24: training course

Q25: introversion and extroversion

Q26: time alone

Q27: have good ideas

Q28: mix

Q29: B/C

Q30: A: True, B: True, C: False

Answers to questions and activities for Unit 3

Topic 1: Learning in context

Business words (page 202)

Q1:

1. product
2. price
3. brand
4. market research
5. promotion
6. development
7. advertising
8. public relations
9. consumer
10. distribution

Defining business terms (page 202)

Q2: 1-e, 2-a, 3-d, 4-j, 5-c, 6-I, 7-f, 8-g, 9-h, 10-b

How I became a businessman (page 203)

Q3:

Having studied for four years as an **1) undergraduate** in order to gain my degree in teaching, I soon learned that in the real **2) world**, once the day to day satisfaction starts to wean, the career prospects and opportunities for climbing the **3) ladder** are limited for all but the elite few. Teaching had been my **4) vocation** for several years though, and I was **5) concerned** about allowing my dissatisfaction to lead me down a different career path which may prove to be a disaster. But it was one morning around that time, when I was **6) scanning** a newspaper article, something **7) caught** my eye, and I decided I had to find out more.

I had been searching for a way to be my own **8) boss**. That was part of the problem. Teaching had given me a sense of **9) responsibility** for others, but I never really felt in control of my own **10) destiny**. This advertisement was calling out to me - 'How to start your own **11) firm**: 3 easy steps to a new life'.

I have to admit, it sounded too good to be **12) true**, so I approached the idea with caution and low **13) expectations**. However, having answered the advert and signed up for the course, I realised that I had a lot more **14) drive** to succeed in business than I ever had as a teacher.

Within three months, the training **15) programme** had helped me set up my own **16) company**, doing something that I had always enjoyed but never realised I could do professionally: photography.

Four years on, I now **17) employ** two members of staff to assist me, and the company has **18) products** and services to cover all kinds of occasions, from children's portraits to wedding packages. Thanks to the internet, we have increased our distribution network and even had a few international

19) clients who have used our services, and this has meant travel to places such as Paris, Rome and Budapest.

Would I go back to teaching? No. I realise now that it wasn't for me. The course brought out the **20) entrepreneur** in me, and I am doing things now in my new career that I would otherwise only have been dreaming of.

Language of business meetings (page 204)

Q4:

1. Opening the meeting
2. Welcomes/Introductions
3. Outlining the Agenda
4. Moving the meeting forward
5. Concluding

Choosing appropriate language in business meetings (page 205)

Q5:

Opening a meeting

- Good morning, ladies and gentlemen.
- Is everyone present? Let's get underway.
- May I begin by welcoming you all to our monthly update. . .

Welcomes/Introductions

- We're delighted to have Alex Smith with us today.
- If we could go around the table and just state who we are and what department we work in. . .
- My name is Michael Lane and I'm pleased to welcome you all to Optec Computers.

Outlining the Agenda

- The reason we are here today is to discuss. . .
- Is everyone happy with the order of the points of discussion?
- Let's get down to business. Point one. . .

Moving the meeting forward

- Any comments on what Jim has outlined there? No? That brings us to. . .
- Next up is an outline of the costs. We turn to Sally for this. . .
- Distribution is the third topic we have to cover today. . .

Concluding

- Let's quickly summarise the main points.
- If nobody has anything to add, that will do it for today.
- Is there any other business to be discussed?

Pre-listening activity: Vocabulay: Definitions (page 206)

Q6: 1-k, 2-g, 3-l, 4-f, 5-b, 6-e, 7-a, 8-j, 9-h, 10-l, 11-d, 12-c

A business meeting (page 206)

Listening transcript

Assistant to Chief Executive (Colin): Good morning, ladies and gentlemen. May I begin by welcoming you all to our weekly update. If we could go around the table and just state who we are and what department we work in then we can proceed.

Jason: My name is Jason Whiteside and I am senior manager in sales.

Anne: Anne Davidson, senior brand manager.

Daniel: Daniel Jones, senior marketing executive.

Colin: The reason we are here today is to discuss the recent launch of our latest E-reader, look at the response in terms of consumer and media interest, and decide on the next step in our campaign. Is everyone happy with the order of the points of discussion? Good... then let's get down to business. Point one, the launch... Daniel, how did the launch go?

Daniel: We were delighted with the response last week in terms of both consumer and media interest. We had an unprecedented turnout, in terms of numbers, and we received reviews the following day in no fewer than six national newspapers, with the response being reasonably positive in each.

Colin: What do you mean by 'reasonably', Daniel?

Daniel: Well, it has to be said the technology writer in UK Today was lukewarm in praise of the E-reader, since he said this model does not add to the earlier version significantly. However, he had also listed the key features of each model and the length of the list itemising our latest model was clearly longer, so his words were a bit of a contradiction. We are pleased that we managed to pitch to the key players and we got the coverage that we wanted. I think we will see that this has already borne fruit, in terms of sales to early adopters.

Anne: If I could just come in at this point and say we have been particularly careful with this product. We have really focussed on the uniqueness of this particular brand. We were expecting this kind of reaction because this is always the burning question with a new model of any existing brand but, as Daniel says, the list of enhanced features speaks for itself.

Colin: Okay... sales team, can you give us your figures please?

Jason: Yes, as you can see from the board here, we have had a good response from early adopters despite the financial climate. The line in blue shows our new model E-Reader, 'Relax', while the red one shows 'E-Reader 3'. As we all know, the economy is not as strong as when we launched our earlier model so the red line does show slightly higher sales at this point in the campaign. In the next four weeks, with the run up to Christmas, we expect this to change and show a significant leap in sales.

Colin: Daniel, where are we going next?

Daniel: The new advertisement will be running as of midday today and the promotion in major bookshops will start tomorrow, so this is phase two of the campaign. Apart from that, I think we

© HERIOT-WATT UNIVERSITY

carry on with what we have been doing and watch this thing grow.

Colin: Outstanding work, everyone! Any comments on what has been outlined? No? That brings us to the end of this morning's agenda. Let's quickly summarise the main points: We have experienced a good response from the media; a cautious remark from one newspaper to be expected. Consumers seem impressed. In comparison to our figures during the launch of 'E-Reader 3', we have a slightly lower uptake from early adopters but, given the state of the economy, we are satisfied with progress so far and expect to see a boost in sales nearer Christmas. The brand seems to offer enough originality to separate it from earlier versions. We now await the TV ad and further promotion to kick in. Is there any other business to be discussed? Let's finish for now and meet again same time, same place next week. Thank you for coming along today.

Q7:

   a) Sales, marketing and brands.

   b) Media and consumer response to the launch of a product, sales figures, next stage of the campaign.

Q8: a) True

Q9: b) False

Q10: a) True

Q11: b) False

Q12: b) False

Q13: a) True

Q14:

- The economy.
- Pitching to important people.

Q15:

- A TV advert/advertisement.
- A promotion at bookstores.

Business reports (page 208)

Sample answer

Western University - Technology Upgrade: Report

This report aims to assess the current technology available on campus and suggest improvements which could be made through upgrades. Recommendations will be presented, including estimated costs and potential disruption to staff and students.

Existing Technology: At present, the university has 610 desktop PCs and 200 laptop PCs. The library contains 300 desktop PCs and the Flexible Learning Unit, another student facility, has an additional 100 PCs. The remaining computers are in staffrooms around the university campus. In addition to computers, there are other types of equipment such as interactive whiteboards which are new and do not need upgrading.

Potential Upgrades: Most of the university's PCs are over five years old. As a result they are slow to start up and incompatible with the latest software. This is having a detrimental effect on student morale and on course work. Some staff have also complained that many of their laptops, purchased almost a decade ago, are now obsolete. It is recommended that we purchase 200 tablet computers to replace the aging laptops for staff, and invest in at least 200 new desktop PCs for student use in the library.

Costs and Time frame: Changes can be phased in over the next twelve months during holiday periods. Further new student PCs can be added next academic year. The estimated total cost for the upgrades will be £120,000. However, it may be possible to recoup approximately 10% of the outlay by selling our old computers to small businesses in the area.

248 words

Business vocabulary (page 209)

Q16:

- Asset
- Commerce
- Contract
- Director
- Overhead
- Profit
- Purchase
- Recruitment
- Sales force
- Slogan
- Stock
- Union

Definitions (page 210)

Q17: 1-i, 2-f, 3-a, 4-g, 5-b, 6-l, 7-c, 8-j, 9-k, 10-e, 11-h, 12-d

Creating sentences (page 210)

Sample sentences

Sample answer sentences are:

a) The new product is going to become the company's biggest asset in the European market.

b) New York remains the USA's centre of commerce.

c) All new employees have to sign and date their contracts.

d) The director resigned hastily when she was caught with the petty cash in her bank account.

e) Transport and other logistical costs will be the biggest overhead we'll have.

f) It looks like the profit we made in Japan will be lost in Canada.

g) Mike is responsible for all the pet food purchases in our European factories.

h) Michelle in HR is responsible for most of the recruitment in this company.

i) Glaxxon are thinking about expanding their sales force. I might apply.

j) We need a new company slogan. "Buy our stuff" just isn't good enough.

k) The majority of our stock is held in warehouses all over India.

l) If you're going to work in this place, my advice is to join the union immediately!

(page 211)

Q18:

e.g. business	Oo
asset	Oo
commerce	Oo
contract	Oo
director	oOo
overhead	Ooo
purchase	Oo
recruitment	oOo
slogan	Oo
union	Oo
advertising	Oooo
consumer	oOo
distribution	ooOo

Reading comprehension: Tax (page 212)

Q19: a. A tabloid newspaper article

Q20:

a) True
b) True
c) False

Q21: cooking the books

Q22: the man in the street

Q23: (the) tip of the iceberg

Q24: a. Slightly biased against the large companies

Listening comprehension: Advertising (page 214)

Listening transcript
How to land a career in Advertising

I'm delighted to have been asked here today to share my experiences with all of you. It may seem a long way off at the moment, but less than three years from now you will find yourself out there in the big, bad world, looking to get a foothold in your chosen career. I would like to begin today by focussing on the two main ways you can get yourself into the advertising industry - agencies and in-house opportunities.

Most major cities in this country have several communications agencies. As the UK's largest city and business hub, London is still where the major companies are located, but that does not mean that there are no good agencies in other parts of the country. Some of the major advertising agencies have regional offices outside of London and many of them offer internships for promising graduates. I actually started out as an intern myself, fifteen years ago now, initially working in a small branch of a major company in York, learning the trade until I was sufficiently experienced and confident enough to apply for a promoted post in London a few years later.

Things have changed a lot since I entered the industry as well. That's one of the most exciting parts of the job - adjusting to, and exploiting, the new methods of communication before your competitors. The internet on a global scale was in its infancy when I started out, but now you are in the fortunate position of being able to apply to a variety of different communications agencies specialising in a multitude of media, such as social media, mobile advertising, as well as the more traditional kinds like PR and direct marketing. You just need to do the research yourself and always try to match up your strengths, your skills set, with the most appropriate available positions. If you have excellent skills in social networking, demonstrate the benefits of this to an employer at interview.

Often, people enter careers in advertising from other fields. Working as part of a design or manufacture team can often have crossover value, and although all of you here today will undoubtedly have a head start with your degree, most agencies are looking for new recruits who, above all else, have excellent communicative skills and a positive, determined attitude.

Advertising is one of the careers in which the job interview really can go for or against you in the first thirty seconds. You have to be extremely confident in yourself while being likeable and coming across as both knowledgeable and capable. Whoever interviews you will probably be able to see if you have these qualities from the way you answer the first question. If you have these attributes, you will also need a working knowledge of who is doing what in advertising just now. Don't be caught out because you're banking solely on your winning smile or charm and persuasiveness. Be informed too. Have your own ideas and opinions. Above all else, be persistent and don't let rejections prevent you from realising your dreams. You need a thick skin to work in this industry, but it is worth it.

Thanks again to all of you and your tutor for inviting me along today. Now I'll be happy to try and answer any of your questions. So speak up and be brave!

Q25: b. It is the main centre of commerce and advertising companies

Q26: a. Discovering new ideas before others

Q27: c. Had limited use of the internet

Q28:

a) excellent communicative skills

b) a positive, determined attitude

Q29:

a) False

b) False

c) True

d) True

Q30: b. An advertising executive

Q31: c. Undergraduate students

Topic 2: Further education

Approaches to education (page 218)

Q1: 1-d, 2-a, 3-e, 4-b, 5-c

Educational definitions (page 219)

Q2: 1-e, 2-j, 3-b, 4-c, 5-h, 6-l, 7-a, 8-f, 9-d, 10-g

Pre-Reading: Steiner - a very particular school (page 219)

Q3: b) No

Q4:

a) Philosophy: All the needs of a child should be addressed. This means: academic, physical, emotional and spiritual needs.

b) Approach to learning: Steiner identified three stages of development in children, all of which he believed should be nurtured. In the early years of childhood the focus is on play and there is an emphasis on learning through activities. The middle years around age 9-14 concentrate on the artistic imagination, while in adolescence developing intellectual understanding and critical thinking are stressed.

c) Organisation: Decisions around learning and teaching are likely to be the responsibility of a group of experienced teachers. Financial and legal issues concerning the schools would probably be the responsibility of a group of trustees.

d) Subject matter: A main lesson of around two hours in which all academic subjects except languages would be taught. Languages are introduced at an early stage in Steiner schools and taught by specialist teachers. Story-telling and craft also feature prominently. The potential of seasons and seasonal festivals is maximised to provide opportunities for learning and teaching.

e) Emphasis: Creativity and spirituality

f) Criticisms of the school: Emphasis on creativity and spirituality could be at the expense of intellectual and scientific pursuits. Some are also suspicious of Steiner's belief in Anthroposophy, a spiritual path that incorporates ideas about reincarnation and which they believe influences the curriculum. Use of television and computers are discouraged which could disadvantage children.

Post Reading: Steiner - a very particular school (page 221)

Q5: play

Q6: adolescence

Q7: individual needs

Q8: involved

Q9: story-telling and craft

Q10: It is thought that ideas associated with this, such as belief in reincarnation, might influence the curriculum.

Q11: This could disadvantage children (they could miss out on information and development of computer skills).

Application forms (page 222)

Model answer

The following answers are given in the original order and provide explanation on why an admissions officer may view the given qualities more interesting than others.

a) In applications for most courses, a good sense of humour is unlikely to convince the admissions board that you are suitable for most courses.

b) The admissions board would want you to have a keen interest in the subject.

c) Sporting ability suggests an ability to work within a team and also determination to succeed and competitiveness, however you would have to make the relevance clear in your application.

d) You will be expected to have appropriate qualifications.

e) It is important to the college/university that you seem likely to be able to manage pressures of studying.

f) The college/university do not want to admit someone who is likely to drop out because they cannot cope with an environment which may be less disciplined than school for example.

g) It is important to work hard in order to keep up with course work.

h) Having friends may mean you are a good communicator and/or have good interpersonal skills but this may also mean that you are more interested in having a good social life than in study - again, wording is important here.

i) It may help to have a family connection, but it could be that you are doing what you think you should rather than following the path that is right for you.

j) It's okay to love parties but the admissions department do not need to know this!

Personal statements (page 222)

Expected answer

The following answers provide explanation on why these points would be suitable or unsuitable for inclusion in a university course personal statement.

a) Yes, even if your work experience is not in the same field as the course which you are applying for this demonstrates self-discipline, initiative and dependability.

b) Yes, as this suggests interest and enthusiasm.

c) Yes. This will show that you have thought about the course and why you are suited to it.

d) If the future plans are associated with the course of study.

e) No, humorous stories are not appropriate.

f) Yes, this can show that you have interpersonal skills and can be part of a team.

g) Yes, this can show that you are willing to take responsibility and are enthusiastic.

h) If the hobbies and interests are relevant and /or indicate strength of character.

i) Yes. This would demonstrate good communicative ability and verbal/written skills.

j) No, this is unlikely to be relevant.

Adjectives to describe character (page 224)

Q12:

a) Having the ability to think in new and exciting ways - imaginative/creative

b) Having the ability to produce something new - creative/imaginative

c) Someone willing to work hard at something they care about - dedicated

d) Excited and interested in something - enthusiastic

e) Someone who shows concern for another who is in emotional or physical pain - sympathetic

f) Willing to take risks and try new things - adventurous

g) Someone who galvanises others to action - encouraging/motivational

h) Someone who wants to know about things - curious

Selecting appropriate content (page 224)

Q13: a - 8 Drama, b-9 Nursing, c-6 Law, d-4 Management, e-3 Engineering

Personal statements (page 225)

Model answer

As the eldest child in my family I always helped take care of my younger siblings. I also enjoyed helping them with their homework. I took this responsibility very seriously. I loved books and used to read aloud to the others trying to make them love the stories as I did.

I believe, alongside my personal qualities, I have the qualifications necessary to succeed in this course. I achieved good results in my school exams, demonstrating that I can meet the demands of formal assessment. In my free time I enjoy reading, cinema and theatre, which shows that I am immersed in the subject I want to teach. The personal qualities that I can bring to this course and to teaching are: dedication, hard work and enthusiasm.

After completing my final year at school, I took a gap year and worked as a foreign language assistant in Ghana. Through this wonderful experience I learned about a new and different culture. I also learned a great deal about teaching, motivating pupils and creating a positive atmosphere in a classroom.

I hope that I am accepted for a place on the teacher training course. Teaching English language and literature is a dream for me. I want to help others develop skills in English and love the language as much as I do.

220 words

Pre-Listening vocabulary (page 226)

Q14: 1-h, 2-c, 3-g, 4-a, 5-l, 6-e, 7-f, 8-j, 9-b, 10-d

Listening for main ideas (page 227)

Listening Transcript

*Margot:*In today's seminar we are going to conclude our series of discussions on different types of school and approaches to schooling. This afternoon we will give our third and final guest an opportunity to describe the school which he represents and explain to us some of the underlying reasons for the educational choices made. Following this we will have a closing session with all speakers, opening the topic up for debate. Our final speaker is Douglas James from Fairways, an inner city school in the north of England.

Douglas: Good afternoon. Well, as Margot has said in her introduction I work in an inner city school. I think it is very important to bear this in mind when thinking about the way the school is run. Our children are from Kirkton, one of the poorest areas in the UK, an area in which there are high levels of unemployment, as well as alcohol and drug abuse problems. Many of our children are extremely well supported at home, but unfortunately we also have some young people who are not supported at all. For some of our children, school provides a welcome break from the chaos that surrounds them at home.
Discipline is very important to us at Fairways. We believe that a traditional, highly disciplined approach to education in our school is the best way to support our young people. We have very clear policies on timekeeping and behaviour. Children understand the rules and know the boundaries and, for the most part, they stick to these rules and boundaries. We do have problems of course,

all schools do. However, when we have a persistent problem we try very hard to establish the root cause of the trouble. We talk to parents or guardians and try to find a solution. We have a member of staff dedicated to working with challenging pupils. This supports their learning. We have fewer exclusions than other comparable schools and I believe this is because of the approach we take.

Another example of our traditional approach is perhaps our policy on school uniform. We believe that a compulsory uniform is a positive feature of the school. Uniforms provide a common identity and support the idea of a shared purpose. We also think that in this age of high levels of consumerism and materialism, uniforms take away the pressure to compete. Parents do not need to invest in the latest fashions and logos. This can be a great relief for people struggling to make ends meet.

Learning and teaching is at the heart of what we do at Fairways. At all times we strive to maintain levels of attainment. In line with this we have introduced a timetabled guidance session which takes place in the first half hour of the school day. This means that guidance teachers have an opportunity to talk to pupils about homework issues, exams, future plans and also any personal problems which might be worrying them and interfering with their school work.

I hope that this short presentation has given you a flavour of Fairways. We endeavour to provide the best conditions possible to support our young people, to furnish them with the skills and qualities that they need to be happy and successful in their lives. Thank you.

Q15: inner city

Q16: Many poor families, children who lack supportive from parents

Q17: Firm line, pupils know rules and boundaries

Q18: Try to support, talk to parents/guardians, dedicated staff

Q19: Compulsory because gives shared identity and purpose, saves parents buying fashionable clothes they can't afford

Q20: At the heart of what the school does, supports pupils through daily guidance meetings

ANSWERS: UNIT 3 TOPIC 2

Listening for detail (page 227)

Listening Transcript

*Margot:*In today's seminar we are going to conclude our series of discussions on different types of school and approaches to schooling. This afternoon we will give our third and final guest an opportunity to describe the school which he represents and explain to us some of the underlying reasons for the educational choices made. Following this we will have a closing session with all speakers, opening the topic up for debate. Our final speaker is Douglas James from Fairways, an inner city school in the north of England.

Douglas: Good afternoon. Well, as Margot has said in her introduction I work in an inner city school. I think it is very important to bear this in mind when thinking about the way the school is run. Our children are from Kirkton, one of the poorest areas in the UK, an area in which there are high levels of unemployment, as well as alcohol and drug abuse problems. Many of our children are extremely well supported at home, but unfortunately we also have some young people who are not supported at all. For some of our children, school provides a welcome break from the chaos that surrounds them at home.

Discipline is very important to us at Fairways. We believe that a traditional, highly disciplined approach to education in our school is the best way to support our young people. We have very clear policies on timekeeping and behaviour. Children understand the rules and know the boundaries and, for the most part, they stick to these rules and boundaries. We do have problems of course, all schools do. However, when we have a persistent problem we try very hard to establish the root cause of the trouble. We talk to parents or guardians and try to find a solution. We have a member of staff dedicated to working with challenging pupils. This supports their learning. We have fewer exclusions than other comparable schools and I believe this is because of the approach we take.

Another example of our traditional approach is perhaps our policy on school uniform. We believe that a compulsory uniform is a positive feature of the school. Uniforms provide a common identity and support the idea of a shared purpose. We also think that in this age of high levels of consumerism and materialism, uniforms take away the pressure to compete. Parents do not need to invest in the latest fashions and logos. This can be a great relief for people struggling to make ends meet.

Learning and teaching is at the heart of what we do at Fairways. At all times we strive to maintain levels of attainment. In line with this we have introduced a timetabled guidance session which takes place in the first half hour of the school day. This means that guidance teachers have an opportunity to talk to pupils about homework issues, exams, future plans and also any personal problems which might be worrying them and interfering with their school work.

I hope that this short presentation has given you a flavour of Fairways. We endeavour to provide the best conditions possible to support our young people, to furnish them with the skills and qualities that they need to be happy and successful in their lives. Thank you.

Q21:

a) Compared to other similar schools Fairways has **fewer** exclusions.

b) Parents often buy fashionable clothes for their children because **they feel they have to compete**.

c) The guidance time is **first half hour of the school day**.

Asking for clarification (page 228)

Q22:

    a) I'm sorry, could you say that again please?

    b) Could you give me an example of that please?

    c) Could you clarify that point please?

    d) I'm sorry, I'm not sure I follow you.

    e) Do you mean ... ?

Word transformation (page 229)

Q23:

Verb	Noun	Adjective
To compare	*Comparison*	*Comparable*
To dedicate	Dedication	Dedicated
To exclude	Exclusion	Excluded
To persist	Persistence	Persistent
To approach	Approach	Approachable
To guide	Guidance	Guiding
To attain	Attainment	Attainable
To interfere	Interference	Interfering
To endeavour	Endeavour	-
To furnish	-	Furnished

Reading comprehension: Etre et avoir (page 229)

Q24: b. A film review

Q25: a. Positive

Q26:

    a) True

    b) False

    c) False

    d) True

    e) False

    f) False

Q27: Getting on with those around you/harmonious relationships

Q28: The school is unusual now which is unfortunate because it is a very positive environment for children.

Listening comprehension: Supportive parents (page 231)

Listening comprehension transcript

Presenter: Recent research carried out in the United States demonstrates that supportive parents can counteract the experience children have in weak schools. Perhaps more importantly, parents can raise the levels of success their children have in exams. To discuss this we have in the studio today, David Wallace, an educational researcher at St Peter's College, and Jenny Watson, head teacher at Stonefield School in Lower Inchley. If we can start with you David, this seems an enormous task for parents, exactly what kind of support is necessary?

David: It is really not such an enormous task Moira. What we are talking about here is the kind of attention which many parents already give to their children. We are talking about helping with homework and attendance of school events, parents' evenings and concerts...

If I can just interrupt you there... many would say that this is a very middle class approach to child rearing. Would you say this a class issue, David?

David: You might be forgiven for saying that this is the kind of behaviour associated with more middle class parents. Previous research has shown that middle class parents do tend to schedule activities for their children, taking them to a range of different types of clubs or sports classes rather than leaving them to their own devices to play freely. You might also argue that this is associated with financial well-being. Interestingly though, the research highlights the importance of talking to children, which we both know doesn't cost anything at all.

Moira: If I could bring you in at this point, Jenny... is it not the job of teachers to get our children through exams?

Jenny: In England, a school with fewer than 35% of pupils achieving 5 GCSE exam passes at grades A-C including Maths and English is considered to be underachieving. Yes, of course grades are a very important part of what teachers do in the classroom, but I do think it is a mistake to focus entirely on exam passes as a measure of success of schools or their pupils. There are also other indicators of performance, such as a positive ethos and good level of attendance, and these can tell us about the quality of the school experience. What I'm saying is that exam results are important, but the school cannot do everything with a child. Those of us in education have long been aware of the role parents can play and now the statistics are backing us up.

Moira: What can parents do?

Jenny: The study revealed that the most important aspects of the parent/child relationship are trust, good communication and active engagement... and I think that the last point there is the crucial one. We see parents from all kinds of backgrounds, many short of money or short of time, but it seems to me that key to the success of the child, in terms of a sense of well-being as well as exam results, is active engagement on the part of the parents.

David: I totally agree with that. Research has also highlighted the fact that parental involvement and a stimulating environment in early years is far more important than parental occupation and income. This is not rocket science; we are talking about play with numbers and letters, craft, games with friends, sport, dance, and of course help with homework too!

Jenny: It seems that what is required is support for parents who may just need a bit of guidance on what they can do. It's also important for busy parents to know that a little effort can go a long way.

Moira: Thank you both very much for coming in to talk to us today.

Q29: A radio broadcast

Q30: Role of parents in supporting children at school.

Q31:

a) David

b) Jenny

c) Jenny

Q32:

Parents can help children in weak schools to **a) pass exams** by helping with **b) homework** and **c) attending events**. Middle class parents tend to **d) schedule activities** for their children which helps in their development but **e) talking**, which costs nothing, also helps. It is not just exam results which show that a school is doing a good job, **f) positive** ethos and **g) attendance** also indicate performance.

BV - #0006 - 210819 - C0 - 210/148/20 - PB - 9781911057291